NIMBLE CHURCH

Why Agility Is Key and Why Upside-Down Is the Real Right-Side-Up

DR. SHAWN KEENER

Overseed PRESS

Nimble Church

Published by Overseed Press
Division of William & James Publishing
581 Washington Street, #3
South Easton, MA 02375 USA

ISBN 978-1-940151-07-6
© 2022 Dr. Shawn Keener

Printed in the United States of America
First Edition 2022

CONTENTS

Start Here

Who is this for?

This book has been written for anyone who is concerned about the current health or long-term viability of their local church. My earnest hope is that pastors, church leaders, and laypersons alike will find in these pages a bright light of hope and practical guidance. Though the practical guidance offered is backed up by theological thought and a coherent philosophy of ministry, the way this book is written should make it accessible to all regardless of their level of or comfort with theological education. Perhaps this is its greatest strength. If it were written primarily for pastors or seminarians, the prospect of implementing any of its practical guidance would be greatly reduced. This is because any turnaround in a church's health requires pastors, church leaders, and laypersons to be working in concert and from the same intel.

The logic throughout this book will be most appropriate for cultural contexts similar to that of the New England region.[1] The six New England states, Connecticut, Maine, Massachusetts, New Hampshire, Rhode Island, and Vermont, share a distinct familial bond because of their common heritage.[2] A strong current of individual independence characterizes these states. It is also possible to say that this region has come to embody postmodern and postchristian worldviews.[3] It seems New England received these worldviews as hand-me-downs from Europe, Australia,

---

[1] Key words, such as *culture* and *postmodern*, are defined in the pages that follow.

[2] J. David Jackson, *New England Culture & Ministry Dynamics: Where You Serve Makes a Difference in How You Serve*, 3rd ed. (Marlborough, MA: Screven and Allen, 2018).

[3] Jared C. Wilson, "10 Surprising Realities of Mission in New England," May 26, 2017, The Gospel Coalition, https://www.thegospelcoalition.org/blogs/jared-c-wilson/10-surprising-realities-of-mission-in-new-england/.

and regions with similar contexts, and that places such as southern California and Arizona are next in line to receive them from New England.[4] Presumably, what this book has to offer will be appropriate in part for other, less similar cultural contexts, but it will make the most sense and fit most smoothly in places like New England.

Since this book proposes that governance and missionality are interrelated, congregations that have the authority to make changes to their polity and organizational structure may be able to apply these concepts more consistently and with greater effect than churches that do not. The chapters that make up this book are synergistic, that is, they are best regarded as essential pieces of a system or theory. Consequently, if a church were to apply the chapters that focus on missionality and strategy but were unable to apply those that focus on leadership and governance, the results would be disproportionately inferior.

Readers from church traditions similar to those of Baptist, Bible, or nondenominational churches will likely find the lines of reasoning in this book more native. This is because my life experience has been almost solely within these three environments. Certain characteristics of these traditions are especially pertinent to the discussion herein: they tend to be theologically and ecclesiologically conservative, they tend to draw a sharp distinction between discipleship and evangelism, and they tend to consider a postmodern worldview dangerous or even demonic. However, with this acknowledged, I have labored to write and reason, to the extent of my ability, in a manner that is simultaneously natural for those in my tradition and readily adaptable by those not in my tradition. This goal may be presumptuous to some degree, so I can only say again that

---

[4] Barna Group, "The Most Post-Christian Cities in America: 2019," June 5, 2019, https://www.barna.com/research/post-christian-cities-2019/.

readers from Baptist, Bible, or nondenominational traditions will most easily resonate with this book.

This book is single-mindedly dedicated to church revitalization. Revitalization is one among many possible answers to the question, "How can our church keep from languishing or dying?" Though the entire subject is something of a new frontier, alternatives to revitalization include church planting, replanting, reopening, revival, dying well, mergers, partnerships, and more.[5] There are many contexts in which these alternatives may prove to be the right fit. Most are capably advocated in books and seminars within the larger conversation about this new frontier. For the most part, however, these alternatives are not discussed at much length in this book, which is devoted to a practical path to revitalization.

Finally, there is no presumption in the writing of this book of finding a universal formula for church revitalization—I know it would be arrogant to think that this book guarantees plug-and-play revitalization success for every church regardless of context. I prayerfully expect that as this book is debated, adapted, and applied in myriad contexts it will eventually be left far behind, having served its purpose of helping to give rise to a kaleidoscope of revitalizing experiments. This book is intended to be a widely adaptable template for a holistic revitalization plan; perhaps for the first time the disparate pieces of such a template are brought together all in one place with this writing. As a consequence, the reader may at times be dissatisfied by the cursory treatment of one topic or another. One obvious example of this might be the scant mention of transitional leadership, a voluminous topic in its own right

---

[5] Tom Cheyney is one of the more prominent voices cataloguing the many alternatives. Tom Cheyney, *Thirty-Eight Church Revitalization Models for the Twenty-First Century* (Orlando, FL: Renovate, 2014).

but incidental to the goal of this book. My concern is to present a complete template as comprehensively as possible. For this reason, the reader may discover many options for further reading in the footnotes. If I have sketched a user-friendly template without sacrificing too much depth in the discussion of its intricacies, I am deeply contented.

I like tech, and I am trying to lose weight by using a wearable to keep me on target. Only two options appeal to me, the Fitbit and the Apple Watch. (Also, I have become a diehard Apple fan.) My success in losing weight hinges upon an accurate accounting of how many calories I am burning each day so I can be certain to regularly undereat. The Apple Watch almost certainly does a better job at this. Its tech capabilities are much higher, and it takes more sophisticated readings. Yet I use the Fitbit because it has one major advantage over the Apple Watch; it has a battery life of nearly a week, compared with the fourteen-hour battery life of the Apple Watch. It will do the job better with less because it will always be on my wrist. This is my justification for a survey-level treatment of many subtopics in this book, in which I hope to lay out a holistic, user-friendly template for church revitalization. Because it offers all the key components in one place and offers a user-friendly experience by referring the reader elsewhere for deeper discussion, it has the greatest chance of being widely adapted and implemented.

Definitions of key terms

Attractional: in common parlance, this refers to a style of church frequently associated with megachurches, with being seeker sensitive, and with exceptionally executed programming for all ages and phases of life. In this book, however, it refers specifically to a strategy of evangelism that envisions nonbelievers finding Jesus and spiritual maturity primarily in a church service.

Autonomous: this describes a local church that is not obliged to obey any ecclesial authority or governance structure outside of herself; according to this usage *independent* is a synonym. Almost all autonomous churches affiliate or partner with other churches. An autonomous church understands Jesus, the Head of the Church, as the only authority outside (and inside) her own internal structure. Most autonomous churches consider the state as an authority so long as the laws of the state are not in conflict with the teaching of Scripture.

Culture: this may be a word that is impossible to satisfactorily encompass in any definition. It is generally employed without nuance in this book in a sense that is comparable to *society* and *worldview*, or even *community sentiment*. Howell and Paris note that common metaphors for conceptualizing culture are a person viewing the world through eyeglass lenses and a fish swimming in a fishbowl. They prefer instead to conceive of culture as a dynamic conversation.[6] While all three of these analogies can be helpful, one of my core motivations for writing is that the church must join in a dynamic conversation with postmodern culture.

Follower: (specific to Mile Marker Six, explained below) technically, anyone who determines to mirror the character of Jesus, as in the definition of servant leadership (defined below); practically, followers refer to the people being guided under the definition of leadership (also defined below).

---

[6] Brian M. Howell and Jenell Williams Paris, *Introducing Cultural Anthropology: A Christian Perspective*, 2nd ed. (Grand Rapids, MI: Baker, 2019).

Governance: this refers to how a church organizes herself to make decisions, maintain internal consistency and Christ-likeness, picture the future, and mobilize her people to action. Very often, in my tradition, this governance is in the form of a body of elders in combination with the pastor.

Incarnational: a model of church evangelism that has grown in popularity over recent decades. Alan Hirsch has been a powerful voice for this model. In the incarnational model, believers who belong to a church expect most evangelism to happen in the community and through the relationships church leaders and laypersons are building with nonbelievers in the course of daily routines. A general theme of this model is the moving of church meetings and functions out of the church building and into public spaces such as coffeehouses and bars.[7]

Leadership: though defined variously in the wider, scholarly discussion of leadership, in this chapter it refers to guiding people from "here" to "there" ("here" is unsatisfactory or even untenable; "there" is better, a leap of faith, and often futuristic).

Liminality: although liminality legitimately refers to leadership from a marginal position or from the periphery in contrast to central, empowered authority, in this book it means the murky, unsettling, fraught-with-danger, and nondelineated zone between the "here" and the "there" referred to in the definition of leadership above.[8]

Members or owners: (specific to Mile Marker Six) the group of people on behalf of whom servant leadership is

---

[7] Alan Hirsch, *The Forgotten Ways: Reactivating Apostolic Movements*, 2nd ed. (Grand Rapids, MI: Brazos, 2016).
[8] Cf Andy Stanley, *Next Generation Leader: Five Essentials for Those Who Will Shape the Future*, 2nd ed. (Colorado Springs, CO: Multnomah, 2006).

empowered and to whom the single, central unit of leadership is responsible.

Missional: has been defined any number of ways. In this book, *mission* and *missional* refer to a simple, two-part concept. First, the missional church identifies and clearly articulates the mission of the church. This identification is drawn from an interpretation of Scripture concerning Christ's Body generally; it includes a context-oriented mission that is unique to each church, identified through specific guidance by the Holy Spirit and through the discernment of the church people, both leaders and laity. Second, the missional church pursues that mission with a near-term expectation of its fulfillment.

Neutrals: this term is used herein to refer to people who have no familiarity with church. They have no knowledge of Jesus, or if they do, he is a two-dimensional character. Jesus and the church are to these people what a Druid temple might be to the average Christian: never in our thoughts, not a place we would think of to go for anything, shrouded in unnerving mysticism, having customs and liturgy we know nothing about, and a place we would feel prohibitively uncomfortable to enter or approach. The term differs from *postchristianity* in that it refers specifically to individual people and not societal prominence.

Postmodernism: there seems to be a bewildering lack of consensus on a definition for this term. Here it is used as an attempt to encompass an array of values that are a direct or indirect reaction to the tenets of a modernist worldview that, among other things, respected a hierarchy of authority and viewed the world through a lens of propositions, absolutes, empiricism, and systems. Defined this way, *postmodernism* began in earnest around the beginning of the twenty-first century and pervades cultures like that of New England. Though it may be more observably prominent in

Generations X, Y, and Z, it has less to do with generational affinities and more to do with a reaction to a modernist world. It refers not to some of the things that might first come to mind with *postmodernism*, such as architecture, philosophy, or literature, but to a worldview common among individual people in a postmodern society.

Postchristian: this term refers to the society, or a person in that society, that has moved away from a once-strong Judeo-Christian basis and ethic. The church no longer has centrality or authority in the postchristian's public life. Postchristian people are biblically illiterate, even if they may still be subconsciously guided by the vestiges of Christian belief from previous generations. Though they may have no fair or accurate understanding of what it means to be a Christian, they may nevertheless consider themselves Christian by default.

Revitalization: this word has been coined within a conversation that has been growing over recent decades. Alternative terms have been suggested, such as *restoration* or *renewal*.[9] *Revitalization* is the process of a well-established but now languishing church becoming intentionally and single-mindedly missional. The focus of this book is how to realistically expect authentic revitalization. *Revitalization* is also appropriate to churches that are growing but for less than the best reasons.

Servant leadership: (specific to Mile Marker Six) though defined otherwise in the wider, scholarly discussion of leadership,[10] here it means being like Jesus by self-emptying, self-sacrificing, and self-giving. The leader is one with the

---

[9] Jack L. Daniel, *Patient Catalyst: Leading Church Revitalization* (South Easton, MA: Overseed, 2018).
[10] Cf. Peter G. Northhouse, *Leadership Theory and Practice*, 8th ed. (Thousand Oaks, CA: Sage, 2019).

people he or she is guiding, commiserates with them, and is a promoter of the qualities of a team sport.

Single, central unit: (specific to Mile Marker Six) the organizational position assumed by most people to have the answers, or the plan, and the leverage to implement it. This unit may be a single person, a simple group, or a tiered group, but (when it is healthy, at least) it speaks strictly as one, acts strictly as one, and enjoys wide freedom to make decisions of its own.

Spiritually stable pastor: a pastor (or any leader of any type who is leading to please an Audience of One) who is humble, hungry, and smart in the execution of that role.[11] A spiritually stable pastor is one who successfully sidesteps the many idolatries that frequently seduce anyone in the pastorate. He is capable of the greatest possible reach, stability, courage, and depth because of a solid footing of his own identity in Jesus.

Zero-agenda discipleship: discipleship that draws people closer to Jesus and Jesus-likeness, regardless of where they may be in their relationship with Christ, and with no angle for the church's gain. In fact, zero-agenda discipleship is calculated to disallow any such manipulation or coercion, real or implied, direct or indirect.

Coming from a reaction

Though the heart of this book is a proactive search for practical steps to revitalization, it is also true that it approaches this from a reaction to certain aspects of evangelical conservatism in my experiences. Perhaps the most prominent of these aspects is a belief that church health

---

[11] Adapted from Patrick Lencioni, *The Ideal Team Player* (Hoboken, NJ: Jossey-Bass, 2016).

has a direct relationship to purity. The thinking often goes that if the church maintains a stance of doctrinal purity and the church people, especially the leaders, maintain lives of purity, then church-wide missionality, effectiveness, growth, and revitalization will be automatic by-products. I sometimes refer to this as *purism*.[12] The correlatives are also held to be true, that truly flourishing churches are so because they are godly and that foundering churches are so because they "have forgotten [their] first love."[13] Purism may sometimes be the result of drawing a one-to-one relationship between godliness and church health.

This kind of thinking has a number of unfortunate consequences. It tends to make a godliness pecking order inevitable. It predictably angles the church toward some degree of legalism. It does this by training us to focus on the wrong things. Rather than fixing our eyes on Jesus, we fix our eyes on our relative obedience.[14] Rather than a narrow attention to missionality, we are drawn into policing one another and developing ranked lists of approved and unapproved actions. Because it places a premium on performance, it hides from our consciousness what is perhaps the grandest theme of the redemptive story—that Christ's work has been finished since Day Six and ever since rest is both the means and result of faith.[15] The correlative that truly flourishing churches are so because they are godly

---

[12] Cf. to the term *puritanism*.

[13] Rev 2.4.

[14] Cf. Heb 12.2.

[15] Cf. Heb 4, especially verse 3; Jhn 15.1–8. A consistent theme throughout Scripture, sometimes forgotten in our soteriology, is that Christ has done all the work from the beginning of time, and our job is to claim it and rest in his finished work for both salvation and discipleship. E.g., Eph 2.8–10. For an interesting discussion about rest as a formational truth for the redemptive story, see Leonard Sweet and Frank Viola, *Jesus: A Theography* (Nashville: Thomas Nelson, 2012); Leonard Sweet, *The Well-Played Life: Why Pleasing God Doesn't Have to Be Such Hard work*, 2nd ed. (Issaquah, WA: Salish Sea, 2021).

encourages church leaders and laity alike to disregard strategy and leadership principles; but surely the Creator wants his people to engage not just their hearts for missionality but also their minds and hands.[16] The correlative that failing churches are so because they have forgotten their first love encourages leaders and laity to associate authentic missionality with a respectable growth in attendance, giving, and momentum. This may lead to disillusionment if authentic revitalization results in a short-term decline in these numbers.

Another consequence of an overdrawn view of the role of purity in church revitalization is that it strongly discourages outsiders from engagement. Younger people and those newer in their faith walk correctly deduce they are a demoralizingly long way from being part of the "in" crowd. Any path toward leadership training or meaningful volunteering requires a navigation through so much red tape and so many performance thresholds that they despair before they start. As a result, the average age of engaged church people grows ever older and the wealth of new perspective, ingenuity, and energy of the new and young is pushed to the edges.

Similarly, placing too much of revitalization's weight on purity tends to send mixed messages about exclusivity to the outside community. Of course, it sends a correct message of exclusivity, that of "a right relationship with your Father can be had no other way than through Jesus." However, it also sends very regrettable messages of exclusivity to the outside community, that of "we're so stuck on the finer points of purity that we can't play well with other churches" and "you'll never belong until you behave." An unhealthy reliance on purity for church revitalization will always, when

---

[16] Cf. 1Co 6.3.

taken fully to its logical extent, end up with a self-righteous party of one.[17]

A second aspect of my experiences in evangelical conservatism against which this book is a reaction is the arbitrary distinction between evangelism and discipleship that is frequently maintained. Presumably, this distinction was a natural result of a belief that initial, regenerative faith always occurs in one self-aware moment, is hyperindividualistic, and is predominantly for eternal result. From this, a careful delineation came to be drawn between regeneration, sanctification, and glorification, with regeneration being further demarcated from justification. Justification, regeneration, and sanctification argued for a discipleship that commenced only after salvation, so that evangelism and discipleship became almost antonyms from the perspective of church strategy and programming. Finally, a biblical understanding of discipleship atrophied into little more than curricula and programming. At any rate, this is my best guess. Regardless, this distinction between evangelism and discipleship seems to have played havoc with church evangelistic strategy. This book argues that point.

A third aspect against which this book is written reactively is an elite view of the pastorate and church leadership. Certainly these roles are elite, and it is not too difficult to argue that point biblically.[18] But, in my view, an unholy alliance has developed between the purism mentioned above and an unhealthy, antiquated view of pastoral perfection. The pastor, the pastor's family, and the church elders are placed on a pedestal, and very often they

---

[17] I have heard an unfortunate remark that IFCA, which stands for Independent Fundamentalist Churches of America, actually means "I Fight Christians Anywhere."

[18] E.g., Jam 3.1; 2Th 3.7–9; Heb 13.7, 17.

unconsciously enjoy the post. An unhealthy power distance widens between church leaders and laity. All of this is discussed at length in the chapters that follow. Again in my view, this has a corrupting effect on two otherwise beautiful fixtures of the church in Baptist, nondenominational, Bible, and similar traditions; the elder board system and the pastor-as-shepherd model both become problematic. In both cases, their beauty is easily salvaged, and this represents a strong secondary motivation for the writing of this book.

Presuppositions

This book presupposes that the churches of New England, or a large minority of them if not the majority, are struggling to survive or thrive. It does not devote much time to proving the point. Even if the point is unfounded, such an error would be no detraction because, as stated above, this book is written for all who are concerned about the current health or long-term viability of their local church. In other words, it is written with those of us in mind who *feel* like our church is in trouble. Further, if the point is unfounded and the majority of churches in New England are doing well, this still does not detract, because this book is written specifically for those that are not. Because of the starkly independent mindset characteristic of New England, and because of the very nature of autonomous or independent churches, it is difficult for anyone to arrive at firm statistics on the collective state of our churches. Anecdotally, however, many church leaders and church people in New England have a palpable sense of a guillotine over our heads, stayed by Christ the Head but nonetheless disconcerting. The New England of our times is renowned for its hard spiritual soil.

This book presupposes that historic churches, a large minority of them if not the majority, are worth resuscitating.[19] New England is still dotted with such churches—in buildings with unobtrusive but inspiring steeples easily recalling a day when the buildings functioned as multipurpose town meeting places. Of course, that is just the stereotype. Many historic churches have little in the way of an impressive façade; they can still claim the descriptor because, though their glory days seem to be in the past, they have enjoyed a long, vibrant life. Because of the baggage and recalcitrance that attends such historicity, many may suppose that church planting, a microchurch, a seeker-sensitive replant, or a full-blown version of the incarnational model is the best answer to historic churches in decline. This conclusion is understandable. Resuscitating a historic church is a particularly daunting proposition, but this book is written out of a conviction that it is many times over worth the risk and labor.

Little argument is made herein that strategy and leadership principles have a place in the church; it is a presupposition of this book that they certainly do. In fact, without this presupposition, there would be no warrant for this book. In tandem with godliness and the Spirit and love, strategy is a good thing in the church more than anywhere else, for who else on earth has a more vital mission? In the same vein, in tandem with holiness and love and servanthood, leadership principles are a good thing in the church. In fact, this book argues that there is a close relationship between governance and revitalization or missionality. Some may fear that the appropriation of leadership principles, sometimes from secular sources, and any talk of strategy in church affairs are incongruent with living by the Spirit as a church. Regarding such concern, this book presupposes, with what I believe is an appropriate

---

[19] For expansion on this point, see Mile Marker Five.

warrant, that all truth is God's truth no matter where it is found.

Outside of some discussion of metrics and growth and the attractional model, this book ignores church size as a factor in its central thesis. This is because I write this book with the presupposition that size is irrelevant to revitalization, and that there is nothing inherently biblical about big or small churches. Everywhere there are churches large and small, whether in imminent danger of closing down or not, that are in need of revitalization. My writing assumes that both small churches and large churches have their pros and cons. Perhaps in most cases they are even called by Christ to be roughly the size that they are. Some churches have been so traumatized by the abuses of the church growth movement of the last several decades that they might even find anticipation of growth undesirable and equate it with compromise of the gospel. This book presupposes that church growth, if authentic, should be an expectation, but, paradoxically, that shrinking numbers may also be a sign of authentic revitalization. Or, to put it another way, Jesus certainly wants his church to grow in numbers and in depth, but, initially, authentic revitalization will typically be accompanied by a decline in numbers. God "wants all [people] to be saved" yet delights to work through a committed few, sometimes even a remnant.[20]

Affirmations

Admittedly, this book may tend to overstate certain positions in the flow of argument. It will push the pendulum too far the other way to allow for a clearer and more distinct point. For this reason, the following affirmations may be helpful before starting.

---

[20] 1Ti 2.4; 2Pe 3.9; cf. Gideon.

The purpose of the church is both inward and outward. Which comes first or drives the other may be a "chicken or egg" scenario. It is crucial to "be holy as [our] heavenly Father is holy," and equally crucial to urgently bring as many to Jesus as possible because the time is short.[21] Loving people into Jesus and going out after them are simultaneous commands—and Jesus and John are both pretty clear that the motivations of love and obedience are two sides of the same coin.[22] God loves his children and desires them to grow up in him and flourish as a beautiful expression of his own creativity.[23] He is not using them merely as tools to accomplish his mission and bring himself glory. And yet Christ does expect an ROI (return on investment) from his church.[24] He does expect her to be on mission and to be the vehicle of his grace to the world.[25]

On that note, this book affirms that the Kingdom of God is both here and not yet, and that though the church and the kingdom may not be perfect synonyms, they have quite a lot of overlap. There is continuity within the Kingdom of God throughout the grand redemptive story between the Old Testament and the New Testament, and between God's purposes through Israel and the church.[26] This book does not relitigate any of these weighty debates, instead completely skipping over such things as covenant and dispensation since

---

[21] 1Pe 1.15–16; Jhn 9.4.

[22] 1Pe 2.12; 2Jn 6; Luk 15.4–6; Jhn 14.15.

[23] Cf. 2Th 3.5; F. LeRon Shults, *Reforming Theological Anthropology: After the Philosophical Turn to Relationality* (Grand Rapids, MI: Eerdmans, 2003); Nonna Verna Harrison, *God's Many-Splendored Image: Theological Anthropology for Christian Formation* (Grand Rapids, MI: Baker, 2010).

[24] E.g., Luk 12.48.

[25] Mat 28.18–20; 2Pe 3.11–12.

[26] Cf. Nicholas Perrin, *The Kingdom of God: A Biblical Theology* (Grand Rapids, MI: Zondervan, 2019); Christopher J. H. Wright, *The Mission of God: Unlocking the Bible's Grand Narrative* (Downers Grove, IL: InterVarsity, 2018); James Bryan Smith, *The Magnificent Story: Uncovering a Gospel of Beauty, Goodness, and Truth* (Downers Grove, IL: InterVarsity, 2017).

they are not germane to the topic of church revitalization and how to get there. The reader may want to interject, or object, on these matters at points in the flow of this book's argument. This book simply glosses over them. Diving into them is likely a distraction or unnecessary complication in the work of finding a path toward church revitalization.

Though this book is written as a reaction, in part, to an overemphasis on purity as the prescription for church decline, I also affirm that it is possible for a little bit of sin to sideline the whole church. The story of Achan comes to mind as a little sin in the camp of God's people causing disproportionately large havoc. Paul quotes an ancient proverb that "a little yeast works through the whole batch of dough" to stress this very point regarding sins of both commission and omission.[27] In other words, purity is clearly important despite its tendency toward legalism.

Although a presupposition of this writing is that strategy has an invaluable part in church mission, the author agrees, in the same breath, that all strategy is worthless unless the Spirit animates it. It is not on us to save the church; the church belongs to Jesus, and even if at times her outlook may seem bleak, this can only ever be a temporary situation.[28] The common tradition of the church has remained remarkably stable over the millennia since Christ.[29] Sometimes it is thought that all we need to do to see church revitalization is return to the church of Acts. An assumption behind this thought may be that the early church was more Spirit filled and that therefore no strategy was needed

---

[27] 1Co 5.6; Gal 5.9. The latter is part of a polemic against teaching circumcision as a means to righteousness, so the sin could be understood as one of omission because relying on faith and resting in Christ's finished work is the issue.

[28] Cf. esp. Rev 2–3, 12, 21.

[29] Cf. Roger E. Olson, *The Mosaic of Christian Belief: Twenty Centuries of Unity and Diversity,* 2nd ed. (Downers Grove, IL: InterVarsity, 2016).

because the Spirit of God was their cloud by day and fire by night.[30] Judging from the book of Acts itself and from the letters to the churches, particularly the one in Corinth, this is a romanticized picture of the early church.[31] Regardless, much has been written about strategy that clearly did exist in the early church.[32] Strategy in the church is not inherently in conflict with the movement of the Spirit, but seems instead to be something God values and calls us to in the Spirit.

The reader should not think that any line of reasoning in this book has any partnership with compromising the truth or the gospel. Perhaps at first blush it may seem so, but it is not the case. This book affirms the authority of the Word of God over our lives in full. Any pursuit of church revitalization that involves shortening the truth of God in order to be less offensive or more attractive to the unbelieving world will surely shipwreck. The forfeiture necessary to enter the narrow gate and follow the narrow road of the gospel is highly offensive to human pride.[33] Our difficulties often arise when we are offensive in other ways, and in so doing needlessly detract from a clear display of the good news of the gospel. The compromise of the truth or of the gospel has no share in attaining church effectiveness, growth, or revitalization.

Finally, I acknowledge, again, that there is no revitalization formula-in-a-box to hand out. There is no one-

---

[30] Num 14.14; the record of Acts is replete with explicit and implicit examples of strategy in evangelism and church life, including Paul's missionary logic, the deliberation of the Jerusalem council, and the events of Pentecost.

[31] Cf. Rev 1–3.

[32] E.g., Michael Green, *Evangelism in the Early Church,* rev. ed. (Grand Rapids, MI: Eerdmans, 2004); Roland Allen, *Missionary Methods: St Paul's or Ours?* http://www.onthewing.org/user/Allen_Roland%20-%20Missionary%20Methods.pdf

[33] 1Co 1.20–2.15.

size-fits-all strategy. The context for revitalization is significantly different between any two churches—even two churches in the same theological tradition in the same town. I have heard it said that in the field of church revitalization we need to leave all formulas and systems and models behind and move on to other, less packaged, solutions. There is great wisdom in such a statement; and yet, if a church is hoping for revitalization, the counsel it will likely find most user-friendly and tangibly productive will be practical steps spatially organized in an adaptable template. That is what I hope to pioneer here.

What is unique about this book?

While the conversation over church revitalization has been expanding for years, it has relatively little in the way of a solid core. A wealth of publications and seminars have chipped away at the puzzle of how to achieve it. The goal of this book is to draw selectively from that wealth in order to bring into a single resource the crucial pieces. The goal is to arrange these pieces in a philosophical order, and perhaps even a chronological one, in a form that is both specific and adaptable. For the typical church leader or layperson, it can be overwhelming to know of, find, read, and combine all the best information on the subject of church revitalization spread so far and wide. This adds just one more major hurdle for individual churches desiring to journey toward it. Even if they would be able to compile the key components, they may have trouble arranging them in steps of the most practical and effective order.

As a further bewilderment for those seeking to find a path toward revitalization, there are other, often more attractive, alternatives. Church planting may be chief among these. An analogy to landscaping may be helpful. If landscapers are tasked with working their magic in an unkempt yard, they can either work with what is already there or remove it all and start with a clean slate. If they choose the latter approach, they might bring in their bobcats, shave off the top few inches of the lawn, and put down all-new topsoil and turf. They might even change the slope and contours of the yard to better address water runoff or some convenience of the homeowner. Certain trees in the yard, perhaps still potentially beautiful, might nevertheless be removed because of the new layout. Starting from scratch like this might be easier, and it might have a very beautiful end result, but the history of the homeowner's yard will be obliterated. The place where the homeowner's children used to play will be unrecognizable. The character of the yard might be sacrificed to develop a cookie-cutter cleanness. If landscapers instead work their magic with the yard as it is, leveraging its history, the end result may be more ultimately satisfying.

The conversation around church revitalization is often enmeshed with that of other closely related options, such as church planting. Since this clean-slate approach may appear more attractive than the difficult task of working with what already is in place, the proponents of planting may add to the confusion and bewilderment of church leaders and laypeople who wish to intentionally focus on revitalization. By bringing together all the most relevant pieces of revitalization in a single resource dedicated only to revitalization, this book may bring invaluable clarity to those searching for a way to revitalize a church.

Absent an adaptable template composed of practical steps, churches may unwittingly opt for a plan long on hope and short on definition. A church may latch onto solutions such as spiritual revival, new programming, or additional ministries, without first going through a discerning process to see if there are more complicated forces constraining the church. Reaching too hastily for something that has worked for other churches may disappoint because it might either be a plan without a path or a path without a plan.

Finally, the currently articulated range of missional models does not seem to quite arrive at the intersection of postmodernists and historic churches. The attractional model is odious to postmoderns and unlikely for historic churches. The incarnational model seems to struggle to find real value in preserving historic churches. Microchurch models have no use for historic churches. The revitalization template attempted in this book sketches out a new model that marries postmodern critiques and contributions with historic churches in need of revitalization. Failing that, this book at least explores a new iteration or extension of the incarnational model that may get us all closer to authentic, biblical revitalization.

Holbrook, Massachusetts

The inspiration for this book came from an analysis of church decline in a small Massachusetts town named Holbrook. This analysis is no more blessed than the countless analyses of so many others in an array of other contexts. Holbrook has six established churches: Lighthouse Baptist, Holbrook United Methodist, St. John's Episcopal, Brookville Bible, Winthrop Congregational, and St. Joseph's Roman Catholic. Most of these have been around for more than a century. Before the COVID-19 pandemic, these six accounted for about two hundred and fifty active church people who lived in Holbrook. Over eleven thousand people in four thousand households live in the town. While it is surely true that some of those eleven thousand are active in churches outside Holbrook, it is unlikely to be many; New Englanders are generally very parochial.

Once, while sitting in a pastor's conference at a nearby church, I heard two of my favorite speakers, Larry Osborne and Carey Nieuwhof, give some common-sense advice: figure out how to draw or connect with those people in your community with whom you already have some sort of a bridge. Capitalize on that, they said. My guess would be that no more than two thousand Holbrook residents fall into that category. That leaves roughly nine thousand Neutrals, without God, and without the hope and life and purpose that we all enjoy in Christ Jesus. It is my hope that this book will be one practical, experimental step toward coming to grips with *why* numbers like this are everywhere in postmodern contexts like New England and *how* historic churches, by God's grace, can change them. My own analysis for the Holbrook area has yielded two primary reasons, for which this book hopes to offer a remedy: that the church has not entered humbly into a dynamic conversation with postmodern culture, and that the people within postmodern culture do not perceive that the church is authentic or, therefore, remotely relevant to their lives.

In writing this book, I seek to answer this question: how can a path to church revitalization be more clearly charted by nimbly adjusting to a postmodern critique? If the reasons I notice in Holbrook, Massachusetts, for the diminishing reach of the church hold true in the wider postmodern culture, then could someone, rather unkindly, concede that the church is tone deaf and committed to obsolete forms of ministry? Is she glacial and ponderous in a world of nanosecond shifts? If so, perhaps she can become deft and nimble by a fresh consideration of her missionality, a dynamic conversation around postmodern insights, and an internal structure that allows her to make quick adjustments. In fact, the reader may become acutely aware during the course of traveling through this book that the church becoming more nimble and the church becoming revitalized are two sides of the same coin.

How to use this book

The template sketched in this book is laid out in a linear path. Real-world revitalization is probably never so neat. In fact, linear neatness in church revitalization may not be ideal, even if it were possible. But for the sake of flow-of-argument for the writer and conceptual clarity for the reader, each successive chapter builds upon the one before. I have attempted to write each chapter so it can stand on its own, and readers may prefer to jump to the chapter that most piques their interest. However, I think this would be a costly misstep for the reader actively searching for a path to revitalization because reading the other chapters will supply additional context for finding that path. Although the linear character of the template offered in this book may not exactly match the reader's real-life situation, each chapter is nonetheless an essential piece of the revitalization template.

Not only is a path to church revitalization not neatly linear, it is undoubtedly only one of many more paths. It is for this reason that I am thinking in terms of a template as I write, a template that may be significantly adapted depending on the context while still retaining the same underlying rationale. As an aid to the reader, each chapter is associated with a milestone, showing progress toward a level of church health that can anticipate the taking root and flourishing of authentic revitalization. Though wide adaptation of the template may make for many choices of paths toward revitalization, these milestones should serve to keep the paths roughly parallel.

Mile Marker One addresses ecclesiology—what missionality means in the church. With the basis of a better agreement on missionality, Mile Marker Two works toward understanding and appreciating a postmodern context. Mile Marker Three is something of a rest stop before the next big climb. It discloses why the journey toward authentic revitalization is a big shift rather than a series of smaller adjustments. Mile Marker Four sketches an experimental church evangelism model that differs from other models, particularly the attractional and incarnational models.[34] Mile Marker Five, a second rest stop after the hard climb of Four, attempts to show how historic churches are not only worthy of resuscitation, but have unique, inherent strengths to be leveraged in postmodern contexts. Mile Marker Six addresses the big shifts in the way church leadership is understood that are necessary for authentic revitalization. Mile Marker Seven argues for a strong link between clarity of governance and revitalization. Mile Marker Eight is a walk through some of the ways in which taking to heart postmodern critiques and contributions might be manifested in church ministry and function.

Probably the most fruitful way to process this book and navigate these Mile Markers is in a group, as opposed to the reader going through it alone. A group composed of both leaders and laypeople in a particular church, working through the book together, will likely have the greatest chance of effecting the revitalization they seek. For this reason, some of the chapters offer Discovery Projects at their close for use in a group context.

At the end of our journey together in this book, the reader will likely assess that most of what has been encountered is familiar and already introduced elsewhere. Most of the assertions and proposals that have found their way into this book have been part of the revitalization conversation for years. Such an assessment should come as

---

[34] Some may consider the microchurch movement to be another model on the same level. But in the context of the way the terms *attractional* and *incarnational* are used in this book as evangelistic pathways, the microchurch model would be better categorized with types of church structure.

no surprise to the reader given that this book is an abridged collation of the many elements of that conversation. The result, if God wills it, is a map that any church in any postmodern context can use to become revitalized.

At several places throughout the book, you will have the opportunity to hear a little of how revitalization might look from the perspective of a church member. Carol Roman is a member of Brookville Bible Church in Holbrook, a church that has gone the whole way through the revitalization process. Her perspectives are as follows:

> I had the privilege of sitting in on Shawn Keener's dissertation presentation, Nimble Church, on April 29, 2021, via Zoom.
>
> If I were to speak with his doctoral team, I would thank them for being such a good team for Shawn—challenging as appropriate but striving to understand not only what he is saying but who he is as a person, a Christian, a pastor. Their assessment of him was spot on; he is the "humble, hungry, smart" person they came to know and appreciate through this three-year journey. I am his friend and co-worker, actually employee, and have known Shawn for over six years. He is a delight as a friend, as a boss, and as my pastor. He is a godly leader, team builder, and visioneer, the qualities that God used in him to bring him to Brookville Bible Church.
>
> I'd like to share some of my thoughts regarding Nimble Church. Some of this is just the way I process—summarizing and elaborating on what may be obvious to another reader, and some of this just tells a bit of the story that's not in Shawn's book—how this has and is playing out here at Brookville.
>
> Nimble Church has three main points:
>
> - A church must be structurally nimble in order to make adaptive (core) changes and to be ready to pivot to the best methods to engage the culture around them.

- Postmodern thought could be called almost foreign to the modernist. Postmoderns have unique "receptors," like a unique language, that Christians need to understand and "speak" if we are to connect with them and show them Jesus. A church must be culturally nimble for this.

- Inverting the attractional model, "gather-connect-go" to "go–connect–gather" is a biblically based church philosophy that is much more apt to "speak the language" of postmoderns, partly because the church starts by going "out," making the outside world the priority. This helps a church be missionally nimble.

Mile Marker One: Church Missionality

Re-seeing

The Greek philosopher Epictetus once said, "It is impossible for a man to begin to learn that which he thinks that he knows."[35] This unfortunate state can befall anyone and not just the especially obstinate or proud. Is it possible for pastors, church leaders, or anyone steeped in years of seminary courses, a Bible study, or a church ministry to think they know what a church is and why it exists and yet be a little off the mark all the while? It could certainly happen innocently enough. The more they think they know, the less likely they are to diligently unearth their own misconceptions on a topic. They stop asking the questions a beginner would ask. Sometimes it is because they are too proud to do so, but more likely it is simply that their investigative eyes have become incurious.[36]

In attempting to solve the riddle of church decline and revitalization, the best place for one to start is by making sure to humbly reanalyze one's understanding of what a church is and why it exists—to go back to the basics and make doubly sure those basics are properly understood. When I was a teenager, growing up in the Appalachian Mountains, I cherished a book titled *Back to Basics: How to Learn and Enjoy Traditional American Skills*.[37] It was chock-full of the skills of yesteryear: lumberjacking and log home building using only hand tools and horses, weaving baskets and making moccasins, and so on. Many of these skills are lost to common knowledge today. The knowledge of a few of them might already be very near irretrievable extinction.

---

[35] Epictetus, "Book II, Chapter 17," in *The Discourses*, trans. Internet Classics Archive (n.p.: n.p., n.d.), http://classics.mit.edu//Epictetus/discourses.html.
[36] Liz Wiseman, *Rookie Smarts: Why Learning Beats Knowing in the New Game of Work* (New York: HarperCollins, 2014).
[37] Reader's Digest Association, *Back to Basics: How to Learn and Enjoy Traditional American Skills* (New York: Reader's Digest Association, 1981).

Against this threat, it was the editors' goal to preserve them in writing. Similarly, I am alarmed to notice the general loss of my finesse in something as basic as handwriting, simply because paper and pen have long since become unnecessary, and now unfamiliar, tools. Perhaps, if the church revitalizer could but sit for a while at the feet of an old timer and review once more the basics of the *what* and the *why* of a church— perhaps then, any previously unnoticed misconceptions might become known and a new ray of hope may illuminate the path to a solution.

The purpose of this mile marker is to make the case that missionality is the best discipleship, and that the duty of planning for both falls ultimately to those responsible for leading the church. Here, *missionality* stands simply for an intentional focus on fulfilling a unique commission through the power of the Holy Spirit and guided by the will of God.[38] On a route to discovering this purpose, I will ask you to reassess for yourselves the answers to two questions: What makes a church a church? and *Why* is a church? Armed with new discoveries from this reassessment, you may then see how to chart a path to church revitalization in a new light. For such a charting of this path to have real viability and clarity, effective church governance is a necessary element. Missionality and revitalization are great to talk about, but without good governance to define and organize them, they may remain little more than great talk. This mile marker concludes with a preliminary application of the purpose— that missionality is the best discipleship, and that the duty of planning for both falls ultimately to those responsible for leading the church.

---

[38] See the section on definitions of key terms in the introductory chapter, Start Here.

What makes a church a church?

Answering this basic question afresh is an indispensable starting point in charting a revitalization pathway. Perhaps within a particular family of churches, such as the Baptist Churches of New England, the answer is fairly uniform. There the reply may be something close to the official version: ". . . a church is an autonomous local congregation of baptized believers, associated by covenant in the faith and fellowship of the gospel; observing the two ordinances of Christ, governed by His laws, exercising the gifts ..."[39] In practice, and also ecumenically, the reply might vary widely even when discussants appeal to Scripture for support.[40] Is it where the Word is preached and the sacraments are administered? Is it something more informally understood, such as a gathering of at least fifty people and something of a group structure? Often, whether intentionally or subconsciously, a church building and property are incorporated into the reply. Perhaps a direct reply from Scripture would be as radically minimalistic as "where two or three come together in my name, there am I with them."[41]

Many would rely on the list of adjectives in Acts 2 to define what makes a church a church.[42] This kind of definition carries a risk—by relying on examples of early church activity for a definition, the activity might be

---

[39] *"The Baptist Faith and Message 2000,"* https://www.namb.net/wp-content/uploads/2020/06/Baptist-Faith-and-Message.pdf.

[40] One beautiful variation is that of the Salvation Army, which does not observe the sacraments in the typical sense but says metaphorically, in the case of communion, "My life must be Christ's broken bread, my love his outpoured wine ... my all is in the Master's hands for him to bless and break." Ben Clapton, "A Salvationist Perspective on the Sacraments," *Ben Clapton* (blog), May 3, 2012, https://benclapton.id.au/2012/05/03/a-salvationist-perspective-on-the-sacraments/.

[41] Mat 18.20.

[42] Act 2.40–47.

confused for the essence of what makes a church a church. For example, it is commonly argued that preaching is a singularly important component of what makes a church a church.[43] But this can quickly be seen to cause problems. What if two or three meet underground in China and merely discuss the Word devotionally, or only pray? Is that then not a church? Or a similar difficulty could likewise arise in the microchurch movement.[44] In some cases, the inquirer might hear a reply based on emotions. One might say, "After COVID, our church doesn't feel like a church anymore because there are only twenty people on Sunday." Or another might say, "We liked that church when there were only two hundred people, but now that there are five thousand, it just doesn't feel like a church should." So if size, structure, activity, and creedal definitions are imprecise, where can a more helpful definition be found?

Without delving into a detailed analysis, we can say that the word translated as *church* in the New Testament means, basically, a gathering of people.[45] The effort by some to make the word a sum of its parts, and in this way arrive at a definition of *called out ones*, might be considered a linguistic fallacy.[46] So a church is a gathering of people who are the Body of Christ.[47] Christ is her Head, and she is his Body.[48] This Body is a church whether gathered physically in one

---

[43] E.g., Mark Dever, *Nine Marks of a Healthy Church*, 4th ed. (Wheaton, IL: Crossway, 2021); Jack Daniel, *Patient Catalyst: Leading Church Revitalization* (South Easton, MA: Overseed, 2018).

[44] For a standard explanation of microchurches, see Neil Cole, *Church 3.0: Upgrades for the Future of the Church* (San Francisco: Jossey-Bass, 2010).

[45] *New International Dictionary of New Testament Theology*, ed. Colin Brown (Grand Rapids, MI: Zondervan, 1986), s.vv. "Church, Synagogue."

[46] D. A. Carson, *Exegetical Fallacies*, 2nd ed. (Grand Rapids, MI: Baker, 1996); see also Moises Silva, *Biblical Words and Their Meaning: An Introduction to Lexical Semantics*, rev. ed. (Grand Rapids, MI: Zondervan, 1995); James Barr, *The Semantics of Biblical Language* (Eugene, OR: Wipf and Stock, 2004).

[47] Eph 1.22–23.

[48] Eph 5.21–33, Col 1.18.

place or united by nothing but the one Spirit.[49] This all has two key consequences: the church is a person, not a thing, and the church has a purpose greater than herself.[50]

Since the church is a person, all other things normally associated with what makes a church a church are, at best, merely helpful aids. This list is long, and includes things such as buildings, staff, giving, attendance, membership, corporate worship on Sundays, and so forth. Since the church has a purpose greater than herself, it may be seen that, in addition to caring for herself such that she allows herself to be beautifully prepared as a Bride, she is preoccupied with fulfilling the purpose she has been given.[51] Since the church is a person and has a purpose greater than herself, the local autonomous church should not think of her autonomy as something that separates her from every other variation of the Body, no matter how near or far, and no matter how dissimilar.[52]

Why is a church?

Scripture is run through with themes that apply color and definition to the purpose given to the church by her Head.[53] Jesus's parting words in Matthew 28.18–20 are commonly accepted as the clearest statement of this

---

[49] Eph 4.4–6.

[50] Cf. Travis Collins, "What Is a Church?" in *From the Steeple to the Street: Innovating Mission and Ministry Through Fresh Expressions of Church* (Franklin, TN: Seedbed, 2016).

[51] Rev 21.2; Pro 31.10–31.

[52] Cf. Andrew Walls, "The Ephesians Moment in Worldwide Worship: A Meditation on Revelation 21 and Ephesians 2," in *Christian Worship Worldwide: Expanding Horizons, Deepening Practices*, ed. Charles E. Farhadian (Grand Rapids, MI: Eerdmans, 2007).

[53] Cf. Paul S. Minear, *Images of the Church in the New Testament* (Louisville, KY: Westminster John Knox, 2004).

purpose.[54] In our English translations of these verses, the word *go* forms a basis for the verbs that follow—making disciples, baptizing, teaching, and obeying.[55] For more than two hundred years, this scriptural section has been known as the Great Commission, yet another, complementary passage may be even more illuminating to some. Peter paints a picture of all humanity awaiting a second, and final, planetary catastrophe.[56] During this pregnant moment of time, as the heart of God waits with awesome patience for all people to come to him,[57] the purpose of the church is stated with succinct clarity: "Since everything will be destroyed in this way, what kind of people ought you to be? You ought to live holy and godly lives as you look forward to the day of God and speed its coming."[58]

In the 2017 adventure-comedy film *Jumanji: Welcome to the Jungle*, four real-life teenagers are magically transported to a parallel universe inside a board game called Jumanji. They are desperate to return to who they were meant to be before they were trapped in the game. Their only way out is to rescue others also trapped in the game so they can all

---

[54] As mentioned earlier, Act 2.42–47 may be best situated in the category of description of the church rather than the end goal or assigned mission of the church. As such it might better be lumped into the conduct passages and a supporting role to the mission as developed below.

[55] These verbs are all participles in the Greek, except for "making" (making disciples), which is the ultimate emphasis of Jesus's commission here. However, for contextual reasons both in Mat 28 and in the several parallel passages (Luk 24.45–49; Jhn 20.21; Act 1.8; cf. Mat 4.19; 10.16–20; 13.38; 24.14), *go* carries some force borrowed from the main "making disciples" verb. Further, as developed below, the discipleship process Jesus intended and modeled seems to emphasize going and doing more than staying and studying. Cf. D. A. Carson, "Matthew," in *Matthew & Mark*, vol. 9 of *The Expositor's Bible Commentary*, rev. ed., ed. Tremper Longman III and David E. Garland (Grand Rapids, MI: Zondervan, 2010), 666.

[56] The first, as Peter develops in his argument, was the Great Flood. Cf. 2Pe 3.5–7.

[57] 2Pe 3.8–9.

[58] 2Pe 3.11–12.

return to their true reality together, to their outside-the-game identity.

Perhaps this could be a helpful analogy for the present age. The church is waiting patiently in a universe parallel to her heavenly home, living in an already-but-not-yet realization of oneness with God and looking forward to the redemption of all God's creation.[59] Jesus left his church in safekeeping, certainly, with his Spirit, but this only magnifies the yearning of both church and God for the day when "They will see his face and his name will be on their foreheads."[60] She, along with all of creation, longs to be restored, in full, to her Groom.[61]

Sticking with the Jumanji analogy for a moment, Jesus provided the path out of this parallel universe through his ministry, death, resurrection, and life prior to delivering his last words in Matthew 28. Since that time, the church has been waiting in a forward-looking posture. She knows her true reality is the heavenly scene of Revelation 19–22,[62] yet endures the faux reality of the Jumanji game, also through faith. What is the singular reason why Jesus, as a Bridegroom, has not yet brought his beloved Bride out of this faux reality and to himself? Peter states with succinct clarity, "The Lord is not slow ... He is patient with you, not wanting anyone to perish, but everyone to come to repentance. Since everything will be destroyed in this way, what kind of people ought you to be? You ought to live holy and godly lives as you look forward to the day of God and speed its coming."[63]

There are two parts to Peter's statement: "to live holy and godly lives" and "as you look forward to the day of God

---

[59] Col 3.1–4.
[60] Rev 22.4.
[61] Rom 8.19–25.
[62] Php 3.20–21.
[63] 2Pe 3.9–12.

and speed its coming." The reason Peter's statement of the purpose of the church may serve to illuminate the Great Commission of Jesus for some hearers is because it reinforces the driving emphasis Jesus intended, that of an outward rather than inward purpose and bent of the church. In Matthew 28, the stratagems for discipleship traditionally conceived by the church and written about copiously are important, but they are conspicuously preceded by the verb *go*.

Peter's "live holy and godly lives," crucial to becoming like Jesus, is not a good enough reason for the Bridegroom to remain patient. It is insufficient but not unimportant. For the church is his betrothed after all, and he is radiating and exhibiting his love and healing ever more brightly as she is being prepared for her wedding day. The words "live holy and godly lives" only embody a sufficient enough reason to delay that wedding day if they are combined with and in support of the greater-than-herself piece. What *is* sufficient for Peter is that all people, by God's own concealed accounting, have not yet been drawn to Jesus. The speeding of the coming of the day of God by bringing all people to himself is the *go* of Jesus's final words in Matthew 28. The "making disciples" and the "live holy and godly lives" follow after the "go" and the "speed its coming"—logically, chronologically, and geographically. Both parts of Peter's statement are crucial, but the latter part is the primary driver.

To better see this picture, it may be helpful to paraphrase 2 Peter 3 by using the elaborate imagery of Hebrews 6.19–20: Jesus, the high priest, goes behind the curtain into the Holy of Holies to mediate for all who believe. Meanwhile, the heart of God, who dwells between the cherubim in the Holy of Holies, yearns to draw all his children to him, finally face to face. He is poised to do so at any moment because of his heart as a Father. But Jesus, the high priest, who does not know the day or the hour when this will occur,[64] pleads with God each day, in his role as the mediator between God and the world.[65] He enters the Holy of Holies that is in heaven, saying, "We yearn for all things to be made new, Father. Just please not yet. Please not yet. There are still so many who are estranged from us."[66] As Jesus emerges from the tabernacle, he says to all his people who are expectantly waiting outside, "I have bought us a little more time. Now go. Hurry! Bring them in!"[67]

How are the "go" of Jesus's last words and the "speed its coming" of Peter's statement accomplished? Of course, they both state the answer: by the power of the Spirit of God manifested through baptized disciples-in-the-making living holy and godly lives. It is accomplished through a biblically astute, thoroughly authentic, and passionately engaged church of Jesus. These are churches that show off a vibrant, generous, and selfless faith capable of cutting through cultural bias, defensiveness, and apathy. They cut through it by mirroring Jesus as he really is, refreshingly distinct from the picture sponsored by institutional religion and the church behaving badly. These are churches that fulfill the promise made to Abraham, the father of all who believe, that the generous and creative God would bless the entire world through him.[68] This is what Jesus refers to when he says, "And surely I will be with you, even to the end of the age" and what Peter refers to when he says, "as you look forward to [the day of God]."

Someone might interject here that discipleship, or Peter's "live holy and godly lives," ought nevertheless to be

---

[64] Mrk 13.32.

[65] 1Ti 2.3–6; cf. Heb 10.12–13.

[66] A paraphrase of 2Pe 3.8–9.

[67] A paraphrase of 2Pe 3.11–12; cf. Jhn 9.4.

[68] Gen 12.1–3; 18.17–18; Rom 4.16–17.

the greater emphasis of the church by some other line of argument. Or someone might object on the grounds that discipleship must be in place prior to evangelism, thinking perhaps that the maturity or Christian education that comes through discipleship must first be in place before a successful evangelistic effort can be mounted. But could this be a false dichotomy, this distinction that is drawn between discipleship and evangelism? Might these two merge to form a single entity rather than two separate things? Several lines of reasoning argue that this is in fact the case, and if it were so, it would handily dissolve the tension in church ministry and strategy that arises from this supposed distinction.

It seems that discipleship is usually thought of in terms of passive learning. Many in my own church tradition presuppose that it entails multiple courses of study, the memorization of key scriptures, the learning of prayers and the other spiritual disciplines, and the proving of oneself in terms of morality and character over time. Being mentored by someone more spiritually mature and honing the skills of sharing the gospel with others are other common components. In some cases, a solid grasp of systematic theology might be considered a requirement of graduation from a discipleship plan. All of these are passive.[69] This list is drawn up with an assumption that discipleship can be categorized separately from evangelism and that it is something, in theory at least, that can be finished first. It imagines that the privilege of evangelism and the certification to move on to evangelism is contingent upon prior attainment of some level of discipleship. But this does

---

[69] I was a realtor for a short stint, and one of the things that stood out to me was the difference between passive and active promotion. Passive was anything easy for an introvert like me, such as mailers, door hangers, and ads. Active was knocking on doors, mingling, and shaping the direction of personal conversations.

not match up very well with the Originator of our word *discipleship*.

Jesus's discipleship of the Twelve was not passive or prior. It was active, and commingled with evangelism.[70] Jesus's disciples were always on the move, learning in real time. Frequently, this learning was at a need-to-know tempo—a patient, hands-on, learning-on-the-job effort. His sending out of the disciples, in Matthew 10, could be an argument for discipleship prior and passive to evangelism, but it may be better to view it as a more advanced level of the active, commingled discipleship through which Jesus had been shepherding his disciples all along.

The Twelve were not the only ones being shepherded through this commingled discipleship ... the crowds were, too. Just like the Twelve, the crowds were being brought into discipleship long before they ever crossed some invisible line of faith. Their discipleship did not begin only after the point of saving faith. As Jesus's discipleship model was roving throughout the countryside and villages, those in the crowds, both pre-faith and never-faith, were also on a learn-as-you-go track.[71] Throughout his ministry, and as he chose his disciples, Jesus was heralding, "Repent, for the kingdom of heaven is near!"[72] His kingdom was advancing with him, going to where the lost and dying and hurting were to be found, searching out the hungry and the harassed and

---

[70] As Mile Marker Two relates, this is precisely what postmodern culture is asking the church to understand. Speaking about Gen Z, Allen Jackson observed, "To serve is to be engaged. Sometimes it's easier to act your way into believing than it is to believe your way into acting." Maina Mwaura, moderator, "What Should Pastors Know About Generation Z? Five Experts Discuss the Ways This Emerging Demographic Is Helping Them Rethink Preaching, Parenting, and Service," *CT Pastors Special Issue: The Integrated Pastor. Christianity Today* Spring (2019): 26. This quote from Allen Jackson, senior pastor at Dunwoody Baptist Church in Atlanta.
[71] Cf. Jhn 6.66.
[72] Mat 4.17.

scattered sheep. His kingdom was not headquartered anywhere except in his person, and wherever the need was in his realm, there his throne moved. Since the church, too, is a manifestation of the Kingdom of God, a realignment of her ideas about discipleship with Jesus's ideas might be in order.[73]

If discipleship is commingled with evangelism to form a continuum instead of two separate things, it might look like a version of the Engel scale.[74] The Engel scale is artificially linear and is too cleanly ordered to match real life, yet it can give a helpful visual representation of a discipleship and an evangelism that are virtually indistinguishable from one another. Adding Hirsch's "missional scale" to the Engel scale may make better sense of both, as well.[75] If –10 on the Engel scale is the farthest possible point from knowing God and 0 is when salvific faith enters, then +10 could be full, on-display missionality. Typically, +10 is thought of in terms of ultimate sanctification just before glorification, like some sort of theoretically attainable graduation from discipleship to evangelism. But if it is instead thought of in terms of full, on-display missionality, then it is the ultimate form of the blending of on-the-job discipleship with evangelism that has

---

[73] Cf. Nicholas Perrin, *The Kingdom of God: A Biblical Theology* (Grand Rapids, MI: Zondervan, 2019). A fuller discussion of any distinction between the church and the Kingdom of God/Kingdom of Heaven is outside the scope of this book. Perhaps most readers would grant that, at the very least, there is a close link between the mission and presence of the church and that of the Kingdom.

[74] Cf. "What Is the Engel Scale?" *Evangelical Alliance,* https://www.eauk.org/what-is-the-engel-scale.

[75] Alan Hirsch, *The Forgotten Ways: Reactivating Apostolic Movements,* 2nd ed. (Grand Rapids, MI: Brazos, 2016), 57. Hirsch suggests a scale of significant cultural barriers to the gospel ranging from m4 to m0, with m0 being "those with some concept of Christianity" and m4 being those "highly resistant to the gospel."

actually been at play from somewhere well below 0.[76] Now, a definition of discipleship might take the form of following or wayfaring with Jesus with the hope of being like him and a purpose greater-than-self of bringing as many others to him as possible.[77]

Someone might estimate that this talk of a missional, greater-than-self purpose for the church reduces her to a utilitarian implement in the great goal of God. This is a natural conclusion from the assertion above that the beautification of the Bride, while a worthy goal in itself, is in a supportive role to the primary task, that of looking forward to the day of God and speeding its coming. Yet that this is true flows from Jesus's own discipleship model. Jesus's disciples weren't meeting several times each week to become more holy and godly and in love with Jesus. They were receiving constant point-of-need mentoring beside Jesus as they carried out what Jesus said was the Father's business on a daily basis. They were allowing themselves to be continually made ready for what Jesus had for each of them to do. In the case of the church, the supportive task (the beautification of the Bride) and the primary task (speeding its coming) converge into one magnificent "Mission Accomplished" at the wedding of the Lamb. John even

---

[76] Andrew brought Peter before salvific faith, and Philip likewise Nathaniel. Jhn 1.41–51. I would argue that there is another significant biblical theme that supports what I am saying here, one that relative to my writing here might better be left as a discussion for another day. It is this: if salvation is not a once-and-done momentary event but is better understood in terms of "us who are being saved," as in 1Co 1.18, then it may be easier to see that discipleship and evangelism are not two but one. This, of course, has the potential to veer into a hot debate over the binary-ness of Calvinism vs. Arminianism, which is why I would like to sidestep it here.

[77] Leonard Sweet argues for using the "transfiguration" in discipleship instead of transformation. Leonard Sweet, *Rings of Fire: Walking in Faith Through a Volcanic Future* (Colorado Springs, CO: NavPress, 2019); cf. Leonard Sweet and Frank Viola, *Jesus: A Theography* (Nashville: Thomas Nelson, 2012), 131ff.

combines the two into a single thought in describing that event: "For the wedding of the Lamb has come, and his bride has made herself ready. Fine linen, bright and clean, was given her to wear." (Fine linen stands for the righteous acts of the saints.)[78]

Jesus says that the goal of vineyards is fruit.[79] A passive discipleship thinks this fruit is the fruit of the Spirit. An active discipleship realizes that it is the grapes, the harvest, of which the health of the branches is in service. Vibrant branches and grapes are both important, but the grapes are easily the most important. Jesus is no-nonsense about this. He who "is love" can be a hard master.[80] Besides, holy and godly lives are not first a function of discipleship but of the work of Christ, as is readily apparent in John 15. Or stated another way, the Galatians 5 fruit of the Spirit is fruit the Spirit produces in us and not so much a product of us working really hard to be good disciples. Discipleship is an identity, not an attainment. It is bound up in a person, the person of Jesus, as Paul declares, "He has brought you into his own presence, and you are holy and blameless as you stand before him without a single fault."[81]

Someone might object that discipleship commingled with evangelism is dangerous, that it lends itself to poor quality control. If commingled discipleship is an on-the-way thing, and not a prior thing, then it is always in an incomplete state and somewhere on a continuum from extremely incomplete to partially incomplete. As a result, disciples are unleashed for evangelism all along the continuum, even before such things as a simple grasp of

---

[78] Rev 19.7–8.
[79] Jhn 15.1–8.
[80] 1Jn 4.16; Mat 25.14–30.
[81] Col 1.22. *Holy Bible*, New Living Translation, 2nd ed. (Wheaton, IL: Tyndale, 2015).

doctrine can set in. It might seem much safer to fall back to a passive and prior discipleship because, in theory, it protects against false understandings of doctrine before the disciples are released to spread the gospel contagion. In fact, this retreat to a guaranteed purism is itself the bigger danger. It keeps disciples in a state of paralysis, teaching them that they will only be qualified to share their faith after they have learned more. And that is a goal for which the goalposts are forever moving away like a mirage in a desert.[82]

This consequence plays havoc not only with commingled discipleship within a local church—it also does the same on a grander scale. The more anxious a local church is to guarantee no possibility of doctrinal error among her ranks, the more isolated and out of fellowship with other churches she will become. As churches distinguish themselves with too much care from one another, the greater, universal-church–wide discipleship/evangelism continuum becomes effectively torpedoed. A watching postchristian world does not have the capacity to appreciate the individualized attempts at doctrinal fidelity. It sees only a church with division and without love, or with a love too impotent to respectfully bridge doctrinal distinction.

The greater-than-self purpose for which Christ commissioned the church is a discipleship that serves

---

[82] Will Mancini cites a revealing list from Jeff Johnson on this point: "Missional discerns and discovers; maintenance discusses and debates. Missional talks and listens to the Lord; maintenance talks and listens to one another. Missional believes the Lord knows what to do; maintenance believes the Lord needs to be told what to do. Missional believes the Lord needs nothing to do something; maintenance believes there is not enough money. Missional believes the Lord is present; maintenance believes the location is bad. Missional believes there is time for the Lord to do something new; maintenance believes the day is past and it is too late. Missional focuses on what we have; maintenance focuses on what we lack." Will Mancini and Cory Hartman, *Future Church: Seven Laws of Real Church Growth* (Grand Rapids, MI: Baker, 2020), 236.

evangelism. This is attested throughout the Bible. Even before the church existed, the purpose of the people of God was clear. The family of Abraham, the theocracy of early Israel, and then, later, the established kingdom, were all chosen and shepherded specifically to carry on the mission of God in the world.[83] They were tasked with adherence to the revealed law of God not primarily for the living of blameless lives, at least not as an end in itself, but so that through their obedience and faith God's blessings might pour out over his people from heaven's floodgates.[84] And from such blessing and set-apart obedience the nations of the world might be drawn to Israel's God. This was the ultimate purpose of Mount Sinai.[85] This was the purpose of God in circumscribing the descendants of Abraham as his chosen ones.[86] They were chosen to draw all people back to him. Israel was to make the near and far-flung people of the world jealous for him whose very name is Jealous.[87]

The jealousy God intended to spawn in the people of the world from his chosen people being holy was not a jealousy for their wealth and good fortune and blessing, and not a jealousy for their rigid and righteous obedience to Mosaic Law. The harvest he wanted was a consuming jealousy from the people of the world for a reconciled relationship with their heavenly Father, whose face and memory they had all forgotten since the days of Cain. God's chosen people were chosen so that they could be a beacon to the nations, a voice to call them home. The chosen people of

---

[83] Christopher J. H. Wright, *The Mission of God: Unlocking the Bible's Grand Narrative* (Downers Grove, IL: InterVarsity, 2018).

[84] Zec 8.20–23; Jhn 5.39–40; Gal 3.8. The point here is not to dive into a dispensational-covenantal debate over distinctions between Israel and the Church, but to identify a missional *modus operandi* of God throughout the redemptive story.

[85] Heb 2.2.

[86] Ezk 16.1–14; Deu 7.7–9.

[87] Exo 34.14.

God were to entice the world to the Lamb of God through a jealousy of their blessing. Of course, this blessing is most often one that is multiple levels higher than mere financial security, physical happiness, or a tranquil life. The blessing that most powerfully draws the world to Jesus is the peace that transcends all common sense in the midst of the fiercest brokenness, the giddy terror of walking by faith, and the obvious inner glow of Stephen that bellows, "He is my very great reward!"[88] It is a blessing content with the Lord's countenance lifted upon his child in peace and graciousness.[89]

Traditionally in the church, when one has sought instructions for how to live holy and godly lives, the conduct sections of the epistles have provided a trove of specifics. Much like the pharisaical use of Mosaic Law, these conduct passages are often used to construct a culture of legalism. Yet they are actually intended as an application of the theological principles and arguments of the first part of their respective epistles, and tailored to a particular cultural context, rather than conduct passages in isolation. What is the general import of these foregoing theological principles and arguments? It is none other than the glory and exaltedness of God and his gift through Jesus of a restored relationship with him. It is a verbal painting of the flourishing of restored human life in Christ. The chosen people of Israel were called to obedience and lives of faith not for the purpose of any distinction of personal holiness but for the purpose of inexorably drawing the whole world to God. Likewise, the Bride of Jesus is called to proper conduct not because of some quintessential perfectness of those particular rules of conduct but for the purpose of endearing Jesus to a culture and people estranged from God.

---

[88] Act 6.15; Psa 73.26.
[89] Num 6.24–26.

As verification of this truth, the conduct passages in the New Testament always include a "so-what" clause.[90] Similarly, Peter's "holy and godly lives" is no end in itself, but rather is in service of Peter's "speed its coming." Becoming wholly like Jesus is conceptually synonymous with the driving concern of God—that all people be reconciled to himself and brought from death to lush, flourishing new life. Anything the church does to nurture "holy and godly lives" finds its highest expression in exemplifying Jesus to the current culture so that its people might turn to him. His children are endeared to him when he sees them living respectfully and inoffensively in light of what contemporary culture considers socially acceptable. They are endeared to him when he sees in his children no offensiveness other than the foolishness of the cross. Everywhere the church goes, every day and in every way, her actions reflect directly on the flag of Jesus the church unknowingly bears and carries for all to see, and her actions either sully it or speed its urgent approach. The people of God in any age reassure the watching world of the legitimacy of Jesus's kingship by the through-and-through authenticity of their honor and integrity.[91]

As the salt of the earth, the church of Jesus makes the delay in the Jumanji parallel universe taste better, until that day when he who is seated on the throne says, "It is done. I am making everything new."[92] This is not the pollyannaish wishing of some extreme form of postmillennialism. This is living fully in the image of God and in his creative nature. This is healing and redeeming our world while we are still in it to make it a better place, to be that blessing of Abraham upon all the peoples of the earth in the near term and to be a

---

[90] E.g., Tit 2.8, 5, 10; 1Pe 3.1, 16. The same rationale accompanies many Old Testament conduct prescriptions.
[91] 1Pe 3.15–16.
[92] Mat 5.13–15; Rev 21.5.

visible part of the already-but-not-yet making of all things new. While planning out his Sermon on the Mount in the made-for-app series *The Chosen,* Jesus says that salt

> Preserves meat from corruption, it slows its decay. I want my followers to be a people who hold back the evil of the world. Salt also enhances the flavor of things. I want my followers to renew the world and to be part of his redemption. Salt can also be mixed with honey and rubbed on the skin for maladies. I want my people to participate in the healing of the world, not its destruction.[93]

The church of Jesus is a healing balm to her cultural context. Perhaps this is why "the salt of the earth" has come in popular usage to mean people with basic, genuine goodness. The church of Jesus Christ goes about her already-but-not-yet daily life doing the ordinary work of the Creator, tending the garden, and creating art and things and beauty just like him whose image they bear.[94]

Andrew Walls lectured extensively on a concept something like this.[95] Just like individual people, he says, cultures in time and space have their origin in Genesis and out of the creative mind of God. Just like people, cultures are corrupted by sin but still retain their original God-ness to some degree. Then in Isaiah 60,[96] and then in Ephesians 3–4 and Revelation 21–22, just like people, cultures and churches

---

[93] Dallas Jenkins, director, *The Chosen,* season 2, episode 8 (Provo, UT: Loaves and Fishes Productions, Angel Studios, 2017).
[94] Andy Crouch, *Culture Making: Recovering Our Creative Calling* (Downers Grove, IL: InterVarsity, 2013); Charles E. Farhadian, ed., *Christian Worship Worldwide: Expanding Horizons, Deepening Practices* (Grand Rapids, MI: Eerdmans, 2007).
[95] Andrew Walls, *The Missionary Movement in Christian History: Studies in the Transmission of Faith* (Maryknoll, NY: Orbis, 1996).
[96] See Crouch.

are seen being built into a beautiful temple of heaven.[97] Each one is a beautiful, very unique brick in the hand of God as he constructs this temple—all things made new, all things made whole, all finally as it should be. As it is in heaven already, the on-task Bride of Christ will work to preserve and redeem culture here on earth in anticipation of the day of God and the true temple that is in heaven.[98]

God so dearly loves his children and brings them into his family, his kingdom, and his church, not to get something out of them but because they are precious in his sight in their own right. But when this truth takes preeminence over the greater-than-self purpose for the church of "not wanting anyone to perish, but everyone to come to repentance" and speeding the day of his coming, it breaks God's heart and smacks of self-concern to an onlooking postchristian world. As in other cases, the perspective of a postchristian world aligns with God's on that one.

One church vividly illustrated the outward priority of church purpose by turning its yearly budget-writing process into a giant, magnetic four-foot by six-foot jigsaw puzzle. The picture on the puzzle was not of a church building but of a montage of local people at various places in town. When church givers claimed one or more puzzle pieces and put them on their refrigerator at home, they were daily reminded that their tithing was not individualistic but communal, that it was not primarily for building and staff

---

[97] Of course, there is no temple in heaven (Rev 21.22). What Walls seems to be picturing here is that heaven is the temple, as a parallel to the Garden of Eden, since where God and his throne are, there his temple is. Cf. 1Pe 2.5.
[98] Heb 9.

but for local engagement, and that this greater purpose was the driver in their own discipleship.[99]

How can the church be nimble?

The discipleship/evangelism continuum reveals the preeminent purpose of the church to be "not wanting anyone to perish" and speeding the day of God's coming. When the church is singularly preoccupied with this purpose, she is running at full steam and full strength. All her systems become healthier, and she becomes more nimble. She becomes lithely adept at adjusting her proclamation of the gospel to a changing culture around her without compromising that gospel. This is the essence of this book. This is church revitalization in a nutshell. Everything else is rationale or how-to.

The revitalization that comes from missional preoccupation can be purchased by any church even though it is unimaginably expensive. Like the gospel, a pearl of great cost, its price is everything the purchaser has and everything the purchaser holds dear. This is why the majority of churches that come to the point of no return in their trajectory choose to simply do nothing—the cost of revitalization seems simply too high. Of course, the cost of doing nothing is infinitely higher, but that cost does not seem as real to them at the time.[100] Mile Marker Three expands on this topic.

A nimble church deftly matches her gospel proclamation to the changing way the culture around her is

---

[99] This was not a pledge drive. No explicit commitment was made by a tither in taking puzzle pieces. Yet doing so benefitted the budget-writing process by giving the tither more to go on than simply estimating an overall budget increase of, say, 3%.

[100] Cf. Rev 2.4–5.

capable of receiving it. This is the pivotal issue in church revitalization. It requires that the church become intentionally focused on missionality, that she know her culture thoroughly, and that she become organized in a way that allows her to be nimble. These statements summarize the content of this book and are the focus of Mile Marker Two and Mile Marker Seven. Buying into a discipleship that is commingled with evangelism on a continuum calls for deep changes in church ministry and the rationale behind it. This is the focus of Mile Markers Four, Six, and Eight. For example, when the church realizes that discipleship happens primarily outside the church rather than within it, preaching loses its outsized role in discipleship, and in evangelism.

Someone may interrupt at this point and say, "All we really need is church revival and Holy Spirit fire." This is an excellent interjection and cannot be discounted. But the kind of missionality discussed above *is* a form of spiritual revival. It takes Holy Spirit fire to be willingly awakened to a realignment of discipleship and evangelism with Jesus's own model. The burden of "not wanting anyone to perish, but everyone to come to repentance" and speeding his coming is itself the initiator of spiritual revival. There is nothing quite like a common white-hot mission to instantly solve infighting. Desperate times make for strange bedfellows. This drove Churchill to embrace Stalin during World War II with the ancient adage, "The enemy of my enemy is my friend."[101] When the church is preoccupied with mission, thereby, in effect, united against a common enemy, everything other than that mission suddenly looks

---

[101] Allen Packwood, "Sir Winston Churchill: A Biography," Churchill College Cambridge, https://www.chu.cam.ac.uk/archives/collections/churchill-papers/churchill-biography/.

inconsequential. This is why church revitalization is usually generated out of a season of corporate confession.[102]

Practically speaking, in the real world of pastoring and church leadership, and the coming together as an entire church to define missionality for the local church, something more than spiritual revival and a change of heart is usually necessary. If a renewed vision to reach the lost and dying in the surrounding community is to result in tangible change, the way the local church governs herself and comes to collective decisions in order to allow for paradigmatic change can make all the difference. It may even be, for some readers, that the earlier discussion of what makes a church a church overlaps with how church leadership structure is defined. For many, the discussion earlier of what makes a church a church lacked an important piece—any talk of a New Testament prescription for church leadership and hierarchy. Whether or not the structure of church leadership helps to define what a church is for the reader, corporate missionality, and revitalization, is rather hopeless without it. Whole-church missionality requires planning, coordinating, visioneering, and culture setting, and these are usually corralled and harnessed ultimately through a leadership structure. Missionality is the best discipleship, and it is mapped uniquely through church leadership.

Excursus

Beginning the church leadership discussion

Leadership structure varies widely among the churches of New England, despite a common heritage. The bulk of New England church polities derive in one way or

---

[102] Cf. Jim van Yperen, *Making Peace: A Guide to Overcoming Church Conflict* (Chicago: Moody, 2002).

another from the Puritan settlers. Escaping persecution in the Old World, they hoped to establish a church that would be "a city upon a hill," acting as a reforming agent for the church they loved on the other side of the pond but from which they were expelled.[103] Lacking authority for their church in the New World, the authority they would have needed to ordain pastors and establish leadership, they contrived ways to achieve the same ends on their own. This led to the birth of congregationalism, autonomous-minded local churches, Baptists, and the beautifully broad array of variations seen in New England today.[104]

My background is in Baptist, nondenominational, and Bible churches. In these, the local church is often governed by a group of elders, numbering three or greater, with five to seven often considered an ideal number. These elders are to be people of God who thoroughly qualify for the role according to the descriptions of 1 Timothy 3 and Titus 1. They are to be those others would seek for sage godly advice and for prayer. They are to handle matters of church discipline according to Matthew 18 and personally oversee each ministry and area of the church, often assigning specific sections among themselves. The pastor is one of these elders, and typically has equal say with the other elders, plus a little extra clout, because of his designation in the group of elders as a "first among equals." Sometimes the pastor is considered the trainer or leader of the elders and has the final say. Two common dangers are present in this setup. The group of elders might be reduced to little more than rubber stamping

---

[103] "John Winthrop's 'City upon a Hill,' 1630," https://www.gilderlehrman.org/sites/default/files/inline-pdfs/Winthrop%27s%20City%20upon%20a%20Hill.pdf.

[104] This is intentionally simplistic due to the line of argument here. There were other factors as well, such as an attempt at theological restorationism. Cf. Francis J. Bremer, *The Puritan Experiment: New England Society from Bradford to Edwards* (Lebanon, NH: University Press of New England, 1995).

the pastor's decisions, opinions, agendas, and actions. Or the pastor and staff might be heavily micromanaged by the body of elders in any matter related to the church.

From the viewpoint of churches in my tradition, the only other class of church officer prescribed by the New Testament is that of deacon.[105] There is a significant lack of agreement about the biblical intent of this role. Sometimes the role becomes effectively interchangeable with the elder role.[106] A general consensus on the deacon role is that it is a worker or a doer, someone who executes the ministries of the church under the direction of the elders. In many cases, the board of deacons functions separately from the board of elders, reports directly to it, and is tasked chiefly with property maintenance and facility improvement. In fewer cases, the domain of deacons extends to the financial guidance of the church.[107] Ironically, despite the tone of Acts 6, the deacon board is usually not considered instrumental in

---

[105] In these types of autonomous churches, the other roles in the five-fold gospel and gifting lists (e.g., apostles) are conceptually included under the categories of elder and deacon. For an excellent discussion of the overlap between roles and spiritual gifts; cf. Linda L. Belleville, Craig L. Blomberg, Craig S. Keener, and Thomas R. Schreiner, *Two Views on Women in Ministry*, rev. ed. (Grand Rapids, MI: Zondervan, 2005).

[106] In one church I served, the elder board consisted of both elders and deacons. In one meeting, (with a board of nine), seven could not answer definitively when asked whether they were an elder or a deacon.

[107] At this point, there is often further confusion or conflation between a board of deacons and an extra biblical board of trustees. For example, Bremer can say that the role of deacon as treasurer goes back to the Cambridge Platform of Puritan standardization in 1648. He quotes Kenneth Lockridge, who stated "The one lay office that was generally maintained was that of the deacon. It was the deacon's task as financial officer to receive the offerings of the faithful, to maintain the treasury of the church, and to provide for the disbursement of funds to the ministers and to the needy of the parish." Quoting Kenneth Lockridge, *A New England Town: The First Hundred Years: Dedham, Massachusetts, 1636–1736 (Norton Essays in American History)* (New York: W. W. Norton, 1985); Francis J. Bremer, *The Puritan Experiment: New England Society from Bradford to Edwards* (Lebanon, NH: University Press of New England, 1995).

either the shepherding of care or the outreach of ministries of the church. And despite the fact that the deacon descriptions come directly from the same passages that describe elders, a discussion about the role of deacon being open to both genders is rarely as much of a third rail as the same discussion about the role of elder.[108]

What the New Testament says about church polity

A straightforward listing of New Testament prescriptions for church polity underscores, however, that the above is only one of many biblically acceptable church polities. Someone may claim that the tradition outlined above is backed by a scriptural mandate. But this would be like guessing the numbers in a sudoku puzzle rather than proving them out.[109] The pastor–elder–deacon setup relayed above is not a bad one, and it tends to align well with church leadership as exhibited in the New Testament. But to claim that Scripture could support no other polity arrangement is to make Scripture say something it does not say. After further consideration, the reader may discover that there is no single governance structure required of the New Testament churches—and that there is therefore also no single structure required of churches today. The New Testament is not very detailed, or even verbose, on the matter of church polity. In fact, there are such a surprisingly

---

[108] This phenomenon is a function of the role of elder being that of a supervisory role of highest appeal over the role of deacon and of the whole church.

[109] Contra mainstays such as Alexander Strauch, *Biblical Eldership: An Urgent Call to Restore Biblical Church Leadership,* rev. and exp. (Colorado Springs, CO: Lewis and Roth, 2003).

few passages in the entire New Testament related directly to the topic that a full accounting of them is possible here.[110]

> Act 11:30 This they did, **sending their gift to the elders** by Barnabas and Saul. [The Antioch disciples sending help to the brothers in Judea]

> Act 14.23 Paul and Barnabas **appointed elders** for them in each church and, with prayer and fasting, committed them to the Lord, in whom they had put their trust.

> Act 15.5–6 Then some of the believers who belonged to the party of the Pharisees stood up and said, "The Gentiles must be circumcised and required to obey the law of Moses." **The apostles and elders met to consider this question.**

> Act 16.4 As they traveled from town to town, they delivered the decisions reached by the apostles and elders in Jerusalem for the people to obey.

> Act 20.16–18 … he was in a hurry to reach Jerusalem, if possible, by the day of Pentecost. From Miletus, Paul sent to Ephesus for the elders of the church. When they arrived, he said to them: "You know how I lived the whole time I was with you, from the first day I came into the province of Asia."

> Eph 4.11–13 It was he who gave some to be apostles, some to be prophets, some to be evangelists, and some to be pastors and teachers, **to prepare God's people for works of service**, so that the body of Christ may be built up until we all reach unity in the faith and in the knowledge of the Son of God and become mature, attaining to the whole measure of the fullness of Christ.

> 1Ti 3.1–13   Here is a trustworthy saying: If anyone sets his heart on being an overseer, he desires a noble task. Now the **overseer** must be above reproach, the husband of but

---

[110] This is not an exhaustive list but a compilation of the most direct and pertinent mentions. I have bolded particular words that may be especially thought-provoking for the reader.

one wife, temperate, self-controlled, respectable, hospitable, able to teach, not given to drunkenness, not violent but gentle, not quarrelsome, not a lover of money. He must manage his own family well and see that his children obey him with proper respect. (If anyone does not know how to manage his own family, how can he take care of God's church?) He must not be a recent convert, or he may become conceited and fall under the same judgment as the devil. He must also have a good reputation with outsiders, so that he will not fall into disgrace and into the devil's trap. **Deacons**, likewise, are to be men worthy of respect, sincere, not indulging in much wine, and not pursuing dishonest gain. They must keep hold of the deep truths of the faith with a clear conscience. They must first be tested; and then if there is nothing against them, let them serve as deacons. In the same way, their wives are to be women worthy of respect, not malicious talkers but temperate and trustworthy in everything. A deacon must be the husband of but one wife and must manage his children and his household well. Those who have served well gain an excellent standing and great assurance in their faith in Christ Jesus.

1Ti 4.13–14 Until I come, devote yourself to the public reading of Scripture, to preaching and to teaching. **Do not neglect your gift, which was given you through a prophetic message when the body of elders laid their hands on you.**

Tit 1.5–9 The reason I left you in Crete was that you might straighten out what was left unfinished and **appoint** elders in every town, **as I directed you. [One may note here that Titus, the appointer, is never referred to as an apostle].** An **elder** must be blameless, the husband of but one wife, a man whose children believe and are not open to the charge of being wild and disobedient. Since an **overseer** is entrusted with God's work, he must be blameless—not overbearing, not quick tempered, not given to drunkenness, not violent, not pursuing dishonest gain. Rather he must be hospitable, one who loves what is good, who is self-controlled, upright, holy and disciplined. He must hold firmly to the trustworthy message as it has been taught, so that he can encourage others by sound doctrine and refute those who oppose it.

1Ti 5.17 The elders who direct the affairs of the church well are worthy of double honor, **especially** those whose work is preaching and teaching.

Heb 13.7 Remember your leaders, who spoke the word of God to you. Consider the outcome of their way of life and imitate their faith.

Heb 13.17 Obey your **leaders** and submit to their authority. They keep watch over you as men **who must give an account**. Obey them so that their work will be a joy, not a burden, for that would be of no advantage to you.

Jas 5.14 Is any one of you sick? He should **call the elders of the church to pray over him and anoint him with oil in the name of the Lord.**

1Pe 5.1–4 To the elders among you, I appeal as a fellow elder, a witness of Christ's sufferings and one who also will share in the glory to be revealed: Be **shepherds** of God's flock that is under your care, serving as **overseers**—not because you must, but because you are willing, as God wants you to be; not greedy for money, but eager to serve; not lording it over those entrusted to you, but **being examples** to the flock. And when the Chief Shepherd appears, you will receive the crown of glory that will never fade away.

One might notice a complete lack of any statement such as "this is how you are to arrange church leadership." In brief, the New Testament (1) assumes that there will be leaders of the church, (2) requires a high bar of character for such leaders, (3) relays examples of a few tasks performed by these leaders, and (4) gives virtually no instruction for what a church organizational chart should look like in all churches. Absent direct prescriptive statements, the most that can be claimed from the New Testament to argue for any particular church polity is precedent.[111]

Common church polities

Since the days of the New Testament, church leadership has generally taken three broad forms—Episcopal, Presbyterian, and Congregational. Brand and Norman split the Congregational category into three, which, if adopted, expands the list to five.[112] The type of polity in effect in a church has far-reaching effects, including how someone is selected for church office and is ordained, what that ordination means, how clergy and laity are related, and all aspects of membership and church discipline.[113]

POLITY	DESCRIPTION	WHO USES
Episcopal	Takes its name from the Greek *episkopos*, which is translated "overseer" or "bishop." Under this view, the bishops have a diocese, in which they make decisions about who will be leaders in the church. ... the Pope (in Roman Catholicism) or Metropolitan (in the Orthodox Church) rule over	Episcopal Anglican Catholic Orthodox Methodist

---

[111] Chad Owen Brand and R. Stanton Norman, eds., *Perspectives on Church Government: Five Views of Church Polity* (Nashville: B&H, 2004); Ted Hull, *Focusing Your Church Board: Using the Carver Policy Governance Model* (Winnipeg, MB: Word Alive, 2015).
[112] Ibid.
[113] Ibid., 5–9.

the bishops of the various dioceses. Thus an extralocal authority leads individual churches.[77]

| Presbyterian | Comes from the Greek *presbuteros* ..., which means "elder." In this view, the members of the church elect elders to a "session" or board of elders. ...The elders of the session run their local church, and some are also members of the presbytery, which governs over the larger church. That is, the presbytery is a group of governing elders who make decisions for all of the churches in the denomination.[78] | Presbyterians

Reformed

Lutherans |

Congregational	Church governance in which final human authority rests with the local or particular congregation when it gathers for decision making. This means that decisions about membership, leadership, doctrine, worship, conduct, missions, finances, property, relationships, and the like are to be made by the gathered congregation except when such decisions have been delegated by the congregation to individual members or groups of members.[79]	Free Churches Church of Christ Bible Baptist
Single Elder Congregational	The number of elders or deacons is not the issue; what is crucial is that the persons meet scriptural qualifications. In the context of elders, who is giving leadership and direction to the church is far more important than how many are involved in this assignment.[80]	Bible Baptist
Plural Elder Congregational	In this polity, God intends the church to have a plurality of elders; the ministry of the Word, the exhortation of the saints, the maintenance of godly discipline, the refutation of false teaching— all these vital aspects of the life of the church are to be	Bible Baptist

undertaken by a body of elders.[81]

Perhaps the house church movement deserves a place on this list, as well. Many have extolled the concepts of the organic church, microchurches, small groups, house churches, and so on. They cannot claim they are prescribed by the New Testament either; they can only state that there is precedent for them in the New Testament.[114] An awareness of world history and church history may cause one, in the absence of a clear New Testament mandate, to refrain from

---

[114] E.g., Neil Cole, *Church 3.0: Upgrades for the Future of the Church* (San Francisco: Jossey-Bass, 2010); Michael Green, *Evangelism in the Early Church*, rev. ed. (Grand Rapids, MI: Eerdmans, 2004); Everett Ferguson, *Backgrounds of Early Christianity*, 3rd ed. (Grand Rapids, MI: Eerdmans, 2003); and similar works illustrate that for various reasons such models were the norm in the first centuries. Peter Bunton, *Cell Groups and House Churches: What History Teaches Us* (Lititz, PA: House to House, 2001); Dave Gibbons, *The Monkey and the Fish: Liquid Leadership for a Third-Culture Church* (Grand Rapids, MI: Zondervan, 2009); Hirsch, *The Forgotten Ways*, and others speak of churches "without walls" and unconventional meeting formats in what, in some cases, may amount to a call to primitivism or restorationism. From a polity angle, Brand notes that "Holiness and Pentecostal churches often see themselves as restorationists in some sense, and ... one has to wonder whether ... the evidence from the New Testament is as clear-cut as it seems on face value." Brand and Norman, *Perspectives on Church Government*.

thinking that such cell group models are definitionally superior to established church models.[115]

If the New Testament cannot be shown to mandate church polity, someone may still parry that one particular polity or another is the most pragmatic. This, of course, is an entirely different argument from the theological one. Yet it is an argument that focuses much more appropriately on the essential question. In the absence of a scriptural mandate, the question becomes not "Which leadership structure is dictated by God for our church?" but "Which leadership structure best supports God's mission in our church's context?" The driver behind how leadership in a local church is structured is no longer "How does the Bible say our leadership must be structured?" but "If our mission is X, is our leadership structure (1) ideal for pursuing it and (2) not contradictory to the few, nonsystematized prescriptions the New Testament *does* give?" If the discipleship/evangelism continuum is convincing, and if discipleship supports the preeminent purpose of evangelism, then it follows that the church leadership structure should serve missionality, and not the other way around.

The question posed earlier, "*Why* is a church?" suddenly becomes paramount. What does Jesus intend the church to do? Surely, in the absence of a clear, full-bodied New Testament mandate for church polity, the answer to

---

[115] My sole reservation about the microchurch model is the lack of any incentive or viable pathway for excellent, well-educated leadership development. The microchurch may have a natural advantage in developing a distributive leadership among its members, yet even microchurch models call for broader oversight, foresight, and organization. This is a tall order to fill out of distributive leadership development. Hirsch may relate unwarranted optimism when he thinks that networks of cell groups have "what is called 'distributed intelligence' throughout the organization," although his next sentence is surely true: "The aim of leadership in the new paradigm is to identify, cultivate, and unleash that distributed intelligence." Hirsch, *The Forgotten Ways*, 256.

that question should dictate the pragmatically appropriate polity in any given context of time, geography, or culture. The polity should serve the mission; the mission should not take its form from the polity. As Andy Stanley has quipped in related discussions, "Date the model—marry the mission."[116]

Leonard Sweet draws a strong analogy here to grapevine trellises.[117] Different types of trellis systems are used in vineyards around the world, such as wire, wood rails, and a suspension apparatus, and any given geographical area often shows a preference for one particular type. But the trellis system, in the end, has no value whatsoever of its own. The only thing that matters is the grapes, and the wine. The fruit is the whole point, the desire of the whole world, and the pleasure of the vineyard owner.

Similarly, in light of the nearly total lack of a universal polity prescription from the New Testament, a polity's value comes not from anything intrinsic but solely from the degree to which it empowers the church to produce full-flavored, one-hundred-fold fruit. There is nothing inherently sacred about any particular church model from a New Testament standpoint, but there is certainly something ultrasacred about the fulfillment of Christ's mission for the church.

The preference for a flat structure in the New Testament

If the New Testament does not prescribe polity, it does appear to prefer flatness in any leadership structure regardless of time, geography, or culture. To hedge against the influence of the leadership models and teachings of the

---

[116] E.g., Andy Stanley, *Deep and Wide: Creating Churches Unchurched People Love to Attend* (Grand Rapids, MI: Zondervan, 2012).
[117] Leonard Sweet, *So Beautiful: Divine Design for Life and the Church* (Colorado Springs, CO: David C. Cook, 2009).

world, any healthy church polity ought to be one that naturally encourages this preference. Clearly, this preference for flatness does not require leaderless decision making by consensus, because plenty is said in the New Testament about the need for church leaders. But if leadership lines of authority are pictured as a spectrum from flat to hierarchical, the New Testament seems to betray a preference for the flat end. New Testament leadership tends to be communal and divinely legitimated (as in Peter's "a royal priesthood"), distributive and inclusive (as in John's "you do not need anyone to teach you"), and symbiotic and self-corrective (as in Paul's "all members of one body").[118]

Among Protestants at least, the priesthood of all believers is claimed on paper by nearly everyone.[119] But beyond the slogan and the words, church governance structures can unwittingly erode, or even disallow, the reality of such a priesthood. Any church polity in service of the "go" and "speed its coming" mission of the church ought to militate against the power distance so common between the laity and the clergy, setting them as equally as possible on level ground with one another.[120] The dismantling of this

---

[118] 1Pe 2.9; 1Jn 2.27; Eph 4.25.

[119] Nor is it original with Peter. It is a new covenant continuation of a canonical theme first codified in Exo 19.6.

[120] Cf. Mary T. Lederleitner, "Communication and Harmony" in *Cross-Cultural Partnerships: Navigating the Complexities of Money and Mission* (Downers Grove, IL: InterVarsity, 2010). The reader may notice that even a flattened, team-based, or cell-based structure requires some leadership group ultimately responsible for decisive decision making, whether popular or unpopular. Bunton's analysis concludes with "Cells flourished when there was a key leader who could communicate vision and articulate the purposes of the movement." Bunton, *Cell Groups and House Churches*, 84. Hirsch's incarnational model, it may be argued, merely pushes some institutionalism down through its network to the lower levels, cf. Hirsch, *The Forgotten Ways*, 47; "But savvy connoisseurs of leadership know that good leaders don't rely on power; they don't impose their will on a group

power distance, a deconstruction of the pastor's and church's reliance on the leverage of authority, is on the order of disruptive change, but one with broad benefits.[121] By asking any parent of teenagers, or any effective developer of leaders, one will likely hear that authority (or empowerment) and responsibility are inextricably tied to one another. A church governance structure that distributes responsibility widely among the laity in the Body of Christ but holds tightly to the authority or empowerment that must accompany that responsibility embraces the priesthood of all believers in word only, and not in reality. As the reader will find in Mile Marker Two, postmoderns are exceptionally adept at perceiving when responsibility is insincerely given in this manner and will refuse to sign up.[122]

A spiraling effect ensues. If it is not genuinely giving away authority with responsibility, a church governance structure guarantees that the Body of Christ will only

---

as a fiat. Instead, the process of exercising authority is far more complex— more consensual and interactive. But after all the fluff is stripped away and the group processes of discussion and receiving input and feedback come to a close, someone must decide. Leadership will always require one person to stand closest to the edge and say, 'Let's jump.'" Dan B. Allender, *Leading with a Limp: Take Full Advantage of Your Most Powerful Weakness* (Colorado Springs, CO: WaterBrook, 2006).

[121] This point is developed more fully in Mile Marker Three. Packard found that dechurched respondents were "clear that the church needs to adopt policies and practices that disseminate power, reduce the role of the pastor as the holder and conveyor of all knowledge, and utilize organizational resources to empower people rather than to control them." Josh Packard and Ashleigh Hope, *Church Refugees: Sociologists Reveal Why People Are DONE with Church but Not Their Faith* (Loveland, CO: Group, 2015), 94.

[122] Packard concludes: "A church can strive valiantly to be participatory or missional, but if it retains a centralized leadership structure that controls money, time, and other resources, the church will never achieve that vision." Packard and Hope, *Church Refugees*, 95.

function through a minority of its members.[123] This is akin to an eight-cylinder engine running on only a few cylinders—a most unhealthy and ineffective condition. In contrast, a governance structure that hopes to satisfy New Testament preference will do everything possible to guarantee that nearly every single member of that local church is engaged in the mission. Of course, according to the analogy Paul uses in his first letter to the Corinthians, each member will be engaged in a different way.[124] Yet what often happens at this point? An intellectual disingenuousness sets in and the bar of expectation for church members' engagement is set low enough to include little more than their prayer and tithing. This steals away the literal power of the all-hands-on-deck intention of Paul's argument. If the power distance has not been dismantled, many of the body parts will intuitively sense that they have no business engaging beyond the supporting roles of prayer and wallet.

Instead, they start to think that they will be fully involved sometime in the future, just as soon as they are properly trained, educated, and equipped. This in turn works to undermine John's teaching to priesthood members great and small: "you do not need anyone to teach you." Someone may object that they cannot be tangibly involved in church mission until they are properly equipped. But John says very clearly, "you have an anointing from the Holy One and all of you know the truth."[125] Church polity should be in service of the "go" and "speed its coming" mission of the church. It

---

[123] Later chapters, especially Mile Markers Two and Eight, recognize that even the very words here hint at the perspective of a bygone, modernist era. A church governance structure that appears to be the repository and dispenser of authority works against church revitalization. Further, Mile Marker Seven attempts to illustrate that any authority a church governance structure has is delegated to it first by Jesus, and from another perspective, by the church members.

[124] 1Co 12–14.

[125] 1Jn 2.20.

ought always to reinforce in the thinking of its people that while their teachers and leaders are present to assist them, they have become equipped to go and obey and speed the coming of the day of God from the very moment of salvation. They are pre-equipped because the Holy Spirit of the God of the Universe now resides in their rib cage. Of course, the discipleship that Jesus modeled with the Twelve would never settle for only this pre-equipping. A disciple never arrives, after all, but simply continues to follow beside the Master—neither running ahead nor lagging behind.[126]

Experienced church leaders may recognize that the focused realignment of a local church with an effective pursuit of the Great Commission could require something considerably more decisive than congregational debate and vote. This would be doubly true if such a realignment necessitates a change in current church polity. A decisive, strategic leadership is required that (1) understands the need for realignment, (2) foresees the steps ahead necessary for its congregational adoption, and (3) possesses the rock solid commitment to see it through to its final end come what may and however long it takes. Without this, the radical change necessary for authentic church revitalization may be unrealistic, or the rare exception. This is particularly true in a spiritually depressed New England, where the church is fighting for her very life and is apt to cling in desperation to whatever worked in the past.

The New England landscape is dotted with once-thriving historic churches now clinging to survival. The church's hope is not a windfall of money or a few families with children or a more professional Sunday package or lofty preaching. Her only hope is becoming missional once again. Practically this happens as she begins to see with new eyes

---

[126] 2Jn 9.

what makes a church a church and to answer the question *"why* is a church?" As she sits at the feet of Jesus and the New Testament, she hears a voice behind her saying, "This is the way; walk in it ... Stand at the crossroads and look; ask for the ancient paths ..."[127] An excellent definition of worshipping God may be that we know we have worshipped when we have God's heart and he has ours. When the declining church looks with new eyes and sees God's all-important, greater-than-self purpose for the church, she will have his heart and he will have hers. When this has occurred, she has already become missional even before she has taken a single action toward it.

Her newfound missionality makes her eager to truly and humbly see the culture around her for the first time in decades. (In Mile Marker Two, this is explored.) She becomes obsessed with being an expert on her zip code. It begins to dawn on her that truly seeing her culture requires that she walk a mile in her culture's shoes and that she respect the culture around her enough to hear its cries and insistence. Like the baby Jesus in Palestine so long ago, she begins to incarnate because she is compelled by love for the heart of God and wants to pass it on to the culture around her. As she becomes more mature and sophisticated in her incarnation, she begins to realize that for that kind of difficult, disruptive change to take hold, her congregation would best be served by a clearly ordered and accountable leadership to shepherd her through it. The power of the Spirit is primed to flow through her, and it is better that this power is not diffused amidst organizational disorder. She grows nimble. She begins to see that missionality is the best discipleship, and that that missionality is mapped uniquely for her by way of her leaders.

---

[127] Isa 30.21; Jer 6.16.

Discovery Projects

1. Consider trying the following trust experiment with your group as you are reading this book. In a group of at least six, designate one person as a Mastermind. The rest of the group can choose between the following body parts: brain, heart, eyes, ears, and hands. If your group is larger, you could also add other body parts for fun, such as nose, feet, and skin (nervous system). Now the Mastermind should call out commands for "the body" to do something, or a short list of things. This may be something like, "go to the water fountain and get a drink," "climb the stairs to the second floor," or anything else. The person who is the brain will need to translate the commands of the Mastermind for the rest of "the body" in clear, small steps. The person who is the heart will discern the wisdom of any compliance, the eyes can speak the way or give instructions to the hands to accomplish a task, and so on. You might also choose to have everyone but "the ears" wear earplugs, everyone but "the eyes" wear a blindfold, and everyone but "the hands" keep their arms crossed. Then debrief with your group. What does this 1 Corinthians 12 example say to churches in which eighty percent of their body parts are passively involved? What could go wrong? How did this experiment make actively involved body parts feel? Or those passively involved?

2. Is it possible that your leadership or ministry teams at church have a rubber-stamping quality or is there an atmosphere that subtly discourages each team member from voicing ideas or opinions? In his classic work *The Performance Factor*, Pat MacMillan tells the story of a real-life situation in the cockpit of a passenger plane out of control and destined to crash-

land.[128] Each member of the instantly augmented *ad hoc* cockpit team begins to work in seamless concert with one another with a shared, solitary, very literal, life-and-death mission in view. Consider reading this illustration together as a group and discussing how the *ad hoc* cockpit story that MacMillan continues throughout his first several chapters compares with your church leadership teams. What is the mission of your church that makes you at once one with the global Body of Christ and unique in your particular context?[129] Is it solitary (focused or simple) enough? To what extent is it shared, compared with the crucial importance of rescuing the people on that passenger plane?

3. Work through the charts on New Testatment references and church polities earlier in this chapter. Is the chart uselessly simplistic, or does it call for some caution in how tightly your church holds to her inherited polity? Under what polity category does your church fall? If you drew a scale of –10 to 10 and asked the question, "To what extent does our church polity facilitate and empower the fulfillment of our church's unique mission?" where would you draw the X? Is there another polity that seems appealing to you for pragmatic reasons? If you imagined yourself having purchased your current church polity online, what kind of review of it would you write?

---

[128] Pat MacMillan, *The Performance Factor: Unlocking the Secrets of Teamwork* (Nashville: B&H, 2001).
[129] For one excellent tool for finding a clear, concise, compelling, contextualized mission for your church, consider the series of books by Will Mancini.

Mile Marker Two: Hearing Postmodern Perspectives

Missionality in jeopardy

There is a persistent undertow that pulls on even the most missional of churches. It is a constant Siren call to settle for comfort's sake and to codify for safety's sake. When those frightfully alone in the world after the Flood were commissioned to be missional, they instead built a centralizing monument at Babel.[130] At the height of their missional potential, the Chosen People busied themselves instead with an onerous, centralizing tribute and self-enrichment.[131] The only way the Jerusalem church became globally missional was through a violent diaspora. Some invisible damage to the believer's image of God-bearing status inevitably motivates him to centralize, control, and fortify the very things that God yearns to give away freely. Thinking of personal liberty, Ronald Reagan famously stated that "freedom is never more than one generation away from extinction."[132] The same holds true for missionality in the church. Missionality is never more than a generation, or perhaps a much shorter time frame than that, away from extinction.[133] It is the double-edged sword of maturity. As she matures, the local church has a tendency to be less and less attuned to the decaying culture around her and more intent on fortifying the position she has gained.

By definition, missionality is impossible for the local church if she does not know her context. Knowing her context is impossible unless she knows the culture around her because true knowledge can only be had in relational

---

[130] Gen 11.1–9.

[131] E.g., 1Ki 9.11–13, Isa 56.10–11.

[132] Ronald Reagan, January 5, 1967: Inaugural Address, https://www.reaganlibrary.gov/archives/speech/january-5-1967-inaugural-address-public-ceremony.

[133] Cf. Walter Brueggemann, *The Prophetic Imagination,* 2nd ed. (Minneapolis: Fortress, 2001) and Nicholas Perrin, *The Kingdom of God: A Biblical Theology* (Grand Rapids, MI: Zondervan, 2019).

intimacy. Nor can she truly value her surrounding culture without recognizing the presence and fingerprint of God in it. She is not likely to see God in her surrounding culture unless she first opens herself to the vulnerability of loving it. This is the point, incidentally, at which the isolationist exegesis of *ekklesia*, or called out ones, may seem like a refuge from the uncomfortable call of God to vulnerably love the broken culture around the church. Yet as is evident from the last chapter, God calls his church to "come out of her" and be separate in the sense of being purely devoted to him—he never intended the church to interpret this as an exemption from missionality.[134] As Paul exclaims, "In that case, you would have to leave this world."[135] And Peter, in alignment with the rest of Scripture, makes it clear that the preeminent reason the church is still waiting in betrothal is to bring as many to faith in Jesus as possible in whatever time remains.[136]

A liminal void

Even now, but certainly in the next decades, the culture of North America is faced with, and wading through, a great and terrifying liminal space. It is liminal because it is unknown, uncharted, and very different from cultural shifts that have come before. It is a treacherous chasm shrouded in a spooky mist, one that no one would want to wander into alone, and yet the many precious people all around the church are left with no choice but to venture in. It is a liminal void. There is no telling where the other side of it will be. There is not even any surety that there is another side at

---

[134] Curiously, the church defined as "called out ones" is typically taken in the sense of Rev 18.4, "come out of her my people," and not in the sense of Mat 9.38, "Ask the Lord of the harvest, therefore, to send out workers into his harvest field," or Mat 28.19 "Therefore, go and make disciples ..."
[135] 1Co 5.10.
[136] 2Pe 3.11–12 and see discussion in Mile Marker One.

which to arrive. It is the sort of epochal shift in culture that has the feel of a portal to some sci-fi other-dimension. There is no way to have the perspective to know for sure, but it may be a cultural shift on a level with the shift from medieval to modern or from oral transmission to writing. The New England church has, for the most part up until now, stood on the departing shore, calling out to the culture around her as that culture wades ever deeper into the liminal void. Yet this is the church's grand opportunity to go with her culture, as Jesus might do, and lead her culture safely to the other side of the hopeless morass. What is more, the New England church has been uniquely equipped by her heredity to do just that.

Church leaders in New England are aware of the mass of the religious heritage upon which they stand. The autonomy that is so common in local New England churches is a uniquely potent quality that positions them to make the difficult, radical changes necessary in church philosophy and function in order to truly walk with culture through the liminal void. Our predecessors knew intimately the generalized adrenaline rush of surviving with nothing but "a dim chance and a bright hope."[137] Cornered by stark necessity, these forebears chiseled a Kingdom-preoccupied missionality in the Bay Colony's rocky clefts. By sheer force of godly will, they erected a novel church polity and standard operating procedures, teasing them carefully out of the Scriptures as best they could manage. The concern was always centered on "laying some good foundation (or at least to make some way therunto) for ye propagating & advancing ye gospell of ye kingdom of Christ in those remote parts of

---

[137] Quoted from the movie *Iron Will*. Directed by Charles Haid (Walt Disney Pictures, 1994).

ye world, yea, though they should be but even as stepping stones, unto others for ye performing of so great a work."[138]

Have these "stepping stones" now been sacralized in gilded settings? Has the four-hundred-year maturing process served to immortalize the chiseled sculpture rather than the missionality it sought to depict? Has the return to local autonomy by early Bay leaders, a return to New Testament precedence as they may have understood it, become an ideal all bound up in itself, fastidiously packaged, and missionally brittle? New England churches may have become like the dwarves in C. S. Lewis's novel *The Last Battle,* so sure of what they think they know that they cannot see either the inherent power for radical change in their breeding or the grand opportunity right before them for which it is so desperately required.[139] Like earnest people dissecting a kitten intent on knowing what makes it so cute, the church in New England may sometimes become so focused on purity and preservation that she loses the whole point of the good foundation laid on Plymouth Rock.[140]

In order for the church to direct her missionality in an informed way, she will have to gain an intimate, incarnational, loving knowledge of the culture around her. If she is to be nimble, she will have to retool and reorganize to be her culture's guide through the liminal void. As she does so, she will come upon a very enlightening surprise—that the source of church decline is so much less about the long list of things to which it is so often attributed and so much more

---

[138] William Bradford, *Bradford's History "of Plymouth Plantation," 1608–1650,* https://archive.org/details/bradfordsh00brad/page/n5/mode/2up, as etched on the William Bradford statue in Plymouth, MA.
[139] C. S. Lewis, *The Last Battle* (New York: Macmillan, 1978), 147–148. First published 1956 by The Bodely Head.
[140] Adapted from Annette Simmons, *The Story Factor: Inspiration, Influence, and Persuasion Through the Art of Storytelling,* 2nd ed. (Cambridge, MA: Basic, 2006).

about the great masses of postmoderns all around her. These postmoderns are, in the main, untapped, untargeted, and maybe even undesired and unseen by the church. If the church is to deftly navigate a path toward revitalization, her renewed focus on missionality will make her heart ache for all those dying without Jesus in the culture around her. New England churches are not, as a general rule, dying because they are compromising the gospel, or because they don't offer enough programming to young families and teens. Instead, as the numbers in my own context suggest,[141] they are dying because they no longer have a close relationship with postmodern people.

As Mile Marker One contended, the church is God's missional tool. The New England church can harness the inherent power of her heritage to address a postmodern culture. Whatever else they handed down to us, the Puritans started us on a path of active missionality. As Carpenter puts it, "Massachusetts Puritans insisted [on being] culturally potent" and "remaining pure but not … insulated and separate."[142] Like them, instead of vainly attempting to take our culture back to where it used to be, or working to force-fit postchristian culture into a Judeo-Christian kingdom, perhaps the church should "have the courage to go with them to a place that neither [she] nor they have ever been before."[143] The New England church ought to be excellently suited to such a daunting task as this for two reasons: its founding and history emphasize the missionality of Mile Marker One, and its ubiquitous independence in local

---

[141] See the introductory chapter, Start Here. Of roughly 11,000 people in my town, at least a full 9,000 appear to be Neutrals, people who have no thought of being religious and no memory of church.

[142] John B. Carpenter, "A New Definition of Puritanism: A Cross-Disciplinary Approach," *Evangelical Journal* 36 (2018): 9.

[143] Vincent J. Donovan, *Christianity Rediscovered, 25th ed.* (Maryknoll, NY: Orbis, 2003), vii.

church polity makes it easier and quicker for it to adapt. Perhaps God has bred the New England church to be staunchly independent, extolling autonomy as a high ideal, precisely because he plans to use these traits in her as tools to leverage the North American church into a mode of meeting a postmodern worldview with the gospel.

New England's historic missional emphasis

The Puritans purposed from the beginning to spread the gospel through the insertion of themselves into the communities around them and throughout the course of daily activities. They had a natural bent toward the common rank and file, being most often of that class themselves. As one historical novelist put it, "many Puritans ... remained in England, but they were those who had much to lose and little to gain. It was the peasants, the lower middle class, and a few adventurers or impoverished noblemen who settled America."[144] In fact, the Puritan experiment in the New World carried always within it a continuous cord of anti-elitism. When this began to erode toward the end of the eighteenth century, the Second Great Awakening returned the church to an obsession with the commoner and his empowerment within the church.[145]

A century later, with some basis in Boston, progressive theology worked to reintroduce the view that Christ's commission for the church lay not only in eternal salvation for all who come in faith but in societal healing and blessing immediately.[146] And since the days when the political

---

[144] Louis L'Amour, *Westward the Tide* (New York: Bantam, 1977), 21.
[145] Nathan O. Hatch, *The Democratization of American Christianity* (New Haven, CT: Yale University Press, 1989).
[146] "The crucial test of the church's witness is its success in maintaining an equilibrium between personal and social regeneration." Gary Dorrien, *The Making of Liberal Theology: Imagining Progressive Religion 1805–1900* (Louisville, KY: Westminster, 2001).

hegemony of the church in New England culture ceased to exist, she has understood the admonition of Jeremiah to the Israelite exiles to apply to her as well: "seek the peace and prosperity of the city to which I have carried you into exile. Pray to the LORD for it, because if it prospers, you too will prosper."[147] New England pastors today stand on the shoulders of a New England church that has since her inception prioritized going out with the gospel, being a healing balm to the community around her, and seeking out the least likely in their communities to make up the Kingdom of God.

Although it is true that a great opportunity now lies before the New England church to be a trailblazer for a reimagined church evangelistic strategy, the history, and prehistory, of the New England church reveals a long preparation of God's providence for this moment. The philosophical core values instilled by the early colonists are strikingly similar to those of a postmodern worldview today, uniquely positioning the New England church to be "men of Issachar, who understood the times and knew what Israel should do."[148] This value set includes the melding of high and low sources of truth to find answers to spiritual questions and the inverting of "traditional modes of religious authority."[149]

New England's long-standing postmodern character

Similar to early New England Christianity, today's postmodern culture is eager to combine any potentially

---

[147] Jer 29.7.

[148] 1Ch 12.32.

[149] Hatch notes that these resulted at that time in the "fragmenting [of the] evangelical ethos," another cause of a New England preference for autonomous church polity.

helpful sources to better understand mystery.[150]
Postmoderns eagerly pick and choose from different sources
in a buffet style to cobble together their beliefs, worldviews,
and answers to life questions. As we will see below, they are
highly suspicious of authority and therefore tend to put
more faith in their own independent conclusions than they
would in authoritative teachings. Postrevolutionary
preachers emphasized above all the "primacy of the
individual conscience," an emphasis shared by the current
postmodern worldview.[151] Although this emphasis quickly
fragments an ostensibly monolithic evangelical facade, it
places all participants on equal ground by valuing a bottom-
up theology. Inverting traditional modes of any authority, let
alone religious authority, is the hallmark of postmodern
values.

In the space of less than a century, however, these
traits of early New England Christianity eroded badly. The
church wandered back into a clerical elitism, effectively
rubbing out these values of individual conscience and
leveling of authority. The privileged position of the Puritan
legacy in New England culture weakened over the century
that followed the Salem witch trials and was finished off by
the inundation of Irish Catholicism that resulted from the
Great Potato Famine.[152] During this same time frame, the

---

[150] "The crucible of popular theology [in early New England] combined
odd mixtures of high and popular culture, of renewed supernaturalism
and Enlightenment rationalism, of mystical experiences and biblical
literalism ..." Hatch, *Democratization of American Christianity*, 35.
[151] Ibid.
[152] One historian stated flatly, "the Salem witchcraft was the rock on which
the theocracy shattered." George Lincoln Burr, ed., *Narratives of the
Witchcraft Cases, 1648–1706* (C. Scribner's Sons, 1914),
https://archive.org/details/narrativeswitch03burrgoog#page/n221/mode/1
up. Smith-Dalton argues that the larger story of the Salem trials was "a
reaction to elite authority (dogma and creed) toward democratic populism

Protestant churches of New England were obliged to acknowledge for the first time and partner with the Roman Catholic Church for the Revolutionary War effort. A congregational church of Puritan legacy was now forced to share cultural space with an enlivened Catholic Church. From antebellum days until the dawn of the twenty-first century, the Catholic Church was ascendant, claiming an ever-enlarging share of the New England faithful. Yet by the present day, in part because of the giant scandals that rocked the Catholic Church, the *Boston Globe* could declare what had already been true of New England religious culture for decades—New Englanders had generally decided that the church was no longer something that added substantial value to their lives.[153]

Re-engaging our culture

Carey Nieuwhof says that "irrelevance is the gap between how quickly things change and how quickly you change."[154] While New England culture has, in a manner of speaking, returned to her postmodern tendencies, the New England church has forgotten that these tendencies were part of her own heritage. She seems to be operating and

---

(the evidence of direct experience)." Maggi Smith-Dalton, *A History of Spiritualism and the Occult in Salem: The Rise of Witch City* (Charleston, SC: History, 2012), 16.

[153] "Church Allowed Abuse by Priest for Years," *Boston Globe*, January 6, 2002, https://www.bostonglobe.com/news/special-reports/2002/01/06/church-allowed-abuse-priest-for-years/cSHfGkTIrAT25qKGvBuDNM/story.html.

[154] Carey Nieuwhof, "Avoid This Big Mistake: Stepping Back into the Past When You Step Back into Your Building," https://careynieuwhof.com/avoid-this-big-mistake-stepping-back-into-the-past-when-you-step-back-into-your-building/.

ministering and posturing as though she still held a
privileged position in New England culture and as though
her authority still holds sway. This irrelevance gap
desperately needs to be closed. The good news that Jesus
Christ, the son of God, has come so that all may have
flourishing, eternal life does not change, and never could.
Compromise on the truth of Scripture is not what is being
entertained here. But the way that the churches of New
England explain it and display it to the surrounding culture
should be constantly adapting, morphing this way and that to
meet the ever-shifting capacity of culture to comprehend
and seize it.

So to be relevant is to fit the explanation of the gospel,
in all its fullness and power, to the current and upcoming
cultural receptors; and to be relevant in this way, the church
can take hold of and breathe back into life the strengths of
her Puritan heritage.[155] She can dust it off and remember it,
find strength in it, and leverage it. It has positioned her for
the variety and flexibility so crucial in making radical catch-
up adaptations at rapid speeds. These radical adaptations
include understanding the liminal void that postmodern
culture has begun to cross so that the church can close the
gap of irrelevance and become the beacon of God's light
necessary to lead a lost culture to the other side.

New England is a spiritually desolate land. The light of
the gospel is here, within easy reach of any who seek it. Yet,
because of the twists and turns of history, it is so hopelessly
unpalatable to the average New Englander that it lies all
about, untouched and untasted. This situation is similar to
that of an outcast in a desert, dying of thirst next to an oasis

---

[155] Ironically, although historically Puritans and Baptists were bitterly
separate, they have always had in common the postmodernesque traits
discussed here. They both extolled individual conscience and leveling of
authority.

that to his perception is fouled to such an extent that he would default to a waterless death rather than sample the pool. In fact, if it were not for the ample availability of the gospel in New England, the land of the Pilgrims could today be considered the home of an unreached people group because of the low percentages of Christians here compared with regions around the world without any Christian witness.[156]

The opportunity this poses for the church is not one of finding new ways of growing churches in size on Sunday mornings and in membership rolls. It is not one of pulling back into the fold unchurched New Englanders with whom the church already has some sort of connection in the past. The grand opportunity is trailblazing a reimagined church evangelistic strategy that obsesses over introducing Jesus in his own right to people with no thought or trigger of God, or of the church, in their lives.[157] These Neutrals represent the lion's share of the New England demographic pie.[158]

---

[156] David Platt defines *unreached people groups* as "those among whom Christ is largely unknown and the church is relatively insufficient to make Christ known in its broader population without outside help." Kate Shellnutt, "Why Missions Experts Are Redefining 'Unreached People Groups,'" *Christianity Today,* April 22, 2019, https://www.christianitytoday.com/ct/2019/may/redefining-unreached-people-groups-frontier-unengaged-missi.html.
[157] This is the subject of Mile Marker Four.
[158] Hirsch's expansion of Ralph Winter's scale of cultural distance would place New England Neutrals in his m2 to m3 category:"People in this group have absolutely no idea about christianity." Alan Hirsch, *The Forgotten Ways* (Grand Rapids, MI: Brazos, 2006), 57. A more common term for Neutrals may be "unchurched" or "nones." *Unchurched* connotes that they should be "in" church, and *nones* connotes that they have an atheistic or agnostic bent. Neutrals in New England would almost always answer affirmatively with "Christian," "Protestant," or "Catholic" on a survey with an option of "None," yet that's as far as their sentiments would go.

The easy temptation, everywhere lauded, is to default to exhortations to one another that pastors must return to preach the Word of God ever more uncompromisingly, that churches must be more welcoming, with better systems of assimilation, that facility curb appeal must be enhanced, and that programming must be run with ever greater exceptionalism. But all this is betrayed by the facts that in New England, the Bible long ago lost its status as a philosophical T-square, the Neutrals never seriously consider seeing the inside of a church, and exceptional programming trips alarms of cynicism and suspicion for the postmodern.[159] The answer lies, instead, in buckling down and doing the hard and dirty work of knowing and valuing the postmodern and postchristian culture so thoroughly entrenched in New England.

Knowing postmodern culture

As mentioned in the introductory chapter, Start Here, the term *postmodernism* or *postmodern culture* is not used here to refer to art or literature or architecture or philosophy, or to a cultural wave that denies the existence of any absolute truths. As concerns the latter, it is not even referring to a worldview, strictly speaking. Instead, in this chapter *postmodernity* or a *postmodern mindset* refer to a laundry list, explored below, of characteristics, presuppositions, and perspectives that can be overlaid on our culture generally and on more recent generations specifically, that is, Gen X, Millennials, and Gen Z. However, it cannot be strictly categorized as generational. Although the younger

---

[159] "Theological T-square" is a reference to Mark Draper, "A Church Historians [sic] Look at the Same Sex Marriage Debate," https://markwdraper.wordpress.com/2013/03/28/a-church-historians-look-at-the-same-sex-marriage-debate/.

generations may have been part of ushering it in, it pervades all generations and all of culture in areas like New England.[160] In some sense, this use of postmodernism or postmodern culture is parallel to the way a variety of other terms are used, such as *nones, dones, dechurched,* and *church refugees.* These populate a field of meaning within the use of postmodernism in this chapter that provides definition to or is symptomatic of that part of a postmodern mindset that intersects with churches, church ministry, and discipleship.

Postchristianity, strictly speaking, is the loss of the church's central influence in society. The complete erosion of any Judeo-Christian ethic as a basis of morality, lawfulness, or societal opinion has brought Christianity to be regarded as something of a foreign, misunderstood religion. Sometimes its most obvious symptom is the utter lack of familiarity the person on the street has with even the most fundamental Bible stories or names.[161] Justifiably,

---

[160] As an example, the respondents to Packard and Hope ranged in age from 18 to 84. Josh Packard and Ashleigh Hope, *Church Refugees: Sociologists Reveal Why People Are DONE with Church but Not Their Faith* (Loveland, CO: Group, 2015), 76.

[161] Allen Jackson remarks, "We used to assume a Judeo-Christian starting line. I wrote a book a long time ago that said, 'Just because somebody is not a Christian does"t mean they're stupid. They have heard of Jesus, they have heard of Christianity, and they have heard the basic points of the biblical story.' But that's not necessarily the case today. It's feasible that, because their Gen X and millennial parents didn't have much to do with the church, their kids may not have heard God's story at all. They don't know the differences between Islam and Mormonism and Christianity. They've vaguely heard of Jesus and Mohammed and Martin Luther King Jr., and Gandhi. But they aren't sure how they all fit together or what country they're from. So their faith is fragmented at best. We in the church use words we think they should know, but they don't. So if we want to help them integrate their faith, we have to stop assuming they have one." Maina Mwaura, moderator, "What Should Pastors Know About Generation Z? Five Experts Discuss the Ways This Emerging Demographic Is Helping Them Rethink Preaching, Parenting, and Service" *CT Pastors Special Issue: The Integrated Pastor, Christianity Today* Spring (2019): 25. This quote from Allen Jackson, senior pastor at Dunwoody Baptist Church in Atlanta.

postmodernism and postchristianity are carefully distinguished in most literature.[162] But in this book, they are combined into a single concept. This is for two reasons. First, they are both considered solely in the light of their bearing on church evangelistic strategy. Second, and very practically, they are heavily overlapped and symbiotic. Both are necessary components, and as they concern church evangelistic strategy neither can be spoken of without the other. And so this book speaks of contemporary New England culture as postmodern and postchristian, even if, for simplicity of writing, one or the other term is used for the whole.

Recalling that irrelevance is the gap between how quickly the cultural landscape changes and how quickly the church adapts to meet it with the gospel, it becomes crucial for New England churches to first grasp, and then know intimately, the sea change of postmodernism so that we understand what cultural receptors there are to fit with the gospel. In some cases, the reader may object that an attempt to know postmodernism intimately is dangerous because it asks us in doing so to fraternize with evil. This objection is only valid if postmodernism is considered an evil entity in itself. But if postmodernism is understood to be essentially amoral and not automatically in conflict with the truth of Scripture, one need no longer fear putting oneself in the shoes, so to speak, of a postmodern cultural perspective.[163]

Alternately, the reader may object that to get to know postmodernism intimately is to risk culture shaping the gospel rather than the other way around. This objection

---

[162] Barna uses a list of factors to classify someone as post-Christian, including "things like disbelief in God or identifying as atheist or agnostic" and not practicing Bible reading, prayer, or church attendance. Barna Group, "The State of the Church 2016," September 15, 2016, https://www.barna.com/research/state-church-2016/.
[163] See the discussion of culture in Mile Marker One.

probably misunderstands the way in which the gospel of Jesus Christ first interacts with and then redeems any culture it comes upon. Andrew Walls illustrates how the gospel has done two consecutive things as it came upon every new culture throughout the history of its transmission. As he describes it, the gospel is not, nor has it ever been, some kind of pure entity walled off from the effects of cultural context. Instead, in every instance of history and contemporary missiology, the gospel first "indigenizes" when it comes upon a new culture. That is, it puts on the clothing of that culture, becomes an authentic part of that culture, incarnates as Jesus did in first-century Palestinian culture, and intimately knows that culture. But the gospel of Jesus Christ loves that culture and its people too much to stop there. Instead, it always follows indigenizing with "pilgrimizing." That is, once it has become one, in some sense, with the culture, it then transforms or transfigures that culture, in God's pace and timing, into something ever closer to the likeness and flourishing vibrancy of the person of Jesus.[164]

One more thing may be said against these two objections. The motif of the Kingdom of God throughout Scripture does not allow the church to shirk God's call to indigenize and pilgrimize in her culture. If "the royal priesthood" are the King's mediators and managers of his realm, then it stands to reason that the King would want his priests to fully understand the current state of affairs in his realm in order that they might address it properly.[165]

There have probably been as many books and articles written on the intersection of postmodernism and the church as there are tentative attempts at defining postmodernism itself. Below we look at the results of two

---

[164] See here Andrew Walls, *The Missionary Movement in Christian History: Studies in the Transmission of Faith* (Maryknoll, NY: Orbis, 1996).
[165] Cf. Perrin, *Kingdom of God.*

research projects published in 2008 and 2015. Neither is intended to discuss postmodern culture head-on and yet the results of both studies handily reveal how people with a postmodern mindset critique or wish to converse with the church. They highlight a dissonance that may be causing the decline in so many churches, a dissonance arising from the gap between how the postmodern mind filters information and how the church has often been proclaiming the gospel.

The dechurched and the postmodern mindset

In 2015, under the title *Church Refugees: Sociologists Reveal Why People Are DONE with Church but Not Their Faith,* Josh Packard and his team published the results of nearly one hundred interviews with dedicated Christians who had given up on church.[166] In this excellent ethnographic work, the authors prefer to call the dechurched people they are studying *refugees* because they are Christians who are virtual exiles from the church, having left only because they felt they had no other choice. These are Christians who are on fire for God and are engaged and active in living as Christians in all the spheres of their lives, but who have given up on the church as a useful vehicle for being missional. "They've opted for relationship over structure, doing over dogma, and creating *with* rather than creating *for.* In short, they've created a new religious home."[167] They've left because of the irrelevance of the churches they know, an irrelevance that comes from the church conducting herself in operation and proclamation in a manner that is little different from fifty years ago, despite the coming of postmodern cultural perspectives.

---

[166] Packard and Hope, *Church Refugees.*
[167] Ibid, 25. Italics his.

As products of that culture, these refugees have experienced church structure predicated on respect for authority in the pastor and church leadership, which flies in the face of their postmodern tendency to be strongly suspicious of authority.[168] A quintessential example of this is one online comment on the "Secret Church" event featuring David Platt on April 24, 2020:

"i'm sick and tired of all these churches being seen on the internet and on tv and heard on the radio and sending out letters asking for money and the leaders of the churches writing books so that people can ignore the bible and read their books. after all.. the leaders will tell you what's in the bible. you don't need to read it. you just need to trust them. read their books. listen to them. watch them. trust them. not God. them. give them money for their coffers and their buildings, which God never told them to build. ignore the fact that paul worked for a living.. and though he did say that ministers should be supported.. is that what is happening? or are they being worshiped? looks like the latter. look, we each have enough trouble of our own. if we want to pray for north korea.. we'll pray for it. but

---

[168] In a private discussion between the author of this paper and an overseas short-term missions trainer, the trainer claimed to see that his most recent recruits, who fall solidly in the Gen Z span, seem to take the postmodern suspicion of authority to a further extent of an even more extreme suspicion of authority. An interesting example of the seeds of this postmodern value in New England is evident in Ralph Waldo Emerson's essays. An anonymous author, writing about Emerson's essays on the CliffsNotes website, says, "In 'The Over-Soul,' he questions not only the authority of the Church, but its faith: 'The faith that stands on authority is not faith. The reliance on authority measures the decline of religion, the withdrawal of the soul.' The more the Calvinists claimed sole authority for religious instruction, the more Emerson and his contemporaries thought them selfish and interested only in their own — rather than their congregation's—well-being." CliffsNotes, "Critical Essays: Emerson, Unitarianism, and the God Within," https://www.cliffsnotes.com/literature/e/emersons-essays/critical-essays/emerson-unitarianism-and-the-god-within

NIMBLE CHURCH: HEARING POSTMODERN PERSPECTIVES

we can't go over there and knock on doors. there is nothing that makes praying for north korea or persecuted christians better when you do it because some christian leader tells you to do it than when you do it because it's something you want to do. and if you don't pray for them, and pray for other things.. like a friend of yours, or an acquaintance.. who is sick, or needs to be saved.. then why should you feel guilty? i don't go to a church, and i don't feel guilty. i mean.. even before the virus i didn't go to one. i do not feel guilty. i follow God. christians are among the largest group of people who do not think. they say they follow God.. but the protestant reformation may as well not have happened. after all.. before then.. people would go to a church and just believe what the leader told them, because they didn't have the word of God in their language. same thing today.. except we are fullon idiots. we have the word of God.. but because we can't stand not being a part of some group.. we ignore what the bible says and just listen to what this christian leader says or that christian leader. dumb."[169]

They see in churches such as the conservative and autonomous churches of New England an inordinate emphasis on proclamation, salvation, and adherence to rules coupled with a tacit dismissal of the value of relationship and community value-added efforts in their own right. Packard states, "They wanted community and got judgment. They wanted to affect the life of the church and got bureaucracy. They wanted conversation and got doctrine. They wanted meaningful engagement with the world and got moral prescription."[170]

---

[169] Caleb Parke, "'Secret Church' Event Hit by 'Cyberattack' Preventing People from Watching It Live," https://www.foxnews.com/us/secret-church-cyberattack-coronavirus-online-virginia.
[170] Packard and Hope, *Church Refugees*, 28.

Postmodernism is all about eliminating or reducing the power distance between authority and the collective, and also about local, global, and regional concern. But the biggest takeaway from books like *Church Refugees* is that the first three values in the postmodern perspective are relationship, relationship, and relationship. It is the way postmodernists come to God, it is the only thing that makes sense out of church to them, and it is the core value that inspires their suspicion of authority and their social concern. Packard's respondents have chosen to work outside the church they still love because it is offensive to them that in the church "people were either doing the things that the person or people in charge wanted done, or they weren't allowed to do much of anything. There was no freedom to truly shape their community."[171] They also "aren't willing to be the mouthpiece of someone else's vision."[172] This is not some veiled form of consumeristic Christianity. It is a cry for authentic relationship.

One of the numerous ways this offers an opportunity to close the irrelevance gap is in the Sunday sermon. The postmodern, wanting relationship and authenticity, wants to be drawn into the message of a sermon and invited to contribute, even to affect where the sermon goes and how it ends up. They will typically prefer the story aspect of an inductive sermon to the delivery or propositional style of the deductive sermon. They want "authentic conversation, wherein both parties are open to being influenced by the other."[173] And in true postmodern style, they hunger for and value the way an inductive sermon allows for loose ends and the lingering of mysteries too great or too hidden to

---

[171] Ibid, 61.
[172] Ibid, 62.
[173] Ibid, 78.

explain.[174] As youth pastor Dan Scott suggests in a CT Pastors interview, "start by engaging them in a conversation: 'Hey, let's talk about this. How does this resonate with you?' That is how they learn. They collaborate. They rarely have a teacher lecture to them for thirty minutes. That only happens at church."[175]

Another major way the postmodern demand for authenticity should affect the church is in the way she emphasizes or covers doctrine. Packard highlights one respondent, Mary, who said, "'The church kept getting in the way of my relationship with God with all of their arbitrary legalism ... so I left." She went on to ask, "Why do we get so hung up on just a few things? Like, tell me how ignoring the poor is *not* a moral failure? Why don't pastors ever have to resign for that?"[176] The researchers heard a lot about the issue of homosexuality when it came to the respondents' frustrations with church doctrine, and they expected to hear a constant complaint of persecution and trauma from the respondents who identified as gay or lesbian. Yet they rarely heard this. Instead, what they heard consistently were complaints such as this: "Can we, as a church, just get

---

[174] A both-and theology appeals to the postmodern perspective. A great example of this done well is Roger E. Olson, *The Mosaic of Christian Belief: Twenty Centuries of Unity and Diversity,* 2nd ed. (Downer's Grove, IL: InterVarsity, 2016). This is often the point of confusion for those who misunderstand postmodernism as an evil entity designed to undermine absolute truth. Far from denying absolute truth, a Christian postmodern perspective is more blended, nuanced, and in some cases agnostic, allowing for mystery and eschewing anything binary.
[175] Maina Mwaura, moderator,"What Should Pastors Know About Generation Z? Five Experts Discuss the Ways This Emerging Demographic Is Helping Them Rethink Preaching, Parenting, and Service" *CT Pastors Special Issue: The Integrated Pastor, Christianity Today,* Spring (2019): 27. This quote from Dan Scott, Director for 252 Kids and 252 Preteen curriculum at Orange Group.
[176] Packard and Hope, *Church Refugees,* 101–102.

everything else right—love you're [sic] neighbor, feed the poor, all that stuff—and *then* talk about homosexuality?"[177]

For the postmodern Christian, it is all about what is going on in the heart, and the transformation of the heart, and so much less to do with what is happening on the outside that aligns with the church's rules. One striking example from Packard's research bears this out well:

> Jeff is a former megachurch pastor who was overseeing digital ministry for a congregation that numbered into the thousands on a given week. He had a long history of working in the church and had reached a point where he was well paid, respected, and influential. Eventually, though, he began to question what kind of an impact his congregation was actually having. The tipping point for him came late one evening after a small group had spent a long time talking about how to respond to a group member who was dating two women at the same time: "On the way home, I just couldn't get over the absurdity of that conversation. I mean, I don't want to condone his actions, as they were clearly destructive relationally, but I knew he wasn't going to change, not in his heart, and I think everyone else there knew it, too. We were just focused on making his behavior conform, thinking his heart would follow. But that's just not how it works. I started putting all of these pieces together, and I left my job and the church when I realized that we as evangelicals were doing lots of lifestyle indoctrination and very little soul transformation."[178]

For postmoderns, the intertwined triad of authenticity, relationship, and story is the prism through which they view all things. They want their faith and their engagement in the church to mean something far more than attendance or giving or church strengthening—they want their engagement

---

[177] Ibid., 104–105.
[178] Ibid., 101.

to be part of something bigger, some grand narrative that doesn't have anything to do with church brand building.[179]

Postmoderns are generally hypersensitive to secret agendas, background motivations, or any kind of veiled guilt trip. They can smell pressure from a mile away. It is their working assumption that when someone asks something of them or wishes to give them something, there is always an angle. Perhaps this is the result of the proliferation of the availability of information, and the advertisements and sales pitches of all types that pervade society. Some of the ways this translates into a New England context is that postmoderns are certain the church wants their money and wants their families in order to fill out their attendance.

Postmoderns tend to see the institutional church as a ball and chain. As they see it, pastors suppress any question of mystery or theodicy, stifle involvement and advancement within the church, and obsess with petty social issues to the exclusion of the great mysteries of life. Even worse, they perceive that the institutional church is preoccupied with self-preservation, systems maintenance, and internal affairs, even as the recent generations brought up under a postmodern worldview are increasingly focused on just the opposite—social concerns, global justice, and community relationships. For the dechurched, and for the postmodern, everything about the attractional mode of church evangelistic strategy screams a selfish resourcing and myopic promotion of an irrelevant one hour per week.

Millennials and the postmodern mindset

In the course of seeking to discover why young people were leaving the church in the mid-2000s, Stetzer and his research team were simultaneously identifying the

---

[179] For one example of this, see Packard and Hope, *Church Refugees*, 103.

postmodern perspective through the lens of those Millennials. The result is their book *Lost and Found: The Younger Unchurched and Churches That Reach Them.*[180] Stetzer made four classifications for this group of people not in any church: always unchurched (never been involved), dechurched (having attended as a child), and two stances toward the church of friendly unchurched and hostile unchurched. There were some eye-opening discoveries. For example, the researchers found that most of the unchurched population over the age of thirty never gave a thought to their existence after death ... it simply wasn't on their top burner.[181] As another example, the research team found that these young people didn't automatically think of the church as a place to go for spiritual guidance, in part because of the postmodern suspicion of authority and the easy access to information with the recent advent of the smartphone.[182]

True to postmodern form, they were very interested in the church "addressing the hard-to-talk-about topics," they despised pat answers, they wanted discussions to be relationally authentic and deep, and they considered "the questions more important than the answers."[183] However, the authors also noted that this hunger "for the unanswerable" was combined with a hunger for emotionally and intellectually challenging worship that placed them within the larger story, "taking people to a place where every part of who they are is connected with Jesus."[184] They wanted community, but community without the pressure of commitment and one that had more spaces for interaction

---

[180] Ed Stetzer, Richie Stanley, and Jason Hayes, *Lost and Found: The Younger Unchurched and the Churches That Reach Them* (Nashville: B&H, 2009), 9–10.
[181] Ibid, 41. Although Stetzer's team was specifically angling to understand "the younger unchurched and the churches that reach them," their data and presentation include the unchurched in all age brackets.
[182] Ibid, 44.
[183] Ibid, 68, 78.
[184] Ibid, 92, 96, 100.

all throughout the week than what the church typically offered.[185]

Of one respondent the authors noted, "she'd always been ambivalent toward Christians, but most of the time she was suspicious and critical. They were hypocrites in her mind. She'd determined there was a significant disconnect between what they said and what they did. If they were so loving, how come she never met any down at the women's shelter, or anywhere else there seemed to be a significant need?"[186] The authors remarked that the value of postmodernism reflected in this statement "was profoundly evident in our research."[187]

What the church can hear

Postmodernism is so notoriously impossible to define or quantify that the term itself is often not considered useful. Nevertheless, a nebulous catching up of the key postmodern values that affect church evangelistic strategy can suffice. As *Lost and Found* and *Church Refugees* indicate, the postmodern and postchristian mind values relationship and authenticity above all. It has a deep suspicion of authority, it embraces mystery, and it places a high value on social and community concern. Conder adds that the "passions of postmodern culture" are "an emphasis on beauty (since knowledge is not inherently good), holism (since truth cannot be ascertained by cognitive inquiry alone), and community (since knowledge must be derived from a variety of contexts,

---

[185] Ibid, 75. In my opinion, postmoderns are very often deeply committed, but their commitment looks much different than what might be typical of past generations. For example, they are generally not interested in becoming a church member, but they might be eager to give their time, money, and skills to something at church about which they are excited or in which they feel empowered and unrestricted.

[186] Ibid, 48.

[187] Ibid, 111.

perspectives, and experiences)."[188] Although he frames these passions in terms of knowledge, for the postmodern true knowledge tends to be experientially based.

Perhaps these values stated negatively will be more meaningful to some readers. Postmoderns are not so much against truth having any absolutes, as is so often charged, but they badly chafe at the certainty and tidiness of modernist answers to everything. For example, systematic theologies and rigorous works of corroboration of biblical events, so cherished by the modernist mind, seem impossibly dry and confining to postmoderns—they want the mystery to remain and are happy to have questions with no ready, or pat, answers. The mystery holds so much more beauty and creativity for them than clearly circumscribed answers ever could. Where the modernist mind wanted authority figures in the church to adjudicate uncertainties and offer answers from their depth of learning, the postmodern longs to arrive at whatever endpoint there may be through the harnessing of communal effort and contribution. And regardless of whether or not postmoderns ever personally commit to follow through on their value of social concern, when they look at the typical church they see an institution that pours most of its wealth and effort into itself, neglecting its community neighbors.

The end result of all this postmodern emphasis on a different way of coming at knowledge, and how it practically intersects with the church, is far more important than the reasoning behind it or how postmoderns got there. Precisely because postmoderns view and seek knowledge this way, and because the church has neither tagged along nor led in this transition, postmoderns have much to say to the church if the church will hear their perspective. In fact, when the

---

[188] Tim Conder, *The Church in Transition: The Journey of Existing Churches into the Emerging Culture* (Grand Rapids, MI: Zondervan, 2006).

church does the incarnational work of respectfully engaging postmodern culture, she hears a veritable pleading from postmoderns to address their critiques and incorporate their insights.

They wish the church could focus on being unassailably authentic. They wish this most because they value relationship above all, and without a secure feeling of authenticity, they feel relationship is a waste of time. They wish the church would be authentic in her outreach and evangelism efforts—that she would be more altruistic, putting the needs of her community above her own desire to grow and flourish. They wish her authenticity would show up in a humility that would allow her to get along with and play nice with others—in politics, with other faiths, and with doctrinally incompatible churches. They don't begrudge the church her doctrinal commitments, and may even find security in the stability and tradition that are part of those commitments. They just want a relational, authentic, humble, and altruistic posture in the way she proclaims them.

Neutrals are highly suspicious of definitive answers to nearly any question and ultrasuspecting of ulterior motives from clergy, the church, or any conversation that delves into faith. They are the world's best experts at sniffing out an agenda from afar off, however honorable it may be. They work from a presuppositional basis from centuries of Puritan, Great Awakening, and Liberal breeding that warns them not to trust authority, particularly church authority, and to cling to autonomy, the individual conscience, and pluralistic self-discovery. If this smacks of transcendentalism,

it is a corroboration for Nieuwhof's observation that
immanence is out of vogue and the transcendental is in.[189]

Generally speaking, New England Neutrals will deftly
deflect any form of direct gospel presentation, whether overt
or covert, before it ever has a chance to reach their minds or
their hearts. On the other hand, from their perspective, any
form of social concern from the church merely dissipates
into the great body of informally understood altruistic
goodness on offer from one and all in New England society.
The only strategy that is able to break through such defenses
and clutter is one that heavily prioritizes relationship, but
relationship that is selfless and vibrant and without even the
slightest, most heavily concealed ulterior motive. This is true
even if the ulterior motive is an innocent concern for the
salvation of their souls.

Church as leader in the liminal void

Greg Epstein, a humanist chaplain at Harvard
University, is a great spokesman for the result in New
England society of the combination of postchristianity and
postmodernism. Because the church has remained blindly
modernist, and has lost her centrality in society without even
fully understanding that she has, postmoderns have had no
other option but to move on into the liminal void without
her. This situation has virtually forced them into the only
option left to them—that they could be "good without
God."[190] As a result, they are wandering through the liminal

---

[189] Carey Nieuwhof, "Five Reasons Charismatic Churches Are Growing
(and Attractional Churches Are Past Peak),"
https://careynieuwhof.com/5-reasons-charismatic-churches-are-growing-
and-attractional-churches-are-past-peak/.
[190] Greg M. Epstein, *Good Without God: What a Billion Nonreligious People Do
Believe* (New York: Harper, 2010). This can be seen as an extension of

void up ahead of the church without the benefit of the Light. And, as a result, the church has lost her ability to witness to that Light in the language New Englanders are able to hear.

The "good without God" optimism plays out something like this: "as long as we are alive we can all still *grow*. Even if we have only one year, one week, or even one *hour* left in our lives, we can still use that time constructively."[191] Today's inheritors of the postmodern and postchristian culture in New England think of church as a handicap, and a waste of time, in pursuing the good God requires. For New England Neutrals, clergy are heavily suspect, church members are unknown, and church buildings are colonial edifices that still elicit some kind of primal, mystical respect or courtesy. Neutrals have no doubts about the possibility of being generally good separate from the church, despite their awareness that their lives and society are in some stage of wreckage. To their way of thinking, there is a God, or at the very least some informally understood altruistic goodness to attain, and Neutrals are confident they will muddle through somehow in satisfying it. In many postmodern contexts, the assumption might actually be that believing in God makes a person automatically less good, but in New England, unique because of her strong Catholic influence, "having faith" is still considered to be an admirable attribute.

Packard and Hope note that "the activities of the dechurched may be ushering in a new understanding of what religious activity means. If this trend continues, it will fundamentally reshape the way Americans experience

---

Ralph Waldo Emerson's joyous exclamation that "every man makes his own religion, his own God, his own charity." Quoted in Dorrien, *Making of Liberal Theology*.
[191] Greg M. Epstein, *Good Without God*.

organized religion."[192] But why should this be the case? Why should the perspectives of the postmodern usher in a newly relevant church activity style? Wouldn't it be so much more missionally responsible if this equation were reversed and the church got ahead of postmodern culture and led the way through the liminal space this culture has already waded into?

Perhaps nothing but blind obstinacy bars the church from leveraging the perspectives of the postmodern for the Kingdom of God. Once the postmodern perspective is intimately understood, it may be readily obvious that the church can faithfully meet the expectation of those perspectives in the proclamation of the good news. It can likewise be seen that postmodernism, far from being an antipropositional bogeyman, is actually a healthy corrective to a North American church that over the last century in many ways became self-concerned and lost her sense of wonder at the explosive creativity and mystery of God. In fact, as a direct result of the church reducing discipleship to a largely self-focused formula and reducing God to a well-constructed box of systematic theology, postmodernism commenced to push the church back to where she ought to be, if it can be said that way.

This can be seen at nearly every point of the postmodern perspective. Stetzer, Stanley, and Hayes remark that where "They are hungry for the unanswerable and want to connect with something that they cannot explain … Faith by its very nature is illogical—it is the belief in the hilariously impossible."[193] Where postmoderns are "interested in living out what the Bible teaches, not just knowing what it says," the church not only can react happily to this interest but can go further by redefining discipleship as a wayfaring relationship

---

[192] Packard and Hope, *Church Refugees*, 69.
[193] Stetzer, Stanley, and Hayes, *Lost and Found*, 92–93.

with Jesus having more to do with acting on faith and learning in real time rather than studying for spiritual maturity in a rigidly set curriculum.[194]

The postmodern mindset can both shame and inspire the church to get ahead of culture in leading through the liminal void with an awesome purpose named by Jesus himself. Reggie Joiner and the Orange Group ask very provocatively,

> What would happen if the neighborhood around your church suddenly decided … your church is somewhere they can build solid friendships, … your church actually helps when something goes wrong in your community, … your church answers the questions they are really asking, your church gives them hope and a reason to believe … What would happen if those of us who are in the church simply decide … we are for our neighbors?[195]

Stetzer and coauthors concluded that the respondents in his research would eagerly volunteer in the church so long as the purpose was something very different from and much grander than the church getting bigger, better, and faster,[196] and that the church should own this and get out ahead of it by "using service [out in the community] as a primary entry

---

194 Ibid, 116. For the wayfaring concept of discipleship, see Leonard Sweet, *I Am a Follower: The Way, Truth, and Life of Following Jesus* (Nashville: Nelson, 2012).
195 The ReThink Group, Inc., church publication, 2016, www.thinkorange.com; cf. Mark MacDonald, *Be Known for Something: Reconnect with Community by Revitalizing Your Church's Reputation* (Houston: High Bridge, 2017).
196 "Bigger, better, faster" is a phrase borrowed from Dr. Tony Blair, one of my mentors in writing this book.

point into the lives of nonbelievers."[197] Kinnaman and Matlock concur, saying, "the ancient call of Christian mission can answer the stifled longings of this anxious age."[198]

In their book *Faith for Exiles*, Kinnaman and Matlock muse, "We often consider our region or city or neighborhood (or Christian school) to be something like a backdrop, the setting against which our—and the other *minor* characters'—lives play out. However, what if we envisioned culture as a character in the story of a person's faith formation?"[199] If this way of viewing the postmodern perspective were taken up by the church and incorporated into both our concept of the discipleship continuum and a radical reinvention of church evangelistic strategy, as we encounter in Mile Marker Four, the church would lead culture in the liminal void and to its far shore rather than the other way around. But without disjunctive, paradigmatic change to church evangelistic strategy, as we find in Mile Marker Three, the result will be great volumes of talk and not much action to show for it. And before that can be done, the church will need the kind of leadership that can "foster relentless discomfort" if she is to ever venture into the liminal void.[200]

Simply put, because of a congruence of a unique New England theological legacy and a postmodern core value set, the church in New England today stands at the edge of a rare opportunity. It is an opportunity to be a trailblazer as an effective witness based on relationship out in the community. A relationship-based witness better aligns with

---

[197] Stetzer, Stanley, and Hayes, *Lost and Found*, 119. Cf. Reggie McNeal, *Missional Renaissance: Changing the Scorecard for the Church* (San Francisco: Jossey-Bass, 2009).
[198] David Kinnaman and Mark Matlock, *Faith for Exiles: Five Ways for a New Generation to Follow Jesus in Digital Babylon* (Grand Rapids, MI: Baker, 2019).
[199] Ibid. *Italics* theirs.
[200] Hirsch, *Forgotten Ways*, 265.

that of the early church than the program-based, attractional model that has been the default for seventeen hundred years.[201] It is one of striving at all costs for better and more relationship building with the Neutrals on their own turf in New England communities. It is one of building bridges of trust that in time will bear the weight of the truth of God's revelation for their lives. As Hirsch comments,

> There is a massive spiritual quest going on in our day and under our noses. People are wide open to the issues of God, faith, meaning, spirituality, New Age religions, etc. This kind of spiritual openness has not existed in broader society and culture for hundreds of years. The problem is that, by and large, the church is not featuring. People are not lining up at our doors, are they?[202]

Allen Jackson, senior pastor at Dunwoody Baptist Church in Atlanta, sees the same opportunity. In a discussion about understanding Generation Z, he says this generation "excites me. Many have never been to church, so they don't have the baggage of 'I don't go to church because it's full of hypocrites.' There's a wide-eyed wonder when the Good News is heard with fresh ears and when it's told with integrity and realism and approachability."[203] So not only can the church join in dynamic conversation with the postmodern community around her, and learn from it, the

---

[201] Cf. Hirsch's discussion of the church since Constantine. Ibid, 58ff.
[202] Ibid, 267.
[203] Maina Mwaura, moderator,"What Should Pastors Know About Generation Z?: Five Experts Discuss the Ways This Emerging Demographic Is Helping Them Rethink Preaching, Parenting, and Service," *CT Pastors Special Issue: The Integrated Pastor, Christianity Today,* Spring (2019): 28.

postchristianity that accompanies it in New England offers a convenient fresh slate.

Postmoderns, in many cases not truly on the church's evangelistic radar, are living and dying all around the church. Their nearly total lack of connection with the church may be the primary factor in church decline. The gospel lies all around them, waiting to rescue them and give them purpose, hope, and life in Jesus. But like the dying man in the desert, unless the church is willing to prepare and present it in a way that is palatable, the postmodern may never taste it and see.

An illustration from Boston Harbor

A few years ago, my friend Dwight came to visit and wanted to go fishing in Boston Harbor. He called around and found a local charter that would take him fishing for striper, a kind of bass. The captain took him well out into the harbor, and then gave casting and reeling instructions, since the captain would be preoccupied with piloting the boat. The lure used was called an umbrella lure, a contraption oddly similar to the mobile hanging over a baby's bed. It was designed to look like a school of feeder fish when in the water. It had a bright red fish dangling behind a school of about seven neon green fish, all about six inches long. The captain trolled the charter boat while Dwight let out these elaborate lures to one hundred feet behind the boat and maintained them at a six-foot depth. The captain hugged the various islands in Boston Harbor, glued to his fish finder.

At first, no catches were made. It became obvious that the captain's extensive network of fisherman friends was wrong about where the striper schools were that day. Nothing at all was on the fish finder. The captain's depth finder read constant within a range of about eight or nine feet because that is the typical striper hangout zone. He tried and exhausted all three locations specified by his intel. Then the captain began to look around with his binoculars. He was looking for seagulls, because they would be looking for feeder fish, as would the striper. They were a tell.

Fishing these areas the day before, the captain said, had netted striper three and four at a time on the umbrella's array of hooks hidden in the neon fish. Dwight then asked the captain to help him find striper that were larger in size. The week before, passengers on one of the captain's charters had caught several striper that were nearly four feet long, all at the tip of a particular harbor island. With the four-hour charter coming to an end, they trolled for about thirty or forty-five minutes all around this area. Curiously, although several large striper were visible on the fish finder, they did not get a single bite. Why? When Dwight pulled the lines in, he found a tiny blade of seaweed on one of the umbrella's neon fish, which was apparently enough to dissuade the striper that were clearly below.

Heralding the gospel and our strategy for doing so are both crucial. Obviously, if Dwight had refused to drop the umbrella lures into the water, content to rest them on the boat rail, no fish would ever be caught. Spreading the knowledge of the relational Jesus is obviously an absolute necessity. Just throwing feeder fish, or worse yet, fake neon fish into the striper schools might bring some relief to the metabolic needs and psychological doldrums of the poor little striper fish, but there would be nothing more, nothing permanent, no real connection of any eternal worth between the vast striper schools and the "rescue" boat. The Name of Jesus can never be obscured.

Nevertheless, the strategy for how revelation of God is introduced in a postmodern and postchristian New England is vastly important, and can mean the difference, by analogy, between five hundred dollars spent aimlessly boating around in the sun and coolers full of fish. Dwight had to cater every tiny thing he did to the fish. First, he had to tailor everything he did to striper, because those were the only fish in Boston Harbor at that time. He had to fish for the type of fish he was among. He had to leave the section of the harbor where he thought the striper were, or where they had been just the day before, and go to the places where they actually were located on that day. He had to carefully factor in the preferences of the striper, the fisherman network intel, the tell of the seagulls, the depth finder, the fish finder, and the captain's gut instincts.

He had to use the right lure, keep it one hundred feet out from the boat and six feet below the surface of the water, and troll the boat at just the right speed in just the right direction. The slightest inconsistency with the preferences of the fish would spook them. If there was the smallest tendril of seaweed on the umbrella lure, the striper wouldn't even deign to investigate. So it is for the Great Commission in New England. The church cannot be a collection of do-gooders without also having a deep-seated hunger for helping everyone gain an understanding of a true relationship with the Son of God. When prompted by the Holy Spirit, the relationships built out in the community are able to carry the gospel in a nutshell, spoken in a personal story or whatever is called for at a certain moment. The difficulty of fishing for New Englanders for Jesus is less about connecting a lure to a "rescue" boat and more about strictly adhering to all the big and little do's and don'ts of Neutrals before they will ever even deign to investigate the lure in the first place.

As much as I love this metaphor for kick-starting the thinking process of missionality, especially because of its familiarity in New England, it breaks down very badly in one particular way. Fishing, of course, has a "gotcha" aspect to it. It is not about the relationship between, in this story, Dwight and the fish. It is downright predatory. So the breakdown at this point in the metaphor is highly unfortunate because these are the very things postmoderns assume about the church: that there is no intention of relationship, that the church cares only for her own needs, and that the church is always "angling" to get something out of them. For a correction, we could look to the metaphor of the shepherd pursuing his sheep, as in Luke 15.3–7. The same expertise and finesse would be in order. The shepherd would have to make a very educated guess about where his sheep might have fallen or become stuck. The shepherd would have to be prepared to get to the lost sheep and be properly equipped to address the sheep's wounds, and so on.

The New England church is in a desperate condition and trying times, but she has four-hundred years worth of lessons and character traits ideally positioning her to trailblaze through the liminal void and out of the crisis. If she is not nimbly adjusting at the present time, she certainly carries the wherewithal to do so. It is a great opportunity that reminds her what is truly important, spawns prophetic voices, highlights the need for genuine discipleship, and incentivizes a renewed unity among church traditions. In a postmodern and postchristian milieu that craves authenticity above all, the present opportunity calls for finally seeing an attractional model in a fully revealing light, and then turning it on its head to cut through and earn the right to the heart of New England.[204] Of course, as we see in Mile Marker Three, the church that sets out on a path to revitalization must first count the cost.

Carol Roman, as was previously mentioned, is a member of the revitalized Brookville Bible Church in

---

[204] Cf. Jeff Christopherson, "Five Benefits of Cultural Opposition," *On Mission Magazine* 22 (2019): 10–11.

Holbrook, Massachusetts. She adds the following perspectives:

Culturally nimble

The culture around us is rapidly becoming more and more postmodern and postchristian. These terms are explained in the book, but I'll briefly describe them here as well.

Postmodern thought embraces skepticism. It embraces mystery over immovable fact. It rejects universal ideas of objective reality, morality, truth, reason, and more. As a result, the modern thinker will have a difficult time understanding the postmodern, and why the postmodern doesn't respond to their logic and verified information. Values that modern thinkers would see as "a given" are often not much of a consideration to postmoderns. Postmoderns tend to be suspicious of others' motivations, but they do value real relationship (that has been earned). As Shawn notes: "The postmodern holds authenticity and genuineness, to the extent that these can truly be achieved, more dearly than any other value."

Postchristian refers to the culture around us having less and less understanding and awareness of Christianity and its beliefs. This includes not only Bible stories which were once common knowledge, but also the values and morals of Judeo-Christian teaching. What were once commonly accepted standards of behavior, of right and wrong, are no longer held by more and more of those around us. The concept of church is an unknown to them. As Shawn has put it, they would have no more desire to enter a church and see what happens in there than we would want to go into a Hindu temple and get to know the traditions.

These two phenomena combined produce a culture that processes the world around them in a way that is completely foreign to the average Christian believer. There is little common ground to start from. What the Christian knows as foundational is mostly irrelevant in the mind of the postmodern/postchristian. This is why the church needs to view itself as the foreign ambassadors that we are, as if we are all workers for Wycliffe, relating to a world that speaks a different language, has different norms, and is quite sensitive about certain topics and beliefs. Shawn describes postmoderns as having "unique receptors" that we need to identify and work with in order to connect with them.

One of the first things to consider is our own feelings about what has just been stated. We don't like it, it doesn't make sense, that's not what the Bible says—how can anyone think and process this way and believe their conclusions are legitimate? Yes, it's hard to understand, never mind relate to. At the same time, it doesn't matter. My feelings, or if I want to go a step further, my being right, my being correct, my being logical, even my being biblical, doesn't matter either. The person matters.

We will also have strong feelings about tempering our speech. Postmoderns are offended by almost anything that contradicts their personal beliefs and worldview. We need to be gentle and thoughtful in our speech, carefully weighing what can be said and what to avoid. This can be upsetting in a country where we are supposed to have freedom of speech—that it seems like one group has that freedom and everyone else is not allowed to say what they believe. It doesn't seem right or fair, but again, it doesn't matter. The person matters.

And what matters is that we, the Church, are willing to go to the ends of the earth, sometimes physically, sometimes metaphorically, to share Jesus with others. If they live in a world of jungle, desert, snow, heat, or if they live in a world of self-delusion, moral relativism, uncertainty, fear—it doesn't matter—we need to reach them where they are. As Christians we are brought into God's family by His incredible sacrifice of Jesus for us. Are we not then called into a life of sacrifice, reflecting the Father's heart and ways, to bring others to Christ? Can we not sacrifice what we often view as our inalienable rights to draw those without Christ into the grace we've been given so freely?

And so, we leave our comfort behind. We are now on foreign soil (although we always have been; it just feels more so now). We need to step into this foreign culture carefully. We need to rethink our approach.

Yes, our approach will look more like that of a foreign missionary, entering a land they've only heard about, now immersed in it, finding it even more unfamiliar than imagined. But the missionary hasn't gone unprepared. The language and customs have been studied; the appropriate clothing has been found both for the climate and the culture; every aspect of life is taken into account—how they can best fit in—to understand and connect with the people there. This will be the only way to have an influence, to make an impact. A more forceful approach will only serve to put a wall up and thwart any attempt to win a real and lasting trust. Picture the kind of response a missionary would get if they arrive and begin explaining how wrong this people's beliefs are, or make sure they know the things they revere are worthless idols and relics. It would be absurd, like walking down the street in India and asking where to go for a good steak.

The foreign missionary does not go in and try to change the culture. They work within the culture. They may not agree with the beliefs and values, but they go in with the people in mind—how they can get to know them, how they can show they care about them, how they can show their intentions are good. And then, at some point, they see God at work, drawing people to Himself, changing lives, bringing hope. It usually takes time.

And so, we are similar—having acknowledged the culture and language, having learned what is offensive to them and what is not, having found ways to connect that are socially natural rather than awkward encounters, we go forward, becoming fully immersed, in the world but not of it.

We're talking about the process of getting to know people, building a relationship with them on their terms rather than our own. And this is not difficult when we are focused on the person—where they are in life, what's going on in their heart, what they wish someone could help them with, what kinds of hopes and fears they have. Even what topics of conversation they find interesting that have nothing to do with their personal life. Listening is key, and letting them monopolize the conversation is almost preferable. But then, to NOT comment on everything, NOT try to solve anything, NOT try to correct them in any way, NOT try to guide them, NOT try to tell them even where they can find peace, as hard as that may be. No, this is the place where we need to tread the most lightly. Where we wait as long as it takes, to build that trust. We wait to hear the person wanting our involvement. It usually takes time.

The point really being that we are waiting for the Holy Spirit to work that trust into the person we're getting to know, and that we are not grasping for control, deciding when and how this person will come to faith. We are giving that agenda completely over to God and having no agenda of our own. Shawn puts it like this, that we are "building bridges of trust that will carry the weight of the Truth in the Holy Spirit's timing."

But where is the gospel? Aren't we called to spread the good news of Jesus to all? Some might even say "Why bother?" if you're not sharing Christ with them as soon as possible. This is where the postmodern's eagle eye for hidden agendas comes into play. Where they could come to the conclusion very quickly that we don't necessarily care about them, but instead care about pushing our beliefs on them or getting something out of them. If this culture prizes authenticity and genuineness above all else, we need to demonstrate those in ways they rarely see. Our love, kindness, and selfless generosity should be what comes to mind when anyone hears our name. This is the language of the postmodern—kind words backed up with kind actions. So if we instead choose to speak a different language, one foreign to this culture, we will not be understood. We will be like "clanging cymbals" to some degree, having all knowledge but not loving them enough to treat their feelings and beliefs with sincere dignity.

It used to be that the Bible and the church meant something to the average person. There was a certain respect for the Bible and a general presumption of its authority. Postchristian/postmodern culture has no reference point like this. It's not necessarily a rejection of the Bible but more that they have no real knowledge of it and why it matters.

This is part of why initiating a conversation about God, or if they know they're going to heaven, will probably be met with a less than welcoming response. Why when we tell them that the Bible says that all have sinned but that God sent His Son to save us, they are not so impressed with "the Bible says so" or even that "God loves you". This applies even more so to morals, values, and behaviors—there is no overarching authority to go to in their world. And they're not open to the Bible being that authority.

Again, they need to "hear their own language" in order to begin seeing that we, the people who say they believe the Bible, are people they actually like and may even consider trusting, and over time may begin to understand that the Bible is a big part of what makes us who we are. So, our reputation is of the greatest importance. Matthew 2:52 relates here: "Jesus grew in wisdom and stature, and in favor with God and man." We will want to be known for good things—things that bring us into favor with others, things that benefit the community we're reaching out to, things that may not seem significant or very "evangelistic" at the time but end up being the things that God uses to show Himself to those who need Him.

Are we being less than "authentic and genuine" to a world that treasures these qualities above all else? No, we do not deny the Truth we hold so dear, but we also do not present it fully until it is ready to be received, until the Holy Spirit makes it more than obvious that He is touching that heart, preparing it for Himself. I say "present it fully" because our actions and attitudes are simply our first utterances of the Truth. The saying, "Preach the gospel at all times. Use words if necessary," comes to mind. This isn't meant to imply that words are never necessary. If the Holy Spirit is the One preparing the way, He will give us the words when the time is right. But until then we need to strive to have no hidden agenda of our own—especially the sort that involves caring about the person but is really more interested in looking for a spot in the conversation to preach the gospel to them or slip in something about God, church, or prayer.

Are we being less than "authentic and genuine" when we are quiet rather than give our opinion about topics we know will upset or alienate others, even when our opinion is backed up by Scripture? Are we giving them the impression we agree with things that are immoral or unbiblical? No, in the same way as before, we don't "fully" present anything to a person who will not understand and who will only be offended. We need to remember that the only things in their world that come even close to an authority to live by are their own feelings and worldview.

Most of our beliefs and opinions are just not necessary to share. They may be quite important, but they can wait. Does the person really need to know this today, right this minute? Most likely, no. Will this be something they will need to understand once they come to faith in Christ? Eventually, yes. But for the time being it is just TMI (too much information). And I'm talking about morals and values straight out of Scripture, never mind things like politics, which should be avoided completely. The Great Commission calls us to spread the gospel, the good news of "God so loved the world that He gave His one and only Son," not to "stand up for this" or "fight against that." The gospel does that on its own, in the hearts of those being renewed by His Spirit.

The idea is to carefully watch our conversation and refrain from offending people, thereby cutting them off from ourselves. This will serve zero purpose and is in fact the exact opposite of everything we're trying to do—connect with a world without Jesus. Which is a very important point. As believers we are literally bringing the Holy Spirit to others as we are in contact with them, interacting with them. Reggie Joiner says, "The best way for a kid to know God is to know someone who knows God." Same with adults.

This approach is not some "cleverly devised scheme" but instead is the approach God uses to bring all of us to repentance—with His kindness. "Don't you know it's God's kindness that leads us to repentance?" (Romans 2:4). If "kind words backed up by kind actions" is the language of the postmodern, we are in a perfect position to show them Jesus as we live out the fruit of the Spirit. Our kind and gentle words, our kind and generous actions, lay the groundwork. God will do the real work in the heart. He sets the agenda and creates opportunities for us along the way to help confirm that He does really love them and have an abundant life in store for them.

And what this approach does for the body of Christ is to give her a mission she can be insanely passionate about but also find incredible rest in.

The pressure is off—we don't have to worry that we "present Christ" in the best way possible, but instead, we just try to "represent Christ" in the best way possible.

The average Christian has been taught all kinds of ways to share the gospel—the Roman's Road, the Four Spiritual Laws, Evangelism Explosion techniques, etc. There is nothing wrong with these tools. But in the postmodern/postchristian culture, they may not speak the right "language." And for the average Christian, there is a good deal of stress associated with "going out to the community to share Christ." Just the idea of this conjures up feelings of dread and thoughts like:

"What will I say?" "How can I bring up the Lord?" "I hope I remember all the verses exactly." "I hope I can be brave enough to tell them the gospel." "I hope they don't see how nervous I am—oh, they will—I'll just stumble over my words!" And the like.

There is such comfort and such joy knowing it is not up to us to win people to Christ. The Lord will lead us to those He is seeking out and develop the friendships He sees fit. I think of Acts 17:26–27: "He determined the times set for them and the exact places where they should live. God did this so that men would seek Him and perhaps reach out for Him and find Him, though He is not far from any one of us." He'll show us how to best express His love in ways that will surprise a world that thinks the church is up to something, with the added surprise that there are no expectations or strings attached—just selfless generosity. And then, we don't tout ourselves. We don't advertise ourselves. We don't even invite people to come to church. We let them know about community events we're involved in. We let them use our building for free. We donate to the causes that matter to them. We come alongside their projects and help them. We make it all about them. But now I'm stepping into the next section about being "missionally nimble." All to say here is that we accost them with nothing but kindness and generosity. No frontal assault with the gospel. I like to call it going in the side door. No one banging on the front door trying to sell you something. No one sneaking in the back door trying to get something from you. Just the friendly neighbor who knows to gently knock at the side door and deliver that cup of sugar you need.

And that's part of the point. We don't want to be delivering a message and then "leave." We want to find openings for real relationships with people. We can't be in a relationship with everyone, but God will show us over time who it is He wants us to get to know better. This point also comes through for those thinking this is about some kind of "social gospel," where we meet people's physical needs and omit the gospel altogether—which also delivers a message that "someone cares about you and will give you practical things you need" but then leaves. We're not looking to be a church who says "be warm and fed" and not bring what they really need—a relationship with Christ by way of a relationship with us. This involves a level of personal commitment that a "social gospel" or even a traditional form of evangelism do not come near to, and don't necessarily want to.

In reality it doesn't take that much personally to hand someone a tract or even talk to them about Christ at length and then more or less forget about that person unless they show up for church. But attending local events that will bring you together with the same people time and again will only naturally bring you into casual friendships with others who also attend local events. Even more so if you and your church are collaborating on an event with the town or a local group. So we're talking about the long term, which will involve some commitment on our part.

And as far as inviting people to come to church—it seems it would be more normal (at least to the other person) to do that only if your friendship is at a point where you might invite them to your home, or at least out for coffee. Coming to church should be pretty far down on the list. We want people to come to Christ, not necessarily come to church. Not that we wouldn't love for them to be there with us! And if they come to know Christ but never come to church—isn't that really ok? We're building the Kingdom, not the church. God will grow our church as He wants. At the same time I think most often the person will eventually crave that fellowship with more than just the few believers he may know outside the church. Another thought on this is that inviting people we're getting to know to come to church may be perceived as an expectation, sort of in return for whatever we're doing to try to bless them. Even when groups use our building for free, we are clear to them up front that there is also no expectation to attend.

But again, I'm getting ahead of myself a little here and talking about mission. Although this does very much relate to how we approach this culture, how we are careful to ingratiate ourselves to others rather than alienate or even just give the wrong impression.

There is something truly wonderful about seeing ourselves in partnership with our Lord. He has entrusted us with spreading gospel, but it isn't a matter of Him commanding us to go into the world while He stays back in heaven watching. He goes with us. He shows us our part and He does the real work. Much of what has been said in being culturally nimble is about trusting Him with even more than we are used to—to not be thinking it's all up to us or else people are going to Hell. We can rest in Him that He is at work within all we are doing to connect with the foreign culture around us. We can't change hearts, but we can trust that God will.

Mile Marker Three:
Counting the Cost

Choosing the more difficult path

The church's preeminent purpose while she waits for the Wedding of the Lamb is a missionality that is eager to bring as many people to Jesus as possible. One church painted this picture vividly using clips from the 1997 movie *Titanic*. In the deathly, icy stillness after the ship disappeared beneath the waves, a few survivors struggled desperately against hyperthermia in the wintry North Atlantic water. They clung to floating remnants of the ship, or dead bodies in life vests, ... anything to stay afloat and alive a little longer. And in that stillness, only two lifeboats ventured back among the dying. While the other lifeboats stayed at a safe, respectable distance, these two searched wearily and rescued anyone they could in the minutes before the icy water brought certain death. In the same way, as the old hymn says, the church is to "rescue the perishing, care for the dying."[205] This is her main purpose before Jesus's return.

When the church looks through the eyes of this missionality to rescue the perishing all around her, she sees the postmodern culture and all those bustling about within it, and her heart is moved to compassion. She begins to love them with a love so strong that she incarnates herself in that postmodern community and culture, despite the knowledge that doing so will require that she change. Incarnating herself in the postmodern community around her will require her to listen to the critiques from that community regarding how she has conducted herself in Christ's Name as a church. She will start to adjust, as but one example, the way she appeals to them in matters of spiritual growth and salvation. Instead of relying on the weight of authority, as she may have been able to get away with in years gone by, she will begin relying more on dialogue, on the humility of not having all the

---

[205] Frances J. Crosby, *Rescue the Perishing* (William H. Doane, 1870).

answers, and on the teaching of authentically lived daily life rather than deductive sermons and propositional assertions. Her heart will break for the dying, she will count the cost, and her love for her neighbors will make her eager to pay it.

This compassion and urgency will show up in strategy, too. As in the example of the striper fishing expedition in Boston Harbor, or the parable of the lost sheep, her compassion and urgency will cause her to become acutely dialed in to the perceptions and interests of those in her zip code. Fully understanding the receptors they possess for hearing and receiving the gospel message on their level will become an all-consuming obsession for the missional church. She will be hyperaware of the tiny bit of seaweed on one of the hooks that is enough to prevent a single bite in waters teeming with fish. She will be preoccupied with making sure the umbrella lure is trolled at just the right depth and at just the right level. She will work tightly with her fisherman's network, and constantly scan the surface to locate seagull tells, in order to make sure that she is zoomed in where the fish happen to be at that moment. Christ's obsession for the lost will become fully hers. And, in contrast to the convenience and biblicality of the fishing analogy, she will see her mission in relational terms, not "catching" terms. She will think of herself as an extension of the Good Shepherd, extending his care and healing, love and rescue— not first to her own members, but first to the whole community in which she has been placed.[206]

This is a church well begun on a path to revitalization. She knows who she is, why she exists, what she is to do, and whom she is to reach. She has counted the cost—but she has only counted part of it. She is too early on a path to revitalization to comprehend the magnitude of the cost, or

---

[206] Cf. Larry Osborne, *Lead Like a Shepherd: The Secret to Leading Well* (Nashville: Thomas Nelson, 2018).

the thanklessness of the task. She has set out on the path and, despite counting a cost, has visions filled with rosy dreams of where she will be when she arrives at revitalization. In fact, she is in much greater danger than she knows at this stage of taking an easier, much less fruitful, path. At this stage she fancies herself as having nimbly adjusted to the postmodern critique by making a few changes in the way she ministers and conducts herself as a church.

What she does not realize is that the cost is many times higher than that. The postmodern critique will call her toward a complete flipping of everything she has ever thought about in terms of weekly church life. The rewards will be great, but they will not be the rewards she expects. As the reality of this higher cost and much more paradigmatic change begins to dawn on the church on a path to revitalization, she is faced with a choice. Is she in or is she out? Is she up for a much harder challenge than she envisioned for an end result different than she seeks? Thank goodness, this is where New Englanders shine. New Englanders tend to embrace a difficult path more eagerly than an easy one.[207]

The temptation is to think that being missional in a postmodern culture means doing what the church has always done, albeit better, purer, and more focused. This is the easier path to revitalization—more of the same but with more vigor and more ingenuity. It is an easier path than the paradigmatic change required for revitalization. But the whole point of the postmodern critique from Mile Marker Two is that something entirely new is being called for. A retooling of current evangelistic strategy will not do in the perspective of the postmodern. That would smack of

---

[207] J. David Jackson, *New England Culture & Ministry Dynamics: Where You Serve Makes a Difference in How You Serve* (Marlborough, MA: Screven and Allen, 2018), 33.

inauthentic listening. Everything about the way the church has gone about her business betrays what appears to be inauthenticity to the postmodern eye. The church may think she can effectively defend the way she goes about her business with a barrage of Bible verses, but in holding to that line she cuts short the postmodern critique and cuts short her own ability to reanalyze what Jesus is truly asking her to do.[208]

The church's status as the purveyor of truth and repository of authority is what has been lost in postchristian societies like New England. But this loss may be a good thing for the church. Although it means less of an ability to sway political sentiment and hold onto a Judeo-Christian ethic in law and custom, it also forces the church to be more winsome and more prophetic, humble, and powerless. The latter sounds a lot more like the Sacrificial Lamb than the former. And the postmodern critique calls for just this sort of transformation in the church—a transformation toward being more winsome, and more prophetic, humble, and powerless ... and self-sacrificing.

A strategic mismatch

As potent a transformation as the shift to postchristianity may be, an equally giant shift comes in the arena of church evangelistic strategy. It may be argued that since the time of Constantine, the default evangelistic strategy of the church has been an attractional one. In the last decades of the twentieth century, an attractional model of church evangelistic strategy began to gain in popularity and prominence. In the decades since it has come to be associated with megachurches, excellently run ministries,

---

[208] Cf. Reggie McNeal, *The Present Future: Six Tough Questions for the Church* (San Francisco: Jossey-Bass, 2003).

vestibule cafes, and seeker-sensitive marketing of all types. God has used this model to bring hosts of people to Jesus, even if some may justifiably question the genuineness or depth of discipleship and conversion under the attractional model.

In the last two decades, many have bemoaned the seeker-friendly excesses of the attractional model and worried about an American-styled consumerism that they detect in this model's discipleship pathway.[209] In some cases, the attractional-model church has become a personality cult of the pastor. In some cases, this has led to high-profile abuses and falls from grace. Regardless of the many possible weaknesses, one thing the attractional model seems to have widely propagated is a heightened attention to the perceived needs of the people in the communities around churches.

An attractional church evangelistic strategy predates and is much larger than the attractional model epitomized in many megachurches and seeker-friendly churches today, however. As mentioned in the introductory chapter, Start Here, the attractional model referred to here is not a style of church or a slick and trendy Sunday worship experience. Instead, the attractional model referred to is a pathway toward discipleship and church involvement or membership. Generally speaking, the church prior to Constantine had to hide its meetings from the public eye. Its evangelism happened in the course of daily life and business and its church services were designed for the thoroughly initiated. Its catechism *before* baptism and induction could be three years long.[210] It did not have church buildings but met in

---

[209] E.g., Leonard Sweet, *I Am a Follower: The Way, Truth, and Life of Following Jesus* (Nashville: Thomas Nelson, 2012).
[210] Clinton E. Arnold, "Early Church Catechesis and New Christians' Classes in Contemporary Evangelicalism," *Journal of Evangelical Theological Society* 47, no. 1 (2004): 39–54, https://www.etsjets.org/files/JETS-PDFs/47/47-1/47-1-pp039-054_JETS.pdf.

houses and catacombs and other borrowed places. Its evangelism happened outside a "church building" and whatever happened inside a church building served as a rallying point, equipping center, and springboard for the evangelism that happened outside the church building.[211]

Ever since Constantine, however, this has all been quite the opposite. Churches became heavily associated with the buildings they built to meet in. Even though most might easily agree that the church is the people of God and not the building they meet in, the church building and campus nevertheless became a strong focal point. Over time, the Sunday meeting lost the aspect of eating together in someone's home that it had in the era before Constantine.[212] It became more formalized and gained stronger liturgy and liturgical props. At some point in the recent past, it picked up the colloquial title "church service."

Now church activity and ministry were housed and took place in the church building. The building itself gained a sacred quality reminiscent of the Temple. It became a hallowed ground in which a long list of things could not happen—their juxtaposition to this hallowed ground began to seem sacrilegious. The terminology of "outreach" ministries became necessary to demonstrate that some church ministry was going to take place off campus or directly engage people who did not come on campus. This terminology became necessary to draw a distinction for such ministries from the norm of a campus-centric focus. Evangelism became a thing that *could* happen in the various spheres of everyday life, but that had its strongest chance of

---

[211] Michael Green, *Evangelism in the Early Church,* rev. ed. (Grand Rapids, MI: Eerdmans, 2004); Everett Ferguson, *Backgrounds of Early Christianity,* 3rd ed. (Grand Rapids, MI: Eerdmans, 2003).
[212] Leonard Sweet, *From Tablet to Table: Where Community Is Found and Identity Is Formed* (Colorado Springs, CO: NavPress, 2014).

happening at the church building, in a church service, and especially in the context of an evangelistic or revival service. It came to be commonly assumed that the best person to evangelize or lead someone to Christ was the church pastor or leadership. Pastors were hired specifically for evangelism, or senior pastors were hired on the basis of their claim to evangelistic gifting. The church building became the Mecca of all things discipleship and evangelism.

It is in this sense that it can be said that the church since Constantine has been an attractional church. This use of the term *attractional* does not include the connotations of catering to the consumerist tendencies of culture or of concert-like worship services or of superior systems and a seeker-sensitive philosophy. Instead, this use of *attractional* refers simply to the concept of expecting the world to come to the church building, rather than for the church to be out amongst the world. Included in that concept is the expectation that Christians must meet at the church building for the church building to be properly considered a church or for those Christians to be active and committed Christians. Further, this concept includes the expectation that those who wish to trust in Jesus for salvation should most properly come to a church service or connect with an established church in order to do so. Since Constantine, the church has become attractional because she has expected her building and her weekly programming to be the focal point of most evangelistic and discipleship activity.

An attractional form of church evangelistic strategy, then, is not about glitz and glam but about a pathway for the discipleship continuum. When defined this way, the attractional church model is an honest, biblical attempt to move people from wherever they happen to be on the discipleship continuum toward a greater closeness to Jesus. It is often framed in connection with some form of missional strategy such as "Come and see" versus "Go and tell." Both are biblical.[213] One seems to reflect more of the intent of Jesus's own discipleship, the Great Commission, and the New Testament. Perhaps since both are biblical, each has its place and call depending on context and culture. But this is the focus of Mile Marker Four.

The attractional pathway for the discipleship continuum has a primary entry point: the Sunday morning (or weekend) church meeting. There are other entry points, certainly, but the front door is the weekly church gathering. An unbeliever, let's call him Taylor, might become interested in Jesus because of a kaleidoscope of factors that the Holy Spirit is using in his life to prompt him toward faith. Some of these factors might be Christians with whom Taylor enjoys a relationship, personally or at work or through family or any other number of contexts. Some of these factors might include a flyer he received in the mail from the church down the road or a radio advertisement he heard for a nearby church. The point is that when Taylor wants to understand more about Jesus and Christianity, in the attractional model, he goes to the church to find it.

The Christians with whom he is in a relationship of one form or another have been generally taught or have been directly called upon to bring him to church. Those Christians might realize that they can share the gospel directly with him, and that he could, at least in theory, become a Christian without ever entering or becoming part of a local established church. But they are under the general impression that the most legitimate and promising place for Taylor to commit himself to Jesus for salvation is at the church. Frequently, in the attractional model, these

---

[213] Jhn 1.46; Mat 28.18–20.

Christians are told something like, "Invite your One."[214] The sermon application in an attractional model is often couched in terms of "and invite them to church." Announcements tout some exciting event or program coming soon and invariably include, "make sure you invite your friends and neighbors." Everything is conceived in terms of bringing people *here*, to the church, because at the church is where all the systems are in place and all the people are prepared to handle the best pitches of the gospel and the best programs for discipleship.[215]

This is why some of the most well-known attactionally modeled churches focus on excellence in weekend programming.[216] Excellence in weekend programming has at least two noble goals, both of which are singularly attractional. First, if the church faithful are being asked to invite their friends and neighbors to church, it stands to reason that the church would do well to have something exceptional for them to come to. Sometimes attractional churches are accused of maintaining this excellence as merely a cover for consumerism or for being the coolest and hippest church on the block. This accusation is probably true in some cases, but for the most part it is unfair. Attractional

---

[214] In early 2019, the Southern Baptist Convention's North American Mission Board rolled out a massive campaign entitled "Who's Your One?" (WhosYourOne.com). I recall a creative device used in a large attractional church to instill this motto that remains a lasting, powerful mental image for me and others; the church handed out a metal paperweight shaped like the numeral 1 and measuring one-fourth by one by one-and-one-half inch that could sit in a high-visibility space at home or in an office.

[215] Cf. Nelson Searcy, with Jennifer Dykes Henson, *Fusion: Turning First-Time Guests into Fully Engaged Members of Your Church* (Grand Rapids, MI: Baker, 2008). The attractional model looks like some of the advancements of the industrial revolution in that it seeks to bring all work to a central location at which something of an assembly line process and specialization in training can be brought to bear.

[216] Cf. Sue Miller, with David Staal, *Making Your Children's Ministry the Best Hour of Every Kid's Week* (Grand Rapids, MI: Zondervan, 2004).

churches want their first-time guests to be greeted with an excellent production so that they will not be distracted by unprofessionalism and so that they will understand that Jesus is so important in this church that no expense is spared to celebrate him and display his glory.

After all, it would be very disappointing if Taylor's friends and family and coworkers, after years of prayerfully waiting, had Taylor join them on Sunday morning for a mediocre, low-energy, unconvincing program. If Taylor brings kids, the attractional church wants them to find bright colors, safe and clean rooms, and a curriculum and programming that helps them encounter Jesus on their childhood level. Taylor should be inspired by the church's excellent curb appeal and signage when he first approaches the church, and greeted by smiling people with name tags who help him park and hold open the vestibule doors for him. He should smell coffee and hear laughter and great music, be escorted to the disparate places to drop off his teenager, his sixth grader, and his toddler. When he is ushered to his seat in the sanctuary, he enters a room and a program with a preplanned ambiance, and he enjoys and engages in an hour of excellent preaching and music.[217]

After his first visit, Taylor will receive in the mail a gift card to a doughnut shop thanking him for coming. A month later he will get a call letting him know that he has been missed. Everything is designed for Taylor to appreciate the gravity of Jesus in his own life and in the lives of the Christians who invited him to come. So, second, excellence in programming is designed to show Taylor that the attractional church takes Jesus very seriously.

---

[217] Andy Stanley, *Deep and Wide: Creating Churches Unchurched People Love to Attend* (Grand Rapids, MI: Zondervan, 2012). Chapter 10, "Rules of Engagement," offers a visual diagram.

The problem is that although the attractional model may be biblical and very well intended, it is a precise mismatch for the postmodern culture in which the church finds herself today. In a postmodern and postchristian culture, most people have no intention of approaching a church for any reason whatsoever. If they become curious about Jesus, they would not think of the church as a good place to investigate that curiosity.[218] They think of the church as either not having the answers, or having all the wrong answers, or having ill-fitted and stuffy answers.

They think of the attractional church as self-centered. It is not difficult to see how they arrive at this conclusion. They perceive that the church has not been concerned about benefiting or healing the society and community around it. Instead, in their memory, the church has been critical and caustic. In New England especially, *church* and *scandal* are associated words. The excellence that is a hallmark of thriving, attractional churches has all the appearance to the postmodern observer of the church herself being consumeristic. The lion's share of money, staffing hours, and emphasis go to making the weekend gathering the best experience that it can be.[219] Taylor wonders why the town

---

[218] Ed Stetzer, Richie Stanley, and Jason Hayes, *Lost and Found: The Younger Unchurched and the Churches That Reach Them* (Nashville: B&H, 2009).

[219] Packard and Hope estimate that as much as 60% of a church's resources may go to the weekend gathering. Josh Packard and Ashleigh Hope, *Church Refugees: Sociologists Reveal Why People Are DONE with Church but Not Their Faith* (Loveland, CO: Group, 2015), 71. Jackson can say, "A healthy church will spend somewhere between ten and twenty percent of its budget [and calendar and efforts] on outreach, ministry, and disciple-making. In addition, ten percent more should go toward supporting missions efforts beyond the church's own efforts. Fixed expenses, including staff, benefits, facilities, utilities, maintenance, etc., make up the rest of the budget." J. David Jackson, *ReNEW: Traveling the Forgotten Path* (Marlborough, MA: Screven and Allen, 2018), 111. Mancini says, "We always probe the question

park is shabby and several people he knows are in danger of losing their homes while the church is busy dumping gobs of money, staffing hours, and focus into excellent weekend gatherings. Taylor wonders why curb appeal is so important to the attractional church in town when he knows the local police cannot fund the opioid prevention programs they wish to run. He doubts the church is tuned into the perceived needs of the townspeople, because the church is too consumed with thinking about her own programming, facilities, and productions.

While this understanding of attractional strategy may be most obvious in thriving, rapidly growing churches that seem to have momentum and everything going right for them, it is just as present in churches that do not make the fastest-growing church lists. Even the smallest, least moneyed churches want to do the best that they can with their weekend services and programming. They want to be an attractive proposition for people to attend, and for young families in particular. They want to offer attractive programming and engaging sermons and music that catch the spirit. They want their buildings to be clean and freshly painted, and they hope their bathrooms do not smell. And no one would fault them for any of this. Nevertheless, these are all concerns that are integrally linked to an attractional church strategy of evangelism and discipleship. The unquestioned assumption is that most evangelism and discipleship will happen at and through the church gathered at the church building.

---

of how much time and energy goes into weekend service delivery. One time [we] queried one of the largest churches in the country, and the staff replied, '95 percent.' That is not uncommon for a church of any size, but ... 'If 80-plus percent of your church's time, energy, and effort goes into making Sunday morning happen, is it a church or a production company?'" Will Mancini and Cory Hartman, *Future Church: Seven Laws of Real Church Growth* (Grand Rapids, MI: Baker, 2020), 101.

Even the things that the attractional church uses to gauge success smack of self-centeredness to the postmodern. Giving levels and church attendance are still the gold standard of evaluating church health, despite the growing discussions around other metrics. The COVID-19 pandemic, despite its unprecedented disruption, has yet to significantly alter this reality. For Baptist churches, conversion and baptism numbers are carefully followed and take on greater importance than giving and attendance. But to the postmodern, these all seem very much like building the brand. Certainly, the church should not be bothered by the postmodern viewing conversion and baptism as brand building. But the church should note that the importance she puts on giving and attendance numbers plays right into the postmodern perception that the church is self-concerned. For that matter, the church may do well to carefully consider that *how* she emphasizes conversion and baptism may send the opposite message she wishes to convey to the postmodern onlooker.

Paradigmatic change

Perhaps then, gaining the heart of God for the lost and becoming intentionally missional requires much greater change than it may have seemed at first. Truly understanding the postmodern critique, stepping into postmodern shoes, and seeing the church from postmodern eyes, inevitably calls the church to a deep, paradigmatic change. It means recognizing that most everything about today's church is founded upon a "Come and see" strategy rather than a "Go and tell" one. It means recognizing that after the church has decided that she will have the heart of God for the community around her, and after she has thoroughly immersed herself in that community to humbly hear and know it, she must allow for the possibility that everything about the way she conducts herself as a church will have to change as a result of this newfound relationship.

Everything she thinks she knows about how to run a church will have to be wholly reevaluated through the lens of the people she is trying to reach with the gospel. She will have to begin to think and act like a missionary rather than like an institution that enjoys a prestigious place in society.[220] James Emery White notes that thinking like a missionary requires first learning the language and becoming a student of the culture.[221] Everything will have to change, the specifics of which become clearer in the next chapter. The point here is recognizing the magnitude of the shift that will be required for a healthy path to church revitalization. The point here is thoroughly counting the cost of revitalization before beginning the climb of Mile Marker Four.

This kind of shift can only be addressed through adaptive change. Adaptive change involves uncharted territory and requires new learning. Its opposite is called technical change. Technical change includes any kind of adjustment or adaptation that does not involve a significant change in the underlying, fundamental system. Technical change may take on significant forms. It may involve sweeping, difficult changes, or multiple minor changes, or a mix of both. What distinguishes it from adaptive change is that it does not ever rearrange or alter the underlying system. Adaptive change, on the other hand, is not concerned with any changes other than paradigmatic ones. It will almost certainly be accompanied by technical changes, but adaptive change is all about fundamentally shaking up

---

[220] Cf. esp. Vincent J. Donovan, *Christianity Rediscovered*, 25th ed. (Maryknoll, NY: Orbis, 2003).
[221] James Emery White, *The Rise of the Nones: Understanding and Reaching the Religiously Unaffiliated* (Grand Rapids, MI: Baker, 2014).

the underlying system.[222] Leonard Sweet uses an analogy of computer programming to describe technical versus adaptive change. In this analogy, technical change is any kind of change to the interface but adaptive change is a switching out or major update of the underlying operating system.[223]

In Mile Marker Four, a rendering is offered of the type of paradigmatic change in church evangelistic strategy called for by the postmodern critique. But the present consideration is this: is the church up for such a change? If the truest form of contemporary missionality requires such radical, paradigmatic change of the very understanding of the church, will the church consider the cure worse than the disease? Will the church opt instead to do the best she can with as much technical change as she can stomach, or will she go all in for adaptive change? Is she willing to submit herself to have everything she thinks she knows about how to "do" church be shaken and redrawn? Will she risk the danger of thinking outside the box regarding missionality and orient all she does around a tireless pursuit of the preeminent purpose of the church, or will she stand in the comfort zone of received institutional knowledge? In short—after understanding "*why* is the church" and after intimately understanding her zip code, and then realizing that giant, adaptive, paradigmatic change will be required to incarnationally transform it—is she in or is she out?

The good news is, if she simply is not able to embrace the adaptive change, technical change might still get her by for a while. The cultural shift to postmodernism, while perhaps having a more compressed timeline than many such shifts in the past, is nevertheless a slow transformation. The

---

[222] Alan Hirsch, *The Forgotten Ways: Reactivating Apostolic Movements*, 2nd ed. (Grand Rapids, MI: Brazos, 2016), 255ff.
[223] Leonard Sweet, *The Gospel According to Starbucks: Living with a Grande Passion* (Colorado Springs, CO: WaterBrook, 2007).

standard attractional evangelistic strategy that has worked well as a general rule for seventeen hundred years will still work now, if to an ever lessening degree.[224] But perhaps, if the church can foresee that within a decade such attractional strategy will be one-hundred-and-eighty degrees out of phase with the community around her, she may be induced to swallow hard and go headlong into the adaptive change required. In this sense, she is willfully entering her own liminal void in order to emerge in short order as a leader of her culture—one that can guide that culture through to the other side of its liminal void. Since this kind of adaptive change generally takes at least five to seven years to take hold and root, willfully diving in now becomes a time-is-of-the-essence thing for the church.[225]

Indications change must come

There are some current indications that such a sense of urgency is warranted. These indications may bolster the church's courage as she prepares herself for an adaptive-level change. One of these indicators, mentioned briefly already, is the growing consensus in the church world that the current gauges of church health need to be replaced. A great number of voices in the church world, growing louder but not yet reaching a fever pitch, are utterly unsatisfied with the metrics of attendance and giving.[226] They are unsatisfactory, not because they have no value but because they create a skewed picture of the actual health of the church. Attendance numbers certainly have some value, because, as Peter says, "The Lord is not slow in keeping his promise" of all things

---

[224] Travis Collins, *From the Steeple to the Street: Innovating Mission and Ministry Through Fresh Expressions of Church* (Franklin, TN: Seedbed, 2016).
[225] Steve M. Cohen and Richard M. Biery, *Ministry Mess Management: Solving Leadership Failures* (Bloomington, IN: AuthorHouse, 2014).
[226] Cf. Leonard Sweet, *So Beautiful: Divine Design for Life and the Church* (Colorado Springs, CO: David C. Cook, 2009).

made new, because "He is patient with you, not wanting anyone to perish, but everyone to come to repentance."[227] Giving numbers certainly have value, at least those that estimate proportional giving; they may be, at least at the individual level, the single most empirical evidence of spiritual maturity.[228]

In the Baptist world, conversions and baptisms have an unarguable value; to the extent that they are spiritually accurate, which might be a rather large caveat, they represent very clear evidence of a portion of the Great Commission. But each of these numbers has been abused, sometimes knowingly and sometimes accidentally, and everyone knows it. Pastors and reporting churches are naturally under pressure to fatten these numbers, and somewhere along the line the depth of meaning of conversions and baptisms becomes shallow. One of the first questions asked when two pastors meet for the first time is, "How big is your church?" It may be that this is very guilelessly asked, but it immediately illustrates a subconscious pressure to inflate.

Further, these metrics skew what may really be going on with a church's health, because they, at best, capture only a few moments along the discipleship continuum. Put another way, they leave completely in the dark what is happening everywhere else along the discipleship continuum. It is like trying to gauge the health of a complex conglomerate from only three or four lines excerpted from the company's balance sheet. A few indicators such as revenue or debt to capital might be in view, but the

---

[227] 2Pe 3.9; cf. 1Ti 2.4; allusion made to Rev 21.5.
[228] Jeffrey Allen Love, *Lord of the Fries: It's Not About Your Money, It's About Your HEART* (n.p.: 2911 Publishing, 2016); Chris Willard and Jim Sheppard, *Contagious Generosity: Creating a Culture of Giving in Your Church* (Grand Rapids, MI: Zondervan, 2012).

company's history, morale, research and development, and a host of other things would not.

For these reasons, and other related ones, a great number of voices are experimenting with entirely new metrics. This is very much in an experimental and developmental phase of a contemporary macrodialogue, but one option that seems to be gaining in favor and rising toward the top is a metric of stories instead of numbers.[229] Stories as metrics may feel disconcerting because of their qualitative versus quantitative nature. Yet they stand a much better chance of getting at and tabulating true life transformation, and they easily lend themselves to capturing every point along the discipleship continuum. They have the added benefit of being much more inspiring and energizing than numbers in a postmodern context, just as numbers may have been more inspiring in a modernist context.

Regardless, this discussion of the need to switch out the metrics of church health voiced so commonly in literature and seminars is an indication that a sharp need for something other than an attractional model of church evangelistic strategy is just around the corner. But it indicates more than that. It is a subtle indication that church revitalization might not translate into bigger attendance and giving numbers. All the work and risk of diving headlong into the paradigmatic change that the postmodern critique calls for may result in a church that looks the same numerically. A church that has embraced with its heart and soul the kind of revitalization pathway proposed in this book might achieve an end result that, strictly by the usual

---

[229] E.g., Leonard Sweet, *The Greatest Story Never Told: Revive Us Again* (Nashville: Abingdon, 2012). Perhaps the reason this macrodialogue about metrics has not yet gained clarity is because it is attempting to figure out a technical solution (metrics) to an adaptive problem (church evangelistic strategy). If an adaptive change in strategy would have come first, the most appropriate metrics might then be obvious to all.

number metrics, downgrades it to a category of declining or plateaued. Yet such churches might justifiably "rejoice that they participate in the sufferings of Christ" if they compare themselves to the earthly ministry of Christ.[230]

Why is that? Jesus had a declining numbers problem too. His crowds in John 6 dwindled to his Twelve, and his Twelve to his zero at the very pinnacle of his earthly ministry. These numbers, of course, did not tell much at all of the story. In John 6 Jesus was divested of all the numbers who were only in it for the food and miracles. And through the course of his death and resurrection, Jesus ended with only a few in number, but they were a few who had been tested and purified, were authentic, and sold out for him. The Bible is rife with instances in which God preferred small numbers of the devoted to large numbers of the lukewarm.

I imagine that most who start down a revitalization path have a picture in their minds of some future year, if they achieve revitalization, in which the church is bursting at the seams and the spiritual health of her members is roaring. While this would be wonderful, it too is a subconscious falling back to an attractional mindset. In reality, an authentic church revitalization may result in smaller numbers in attendance and less happening at the church itself, making the sense of momentum and critical mass for ministry feel lackluster. The church may end up being more spiritually healthy and more missional than ever but without the number metrics to give it credence.

When our son, Gabriel, was born with "multiple fetal anomalies" and barely clinging to life, we realized immediately that bringing this sweet baby back to our home was not going to be anything like what we had imagined. At the time, my wife and I were encouraged by an analogy that I

---

[230] 1Pe 4.13.

have since realized is commonly mentioned in the world of disabilities. Preparing for Gabriel's birth was like planning a vacation to Italy. We could imagine all the wonderful sights and sounds. We would get on the plane, ticket in hand, and our excitement would be off the charts. But, then, as we deplaned, we realized to our great shock that we had landed in Holland instead of Italy. It was not a bad place to be because Holland has its own many excitements, but it was not at all the place we were anticipating.

Something very similar may be what God has in store for the church that begins a path to revitalization. Those working so hard for revitalization and anticipating the beautiful scene on the other side of the process may find that they somehow landed in Holland instead of Italy. They may find that at the end of revitalization they are more alive in and aligned with Christ than ever as a church but undeniably poorer for it in terms of giving and attendance.

A second indication that adaptive change might soon be the unquestioned prerequisite to a thorough revitalization is a lack of satisfactory assessment tools. In my local context, among those who work toward spreading church revitalization, the Natural Church Development system of gauging church health and health improvement opportunities rates high in popularity.[231] One reason is probably because there are very few other long-reviewed options. Another reason is because it tends to be very quantitatively based. Yet another reason, which is of the greatest interest in this discussion, is that it is primarily based on attractional presuppositions. The growing tepidity with

---

[231] Christian A. Schwarz, *Natural Church Development: A Guide to Eight Essential Qualities of Healthy Churches,* 7th ed. (St. Charles, IL: ChurchSmart, 2006); cf. James S. Harrell, *Church Replanter* (South Easton, MA: Overseed, 2014). Lifeway's *Transformational Church Assessment Tool* is another; https://tcat.lifeway.com.

which revitalization consultancies employ assessment tools such as Natural Church Development may be an indication that adaptive change is due for the attractional model.

Another indication that may bolster the church as she summons the courage to accept adaptive change is the unprecedented generational changes currently occurring. First, they are unprecedented simply because of their number—for the first time in history, five generations are interacting at the same time compared with the three that coexisted ever before. This is mainly due to longevity and affluence.[232] But it has the effect of magnifying the postmodern demand for authenticity in the way the church goes about evangelism and discipleship. It also magnifies the postmodern demand for narrative and experiential truth in the way the church evaluates her own health and growth.

Jack Daniel hints at this generational magnification when he uses the analogy of restoring old cars, a personal hobby he enjoys. He notes that when he restores old cars, he brings them back to their old glory but not necessarily with the same parts or detailing.[233] In the same way, contemporary generational magnification of the postmodern critique hungers for the refurbished old glory of the church but with swapped out fundamentals and a more tightly delineated purpose. Five generations sharing the same cultural space has a blending effect of valuing the traditions of the older generations while wanting to heavily update them for the current time or the future.

Malcolm Gladwell comes at this same indication from a different angle. He compares two versions of the fable of

---

[232] Haydn Shaw, *Generational IQ: Christianity Isn't Dying, Millennials Aren't the Problem, and the Future Is Bright* (Carol Stream, IL: Tyndale, 2015).
[233] Jack L. Daniel, *Patient Catalyst: Leading Church Revitalization* (South Easton, MA: Overseed, 2018), 1ff.

the Tortoise and the Hare. In the version most North Americans would know, the tortoise wins the race through persistence and dedication. The moral is "Slow and steady wins the race." But another version, commonly encountered in cultures with a history of oppression and slavery, has the tortoise winning the race through an ingenious combination of trickery and deception. The moral here is "If we work together, even though we may have to resort to mischievery, we will overcome." Gladwell's point is that underdogs can have better odds at winning than their well-situated colleagues.[234] The postmodern critique calls for something very similar from the church. The contemporary generational magnification asks the church to cross the same missional finish line that she has had for two thousand years, but to do it another way. It asks the church to win the race from a position of powerlessness, ingenuity, and relationship rather than through the attractional means that have been standard for so long.

Choosing the path of revitalization

As the church determines to embrace adaptive change on her quest for missionality and revitalization, she must understand that the stakes are high. She must click the "Agree" checkbox and sign on the dotted line, knowing she cannot go back. Once she continues down the adaptive revitalization path, something of a game of chicken inevitably develops—will one and all in the church hold tightly to their commitment to the adaptive change come what may, or will they "blink" first and skitter off instead onto a vastly easier pathway of technical change? Because of certain power dynamics ubiquitous in the local church, it quickly becomes a situation more like a heart transplant

---

[234] Malcolm Gladwell, *David and Goliath: Underdogs, Misfits, and the Art of Battling Giants* (New York: Little, Brown, 2013).

patient who was in such poor health before the operation that he did not rightfully qualify for a good heart. The question becomes, will the good heart "take" and bring the sickly man back to health, or will the trauma be too much for the patient's system for him to survive? The procedure that was absolutely and urgently critical to save the patient's life has very good odds of being the very thing that kills him.

Jim Harrell of Overseed, a church revitalization training agency throughout New England, identifies four stages of church decline. Thinking of Nehemiah rebuilding Jerusalem, he labels the first two Stage 1: Need People and Stage 2: No Gates. Both call for revitalization. He categorizes Stages 3 and 4, each with greater dysfunctionality, as requiring replanting.[235] There has been much debate over what terms to use for revitalization among those with that concentration. Some use *revitalization* and *replanting* interchangeably, and a variety of other terms have been proposed.[236] *Revitalization* has general, if temporary, acceptance as a term to denote a dying, historic church turning around and gaining missional focus, critical mass, and new long-term health. *Replanting* is generally taken to mean completely restarting the church by various methods.[237]

The point here, in this chapter in a book devoted solely to authentic revitalization, is threefold. First, by God's grace, any church can revitalize, no matter what stage of decline she may find herself in. The situation is never too dire if she is willing to walk by faith, not by sight, and if she is

---

[235] Harrell, *Church Replanter*. Harrell uses "replanting" as a hard reset form of revitalization.

[236] E.g., Daniel, *Patient Catalyst*, proposes "restoration," 1ff.

[237] Tom Cheyney has identified many different options. These may be found throughout his writings, but a good place to start is *Thirty-Eight Church Revitalization Models for the Twenty-First Century* (Orlando, FL: Renovate, 2014).

willing to fully commit herself to the harrowing process of true paradigmatic change in response to the postmodern critique. The difficult, lengthy, and high-risk revitalization process returns great rewards, the greatest of which is a continuity of her historic identity, reinvigorated and vibrant, as God's candlestick in the community in which God has placed her.[238] Second, replanting is probably an easier route in most cases because, comparatively anyway, it offers the luxury of starting from a blank slate. It likely has a higher success rate. But it sometimes comes at the cost of capitulation and a truncating of the rich history the church has to offer.

Third, the church must pick one: technical/incremental change or adaptive/paradigmatic change. This is one of those rare instances where the choice must be binary. Adaptive change does not allow much room for a continuum. Both will be worthwhile and will undoubtedly serve the church well in her postmodern context. But the postmodern critique will inevitably judge a technical solution as disingenuous and inauthentic. At best, a technical solution will deny the immense potential for powerful change possible through a paradigmatic course of revitalization. Many churches, fully committed to an underlying attractional model, and executing that model exceptionally, attempt to make a response to the postmodern critique an add-on to their attractional strategy. They have recognized elements of the postmodern critique, and because of their desire to engage the community around them, simply tack on community service programs. These are effective for their name recognition in the community, and they show the hands and feet of Jesus well.

---

[238] Rev 1.20.

But they miss the true power available through the more difficult path of a paradigmatic change that will result in a revitalization that will be far more native in a postmodern milieu. This sort of technical change is incredibly appealing. To churches that are currently thriving under an attractional model, the prospect of deconstructing what seems to be going well to gain a more authentic evangelism and discipleship seems needlessly painful and unwise. To churches that are at death's door and already in the farthest stages of decline, simply throwing in the towel and starting over seems the best option by far. Starting over or limiting revitalization to technical changes may be what a majority of churches will elect to do as they are increasingly forced to respond to the liminal void, but a resolute commitment to revitalization through a paradigmatic change in response to the postmodern critique and with a solitary focus on Christ's missionality is by far the more potent, more native, more effective path.

An example of technical change masquerading as paradigmatic change is the church's response to the COVID-19 pandemic. In the church leadership circles of North America, many have seen a silver lining of opportunity within this health crisis. They have stated that the church must "pivot" by accepting that physical church attendance will become ever less important and that an online presence will become paramount.[239] Such may be the case, but the arguments that are offered in support betray nothing more than technical change in a church evangelism strategy. These arguments center around a generational preference for online content, unique clicks, and IP addresses, and how to ensure that online followers connect with the church

---

[239] A leading example is Carey Nieuwhof, e.g., "Eight Ways to Lead in the New Digital Default Church," https://careynieuwhof.com/8-ways-to-lead-in-the-new-digital-default-church/.

through giving and other means. The excitement around making church digital may be the start of good development, but one thing it is not is any kind of paradigmatic shift away from an attractional model of church ministry and evangelism.[240]

All that has happened in this case is that the locus of attractionality has moved from a physical location to a cyber location.[241] Just as much money, staffing, and focus as before are spent on excellence and whatever stands in the place of the weekend gathering. The expectation remains unaltered that the sacred place is the central location of the church and that all evangelism and discipleship survive through an online umbilical cord to the mothership. The metrics of attendance and giving become even more important for a cyber attractional church than they were for a location-based one. Faced with the golden opportunity of the great disruption throughout 2020 brought on by the pandemic, many churches are seizing upon a grand technical fix when they could have used the opportunity for a paradigmatic one. They have not fundamentally changed the way they do church. They have not materially altered the church evangelistic strategy they have received from their

---

[240] E.g., Carey Nieuwhof, "In-person attendance v. online attendance and the emerging trap of doing nothing well," https://careynieuwhof.com/in-person-services-v-online-services-and-the-emerging-trap-of-doing-nothing-well/.

[241] This was already in the works before the pandemic, in that even committed churchgoers were attending far less frequently. Some small surveys suggest that committed Christians were attending their member churches an average of 1.6 times per month. David Murrow, "Why Is Church Attendance Declining—Even Among Committed Christians?" March 7, 2016, https://www.patheos.com/blogs/churchformen/2016/03/why-is-church-attendance-declining-even-among-christians/; Tom May, "Column: Counting the Blessing of Those Who Minister," *News and Tribune*, May 4, 2019, https://www.newsandtribune.com/opinion/column-counting-the-blessing-of-those-who-minister.

modernist predecessors. They have simply moved their attractional operations online.

Perhaps the reader's appetite is by now whetted for an example of what a paradigmatic change in response to the postmodern critique might look like. Mile Marker Four is solely dedicated to sketching out one option. But the stage of decline or health of any given church has great bearing on her appetite for paradigmatic change. It may even be that churches that are doing well enough and do not find themselves in the more desperate stages of decline have a disadvantage. Such churches may never have the requisite motivation to enter into a complete overhaul or swapping out of their operating system. The pain of being in their present condition might not be high enough to make the risk seem worthwhile. It may be inordinately easier for them to limp along as they are. A few technical changes might sufficiently slake their sense of urgency about the effectiveness of their witness. But the churches that are truly desperate, that are staring certain death in the eyes—this might be their very great advantage. On the one hand, they have nothing to lose. On the other, the pain of staying just as they are is truly unbearable. For them, doing nothing, or merely making some technical or incremental changes, is not even an option on the table. They do not have the time and they know it in the marrow of their bones.

Change only occurs when the pain of staying put exceeds the pain of moving on. If the pain of staying put is equal to or less than the pain of moving on, change is very unlikely to happen. In the middle of a July night in 1988, a fire erupted on the Piper Alpha oil rig in the North Atlantic. Some routine pump maintenance had been underway, but because of a shift change and some communication errors, somebody turned the pump on. It is still the deadliest offshore oil rig disaster in history. The survivors' stories are truly terrifying. As the workers raced around trying to escape the fire that was engulfing the platform, they were faced with two options: go to a fireproofed escape room on the upper levels of the platform and await rescue, or jump one hundred and seventy-five feet into the turbulent North Atlantic Ocean in the middle of the night, one hundred and twenty miles from shore. There were two hundred and twenty-six people on the rig at the time of the explosion, and only sixty-one survived. The fireproofed escape room probably seemed the saner option in the moment, even though it was enclosed in an oil platform that was seriously compromised. Yet the only workers who survived were those who hurled themselves into the ocean. The pain of staying put so greatly exceeded the insanity of the one-hundred-and-seventy-five-foot jump that they opted for the latter.[242]

A renewed missionality for the church will not find its most potent expression in doing the same things better. A greater sense of "*why* is the church" will find an unsatisfactory match with a postmodern culture's receptors for the gospel message if the church's path to revitalization is one of technical or incremental change. The attractional model of church evangelistic strategy that has been the standard for at least the last two hundred years has suddenly become a swing and a miss with the advent of postmodernism and postchristianity. Some other strategy must be employed if churches in that culture, such as those in New England, are to arrest their decline and connect with the vast majority of people in their community that do not even know the churches exist.[243] What is needed, and what is

---

[242] "July 6, 1988: The Piper Alpha Disaster," *The Maritime Executive*, https://www.maritime-executive.com/article/july-6-1988-the-piper-alpha-disaster.

[243] An example of others noticing this is Carey Nieuwhof, "The Western Church Needs a New Evangelism Strategy: Five Promising Options," https://careynieuwhof.com/the-western-church-needs-a-new-evangelism-strategy-5-promising-options/.

proposed next, is an evangelistic strategy that takes seriously the critiques of postmodernism and adaptively alters the attractional model. This kind of adaptive change may seem an almost insurmountable form of change to the church in decline, but the potential rewards for accomplishing it are rich and many. The church that commits herself wholly to such adaptive, paradigmatic change can, by the grace of God, achieve it. The question for the church facing this difficult revitalization path is this: are you in or are you out?

Mile Marker Four: Pathway Inversion

A critical point

This book is designed to apply theory to a great problem facing the church, and out of that theory to offer practical applications for the real-world contexts of local churches and their leadership. The great problem the church is facing is that Neutrals are becoming an ever larger group and the church's best laid plans for evangelism and ministry seem to have little hope of arresting this trend. The decline in church numbers, the absence of Millennial or Gen Z commitment, and any other ominous trend are probably only symptoms of the greater problem and likely have no life of their own. But a missionality born of a dynamic conversation with postmoderns that re-engages them with the church—that has the potential to bring the church decline in places like New England to a halt.

A well-considered and well-stated mission tends to unite and inspire. Denominational disagreements and local internecine wars vanish when a clear, focused, compelling, courageous missionality is driving the church.[244] Actual, authentic church revitalization is the perfectly formulated antidote to the whole plethora of problems currently facing the church in North America because it addresses the core, underlying problem from which all the other problems spring.

A path to church revitalization may be clearly charted by engaging the critiques of postmodern culture, mile marker by mile marker. At Mile Marker One along that path, the objective is to see afresh the missionality Christ intends for his church. Incarnationally walking with contemporary postmodern culture may be thought of as Mile Marker Two. Mile Marker Three could equate to appreciating and

---

[244] Cf. Pat MacMillan, *The Performance Factor: Unlocking the Secrets of Teamwork* (Nashville: B&H, 2001).

accepting that paradigmatic, adaptive change is the prescription. At Mile Marker Four, theory begins to convert to practical steps for real-world contexts.

I remember visiting Niagara Falls as a young child. I was fascinated by an invisible line upstream from the falls referred to as "the point of no return." If a swimmer or watercraft were to cross that invisible line, there was no possibility of rescue. It was simply too late—game over. Churches far along the path of decline face a similar invisible line, and the closer they get to that line, the more keenly interested they seem to be in actual, practical steps and the less in theory, however good it may be. "Understanding missionality, postmodern perspective, and the paradigmatic nature of any solution may be all well and fine," they may say, "but what are we actually going to do differently that could bring in the lost and the young families, and remove any threat of closing our doors?" Mile Marker Four is the turning point from theory to practice on a path to church revitalization. It is the point along the journey at which the theory and theology of the previous three chapters begin to take on a discernible, tangible form. For churches that decide at Mile Marker Three that, faced with the prospect of adaptive, paradigmatic change in their quest for missionality they will go all in and go for broke, find at Mile Marker Four that everything they thought they knew about how to conduct themselves as a church turns upside down.

The unifying mission of the church is to draw those who are not in Christ to Christ. In a postmodern and postchristian culture, particularly one as deeply so as New England, the overwhelming majority of those who are not in Christ are those who have no familiarity with or connection to Jesus or his church whatsoever. To reach them, the church earnestly embarking on a path to revitalization must do anything necessary. As Craig Groeshel is fond of saying, "We will do anything short of sin to reach the lost."[245] Such a church is willing to lose large aspects of her identity to reach them—all her identity, in fact, except that which is found only and simply in the person of Jesus.

This church gladly forfeits her music style preferences, dress codes, unwritten rules, and other sacred cows. She embraces ingenuity in her model of church ministry and rearrangement in her evangelistic strategy. She is fixated on engaging that segment of the population around her that has the greatest distance from church and gospel. For this reason, she finds transfer growth wholly unsatisfactory. The church willing to lose her identity to gain a clearer mission is not lured by the models of attractional churches all around her, because she has a wholly different goal. Her missionality focuses her inexorably on those who have no familiarity with church, no childhood acquaintance with church, and no learned expectation that church has anything to offer them. This church's mission is not to reach the low-hanging fruit of those more easily drawn to an attractional church, but to reach those with whom the church has no bridge whatsoever.

In April 2019, the world was reeling from the shock of the extensive destruction of the Cathedral of Notre Dame and was awestruck by the irrevocable loss of nine hundred years of history. This reaction was symbolic of the angst experienced at the time by the entire western church as she slowly began to realize that the esteem in which society had held the church for seventeen hundred years was no more. Regardless of whether or not the proposals offered in this book are proven to be sufficiently viable or biblical, a proactive answer to this irrevocable loss of seventeen hundred years of how to "do church" will require courageous

---

[245] Craig Groeschel, *It: How Churches and Leaders Can Get It and Keep It* (Grand Rapids, MI: Zondervan, 2008).

thinking, adaptive leadership, the suspension of presuppositions, and a surrender to the whisper of the Spirit. In 2006, realizing the import of this moment, Alan Hirsch said,

> I have to confess that I do not think that the inherited formulas will work anymore ... The tools and techniques that fitted previous eras of Western history simply don't seem to work any longer. What we need now is a new set of tools. A new 'paradigm'—a new vision of reality: a fundamental change in our thoughts, perceptions, and values, especially as they relate to our view of the church and mission.[246]

But this moment, as fear-inducing and traumatic as it may be, is clearly God-ordained, a key movement in the unfurling of God's grand redemptive plan. Almost three quarters of a century ago, Hendrick Kraemer heralded what he could sense was ahead, saying, "Strictly speaking, one ought to say that the Church is always in a state of crisis and that its greatest shortcoming is that it is only occasionally aware of it. ... [it] has always needed apparent failure and suffering in order to become fully alive to its real nature and mission."[247] In the same vein, David Bosch observed that

> for many centuries the church [in the West] has suffered very little and has been led to believe that it is a success. Like its Lord, the church—if it is faithful to its being—will, however, always be controversial, a 'sign that will be spoken against' (Lk 2:34). That there were so many centuries of crisis-free existence for the church was therefore an abnormality. Now, at long

---

[246] Alan Hirsch, *The Forgotten Ways: Reactivating Apostolic Movements*, 2nd ed., (Grand Rapids, MI: Brazos, 2016), 16–17.

[247] Hendrick Kraemer, *The Christian Message in a Non-Christian World*, 2nd ed. (New York: International Missionary Council, 1947), https://archive.org/details/christianmessage00krae.

last, we are 'back to normal' .... and we know it! And if the atmosphere of crisislessness still lingers on in many parts of the West this is simply the result of a dangerous delusion. Let us also know that to encounter crisis is to encounter the possibility of truly being the *church*.[248]

The proposal offered herein will undoubtedly fill the bill for controversiality, and it is offered with the anticipation of encountering 'the possibility of truly being the church."

Leaving an old model

For decades, an attractional church model has dominated the thinking about North American church growth, but the new postmodern and postchristian milieu requires an extreme inversion of the attractional strategy. As in other areas, the postmodern worldview forces a healthy corrective, here reminding the church of Jesus's own model of missionality and the model of the early church. This inverted, kinetic model stands in direct opposition to the attractional model and also differs materially from an incarnational model of church missionality.

The attractional model of church growth has proven effective and powerful in spreading the gospel and putting large numbers of people on the path of discipleship. Even though its heyday may have been in the 1990s and 2000s, it is still often held up as *the* way to "do church" for any church wanting to grow and to engage the culture effectively. As discussed in Mile Marker Three, the attractional model devotes inordinate amounts of resources to making the weekend gatherings everything that they can possibly be, with the goal of exceptionalism and excellence. This

---

[248] David J. Bosch, *Transforming Mission: Paradigm Shifts in Theology of Mission*, 20th anniversary ed. (Maryknoll, NY: Orbis, 2011), 2–3. Italics his.

resource allotment is across the board, in personnel, budgetary line items, organization-wide focus, measurements of success, and use of volunteers. Attendance, volunteering, and engagement in these weekend gatherings is a large part of the calculus in determining if a church member is in good standing. There are other key elements in "doing church" in the attractional model, such as connections through small groups, service to the community, discipleship classes, and an emphasis on *foreign* missionary work as outreach, but the overpowering piece that makes the attractional model the attractional model is the heavy emphasis on making the weekend gatherings the highest expression of church life.

As a review in order to set my proposed model in stark relief, I can say that there is a powerful and effective reason for this: the weekend gatherings are thought of as the front door, the giant, impossible-to-miss main door into church life and into an introduction to Jesus and his way. In other words, (1) attendees of an attractional model church are urged to build intentional-for-the-gospel relationships with those in their various spheres of influence who do not yet trust in Jesus. Then, (2) in his time, the Holy Spirit will open up an opportunity for attendees to invite them to come to a weekend gathering at their attractional church ("we can sit together," they might say). Finally, (3) the exceptionally well done weekend gathering will unveil Jesus as these guests have never seen him before and church as they have never known it before. After attending for some time, (4) these newcomers will take the "next steps" to get more involved in the church community.[249] Sometimes, it can have such a transactional feel to it, or maybe even that of an assembly

---

[249] These next steps are typically a newcomer's class or Alpha course, plugging into a small group, or volunteering in some capacity in the weekend gathering.

line. There is also reason to think that it subliminally encourages Christians to develop relationships at least in some sense *as a means* to make them Christian and add them to the church. This is the very kind of thing that makes postmoderns so wary.

Often, this strategically conceived pathway of being invited by a friend to come to a weekend gathering, beginning to belong to the church community, and paying it forward through volunteering in the weekend gathering is expressed simply in three words. "Gather, connect, serve," "worship, grow, go," "belong, believe, become," and "lead, train, send" are a few examples. The large corporate gathering is the first and most prominent piece, a belonging or discipleship piece typically follows next, and a volunteerism piece is the final stop, or, more accurately, the last step in a pathway that is conceptually cyclical.

The attractional church movement has been frequently accused of fostering consumerism, and the terms "seeker sensitive" and "attractional" are often used synonymously.[250] They are two sides of the same coin. By dedicating every resource possible to making the worship experience exceptional, the attractional model unwittingly plays right into the consumer mentality. Sometimes this is intentional in the attractional church, or uncritically adopted; in most cases, it is wholly unintentional, adopted without sufficient introspection to reveal its flaw. By making the weekend gathering the Mecca where personal evangelism reaches fruition, the attractional model is accidentally saying that the customer needs to be satisfied every time, or the customer's needs must be met every time, and that good follow-up and customer retention are indispensable. It is just as accidentally sending subliminal

---

[250] E.g., Hirsch, *Forgotten Ways*, 35, 42-43.

messages to its members that they are less than qualified to lead others to faith on their own.

Recently, I took my daughters to a favorite restaurant for breakfast. The service personnel were new on this occasion and the service fell well short of the usual excellence to which we had become accustomed. Actually, it was pretty awful. This poor experience could have been enough to keep me, as a consumer, from coming back again. This kind of thinking is the same kind that leads to attractional church "speak." This is why church leaders in the attractional movement are incessantly reminded to make every church experience excellent, to do so within the first ten seconds after a guest enters the doors, to put a gift card in the mail to each first-time guest first thing Monday morning, and to have myriad assimilation systems in place. This is why guest services are considered such a necessity, not so much because they stand on their own as a concept but because of the terror that strikes every church leader's heart: "If they have a bad experience the first time, they'll never darken the door again."[251]

The attractional church has not set out with a goal of fostering a consumer mindset, but she has accidentally fallen backward into it, despite her good intentions, because of a questionable biblical strategy.[252] This accidental

---

[251] This is also the primary motivation for many churches that pull out all the stops for Easter. Because Easter weekend had the highest attendance statistically for many years, it stood to reason that it was also the most important weekend on which to showcase attractional excellence. As an example, I received an email from a church growth organization ahead of Easter 2019 proclaiming Easter "the Super Bowl of church services."
[252] Another indication of something amiss in the appropriateness of this strategy is the jealousy and depression it seems to invite into the larger church of Jesus. "The vast majority of evangelical churches, perhaps up to 95 percent, subscribe to the contemporary church growth approach in

consumerism, much more dangerously, then becomes extended to the overall discipleship journey as well.[253] Incidentally, this is the spawning ground for so many of the ailments of the North American church. One example is one-upmanship. Under this accidental consumerist mindset that springs from the very DNA of the attractional church, even the purest and humblest of church leaders can find themselves justifying subconscious efforts to make their buildings or programs or worship experience, or themselves as pastors, better than those of the next church.[254]

One reason the attractional model likely became so effective around the turn of the century is its emphasis on relational evangelism. Whether this came about as an attempt to meet postmodern values or postmodern tendencies simply infiltrated the church and her leaders may be unimportant; what is important is that this emphasis on

---

their attempts to grow the congregation, in spite of the fact that successful applications of this model remain relatively rare ... it doesn't seem to work for most of our churches and for the majority of our populations. In fact, it has become a source of frustration and guilt, because most churches do not have the combination of factors that make for a successful application of the model." Hirsch, *Forgotten Ways*, 36.

[253] "Sitcom content makes the assumption that things can be resolved at the end of church. It seeks to leave an audience with some key, practical steps to having their best life now. ... Sitcom content often has a good intent. But most content like that is based on the idea that good teaching can't simply introduce a problem without providing sound solutions for life application. Whether right or wrong, most young adults see this type of content as lacking *depth*." Ed Stetzer, Richie Stanley, and Jason Hayes, *Lost and Found: The Younger Unchurched and the Churches That Reach Them* (Nashville: B&H, 2009), 95.

[254] Occasionally, someone stepping away from what is sometimes described as the hamster wheel of the attractional machine will describe a haunting feeling that there must be something more to *ekklesia* than what the attractional model has on offer. "One of the more obvious signs is the sense of holy discontent among Christians of all ages and classes ... Even the boomers are asking, 'Has it all come down to this? Attending church services, singing songs to God, and attending cell groups? Is this really what Christianity is all about?'" Hirsch, *Forgotten Ways*, 268.

relational evangelism stood in stark contrast to some of the more transactional forms of evangelism stressed in the modernist era. A few examples might be cold witnessing, street preaching, handing out tracts, offering apologetics, making an unassailable case, as in Josh McDowell's *Evidence That Demands a Verdict,* and the entrenched linear feel of the Four Spiritual Laws.[255] But the attractional model pioneered a return to relationship in church evangelism. At the very least, this coincided with the advent of the postmodern worldview, filling the hunger for mystery and relationship which that worldview highlighted in society and in the church. The attractional model is, in its own way, every bit as missional and intentional about relational evangelism as the incarnational model or the kinetic model proposed below. The important distinction, however, is that the locus of relational evangelism in the attractional model is solidly in the all-important weekend gathering where relationship is subordinated to the big event.

A second reason might have been the attractional model's eagerness to compete with the excellence of attractions in the everyday life of wider culture. In the vein of Larry Norman's 1972 release "Why Should the Devil Have All the Good Music?" the attractional model puts such disproportionate emphasis on excellence in the weekend gatherings because it is eager to show church invitees that the worship of God can be well done, with a professionalism that stresses the importance of fellowship with Jesus in the lives of the churchgoers. The attractional model desires to show that God is important enough and church is important enough to put the best talent, time, and resources into making the worship gathering as good as any mainstream concert, or better. How could it be thought of any other way?

---

[255] Josh McDowell and Sean McDowell, *Evidence That Demands a Verdict: Life-Changing Truth for a Skeptical World* (Nashville: Thomas Nelson, 2017).

If Jesus is the most important thing in life, then that ought to be obvious to any guest simply by how much effort is exerted in making the weekend gathering excellent in every way. Excellent in every way includes signage and advertising before a guest ever enters the parking lot, parking attendants and valet service and close-in spaces for mothers with child, smiles and friendly welcomes at the door, an inviting aroma, ambiance and cleanliness upon entry, seating attendants, ease-you-into-the-mood opening songs, delightfully fun and safe children's areas, and so on.[256]

But there has come to be in recent years a huge problem here.[257] Postmodernism has moved on and diverged from the conditions that originally gave rise to the attractional model of church growth and evangelism. Postmodern culture has grown highly suspicious, and with good reason, of the true motives of the attractional model, and even more so of its results. This divergence and suspicion is likely to increase in the years to come until in the near future the attractional model may cease to be effective in cultures like that of New England. The best of the attractional church sincerely longs to approach society

---

[256] Andy Stanley's "Rules of Engagement" funnel is a great example. Andy Stanley, *Deep and Wide: Creating Churches Unchurched People Love to Attend* (Grand Rapids, MI: Zondervan, 2012). Another good example is Sue Miller, with David Staal, *Making Your Children's Ministry the Best Hour of Every Kid's Week* (Grand Rapids, MI: Zondervan, 2004).

[257] "While Christendom as a cultural, religious, and political force operating from the center of society was basically eliminated in the modern period, our current imagination of church nonetheless remains fundamentally the same. In the late twentieth century the best missional thinkers and strategists are beginning to recognize that the game is up. This recognition has been partly due to the fact that Christianity is in massive, trended decline in the West but paradoxically is on the increase in the developing world. There is a sense of dread that somehow the church in its current and predominant mode is not going to cut it. As a result, in the last few decades there has been a sense of unease and a roaming of the collective mind in search of new answers." Hirsch, *Forgotten Ways*, 267.

altruistically, seeing one life at a time transformed and healed through an invitation to church and an introduction there to Jesus; however, postmodern culture has begun to regard this altruism as little more than a thinly veiled narcissism.

Where the attractional model proponent extols excellence, the postmodern sees gaudy opulence. Where the attractional church calls for a sacrificial investment in the church's mission, the postmodern suspects a pyramid scheme for the church as an organization, and maybe even for the senior pastor and executive leadership.[258] When the attractional leader advocates for service, the postmodern hears self-advancement of the organizational machine. Even if most attractional churches pursue the one-on-one invitation and life transformation with genuine zeal, it does not matter, because they are on the wrong side of the perception equation in our current culture as it ages into postchristianity and postmodernity.

Shifting to a new model

A proactive shift on the part of the North American church will be necessary to deftly navigate this sea change within postmodern culture. Any delay in recognizing the need for this radical shift and executing it not only further estranges the church and her all-important good news from society at an ever-quickening pace, but increasingly erodes and effaces the path of discipleship modeled by Jesus in the hearts of believers and unbelievers alike. Mile Marker One asserted that the first and primary act of obedience to the Great Commission is going. So at the very least, the "come

---

[258] Once, when I was working on a paving crew in the parking lot of a large attractional church, one worker offered a sentiment popular among the whole crew, "You know what happens here on Monday mornings? That's when all the Brink's trucks show up."

and see" *modus operandi* of the attractional model should be replaced by a "go and be" course of action. This is precisely the pivot point at which the church shifts radically from the attractional model to one that is incarnational or kinetic.

The radical shift required is a simple inversion, one that is logically simplistic but infeasible in the reality of a North American church.[259] Instead of "gather–connect–serve," the inversion calls for "serve–connect–gather." In the attractional model, walking through the giant, can't-miss front doors of the church gives people the feeling they are answering an invitation to go inside and attend an attractional weekend gathering. In an inversion of that model, the front doors of the church offer people a chance to establish a burgeoning rapport with Jesus and the church and then go out to extend it to the local community and form intentional relationships that are the result of serving in the community. It is important to note at this juncture that the definition of *serve* in the two strategies is different. In the attractional model, serve *may* mean projects and benevolence in the community, but it often almost exclusively means volunteering *in* making the weekend gathering a thing of excellence. (In the Attractional Model graphic on the next page, the return arrow shows the direct link of "serve" to ensuring weekend gathering excellence.) But in the inverted model, serve *may* mean volunteering in a weekend gathering, but it almost exclusively refers to projects and benevolence *out in* the local community.[260]

---

[259] Of course, without the power and calling of the Holy Spirit, it is not only infeasible, it is farcical. This book hopes to point the way to making something infeasible have a good chance of success.

[260] Stetzer's research team came to the conclusion that this change in definition must be made: "Among unchurched young adults, service (a tenet of responsibility) was cited as a major reason why they would

The middle step of both strategies is a connection piece that emphasizes belonging, and it is usually a constellation of programs with a small group philosophy as a nucleus. And where "serve" is the final, pay-it-forward step of a conceptually cyclical attractional model, in the inverted model the final, rallying, and equipping step of the same conceptual cycle is instead the weekend gathering. Now, however, the weekend gathering tends to have a rally-like flavor to it, equipping, energizing, and encouraging the faithful in what God has done out in the community in the week past, what he is now doing in their hearts today, and what he will do out in the community through their obedience over the week ahead.[261] So the weekend gathering acts as a springboard, or an equipping session, for continuing involvement of the believers in the community (shown by the return arrow in the Kinetic Model graphic below).

In my own context, an ongoing experiment from which this paper draws inspiration is unfolding and has been for seven years running. The three words used in this experiment are care–connect–celebrate. Imperfect spheres of connotation and unwanted baggage might plague these words, but they still manage to crystalize for church attendees that the impossible-to-miss front doors of the church are relationships built and relational stock accrued while blessing the community in some way.[262] And they stress that the weekend gathering has been demoted from its heretofore ecclesial primacy. Although the weekend gathering is indicated by the word "celebrate," it is still the

---

consider (or not consider) being part of a church. Knowing this, we must focus our efforts toward establishing social action as a major element in the strategies and programs of our churches." Stetzer, Stanley, and Hayes, *Lost and Found*, 117.

[261] Cf. Stetzer, Stanley, and Hayes, *Lost and Found*, Chapter 6.

[262] Because of this, in recent years we have modified these words to be Community Value (instead of Care), Connecting Spaces (instead of Connect), and Collective Worship (instead of Celebrate).

place for so many other *C*s, such as conviction, comfort, confession, contrition, communion, and so forth.

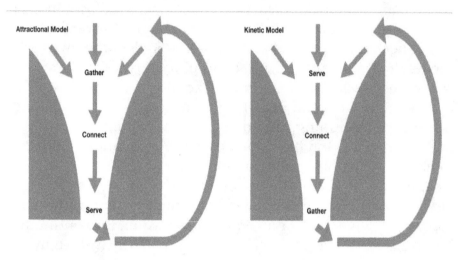

The inversion advocated herein is little more than a flip-flopping of two words, *gather* and *serve*, at least on its face. But the implications are deep and paradigm-shattering. With *gather* as the final step instead of the first step, all manner of long-accepted North American ecclesiology is undermined. The implications border on scandalous for many Christians. Church leaders and communicators no longer urge their hearers to "invite somebody to church," or at least not with anywhere near the intensity they used to have.

Churchgoers are willing to accept poorer-feeling, less-well-done weekend gatherings because they understand and agree with the results of a mathematical equation that puts time, effort, expertise, and funds in service of relationship and rapport building in the community. They are willing to do so even at the cost of a not-so-excellently-done weekend gathering. The old nickels-and-noses metrics are no longer relevant because attendance at the weekend gathering is no longer the primary or most visible expression of membership or involvement.[263] Having a less-well-maintained church campus, far from being the admission of spiritual apathy that it would be under the attractional model, is now a badge of honor; it is a billboard indicating that dollars and resources are being diverted in a selfless manner away from the accoutrements of a central headquarters and toward the neighbors and community in the local church's own backyard.

A core estimation of discipleship moves from classrooms and Bible studies to the act of going in "serve," with the belonging of "connect" and the equipping of "gather" following in tow.[264] The follow-up systems and assimilation strategies for first-time guests and new regular attendees so commonly considered crucial to church growth

---

[263] What if the giving and attendance metrics actually trend down with the successful implementation of inversion? As Kelly notes, this is often the case: "For the most part they are small projects, learning as they go, making mistakes and struggling to stay on track. Some are dipping their toes into postmodern waters, others wading waist-deep, others still diving deep and staying under. Their shared commitment is to ask what it will mean for the Christian faith to be rerooted in the emerging cultures of the transitional generations. As such they are a measure of the Western church's potential for rebirth. ... Experimental groups seeking to engage the Christian faith in a postmodern context will often lack the resources, profile or success record of the Boomer congregations. By definition, they are new, untried, relatively disorganized and fearful of self-promotion. They reject the corporate model of their Boomer forebears, and thus do not appear, according to existing paradigms, to be significant." Gerard Kelly, *RetroFuture: Rediscovering Our Roots, Recharting Our Routes* (Downers Grove, IL: InterVarsity, 2000). I often hear this retort supplied by Hirsch from other pastors regarding an attractional inversion to a kinetic model: "I have often had the field criticism of the EMC in the guise of pragmatic questions like 'Where is it working?' or dismissed in phrases like 'When I can see some success, I might consider it.'" Hirsch, *Forgotten Ways*, 269.

[264] "Our churches must teach that service and missions are foundational to our faith from day one, as opposed to being the 'bonus round' that we can access only after we've worked through the rest of the spiritual developmental checklist." Stetzer, Stanley, and Hayes, *Lost and Found*, 118.

now mostly miss the point.[265] The visibility of the pastor and the importance of pastoral care duties traditionally central to that role diminish precipitously, because the pastor and top leadership are now needed less for actual "doing" and more for publicly painting pictures of Great Commission goals, keeping the entire organism of the church on the same page with regard to communication, and organizing teams to facilitate active involvement of every possible church attendee in "serve."

It is no longer so crucial that the pastor be an excellent orator or a charismatic preacher. Why? Because the weekend gathering is now primarily a rallying and equipping session for believers and less a catch-them-and hold-them church service. By the same token, it becomes less of an absolute necessity to attract and supply the best musical talent at significant cost. The weekend church service is just not that crucial anymore. It is no longer the attractant. In a kinetic model the attractant to a church is the relationships, priestly blessing, and selfless activity of her people out in the community.

Service in, with, and for the church's local community becomes the highest goal of the church, and, in a manner of speaking, the solitary reason for the church to exist. It may be interesting to note that where the advent of the attractional model coincided with the postmodern worldview's emphasis on relationships, its radical inversion might coincide with a cultural obsolescence of schedule availability on Sundays and weekends. At the very moment that the church in New England might choose to begin to invert the attractional model and place importance on going

---

[265] In many circles, Nelson Searcy is the bible on assimilation systems. Nelson Searcy, with Jennifer Dykes Henson, *Fusion: Turning First-Time Guests into Fully Engaged Members of Your Church* (Grand Rapids, MI: Baker, 2008).

out by deemphasizing attendance at weekend gatherings, the New England culture has already reached a point where at least thirty-four percent of New Englanders work on weekends. Frequent weekend vacationing is also becoming the norm, and families with teenagers must choose between no extracurricular involvement or no church attendance.[266]

Difficulties in implementing the kinetic model

There are a host of ways the kinetic model upsets the status quo. Although it is now in vogue to discuss moving away from measurement of the old metrics and toward the collation of redemptive stories instead, an inversion of the attractional model further complicates this discussion.[267] Now even if the collation of stories is embraced as a primary measurement, from where do those stories originate? From

---

[266] https://www.bls.gov/news.release/atus.t04.htm. As already mentioned in a previous footnote, I have read in a number of online posts, but cannot verify, a claim that currently dedicated churchgoers attend their home church an average of 1.6 times per month nationwide. Personal communication with several purveyors of this statistic indicates that it is the result of at least two churches, one in Arizona and one in Oregon, taking internal polls. This number tracks with the author's anecdotal observations and is very likely lower still for the New England area because of its heightened weekend vacation culture and a larger-than-average medical profession segment of the workforce. Carey Nieuwhof lists some reasons for this trend as greater affluence, higher focus on kids' activities, more travel, blended and single-parent families, online options, the cultural disappearance of guilt, self-directed spirituality, failure to see a direct benefit, valuing attendance over engagement, and a massive cultural shift, https://careynieuwhof.com/10-reasons-even-committed-church-attenders-attending-less-often/; cf. Reggie Joiner, *Zombies, Football and the Gospel* (Cumming, GA: Orange, 2012).

[267] Sweet talks of the ABC, Attendance, Buildings, and Cash, metrics in Leonard Sweet, *I Am a Follower: The Way, Truth, and Life of Following Jesus* (Nashville: Thomas Nelson, 2012), 83. In the BCNE (Baptist Churches of New England), a baptism count is all-important, and although membership and membership transfers are also monitored, baptism is accepted as indisputable proof that the invisible church is growing, has plateaued, or is declining numerically.

actual life transformation in or as a result of a weekend gathering or small group, or from unbelievers in the local community who may be barely beginning a journey as a –10 on the Engel scale?[268] If the latter, the capturing and promotion of these stories becomes that much more tricky.

If the centrality of traditional worship and Christian education is removed, where will biblical depth and a full understanding of theology and doctrine be accessed? Will it not also blur the church's identity if the church spread throughout the community is more highly valued than the church gathered? If the central reason for the existence of a local church becomes building rapport for the Name of Christ in the community and building long-term, messy relationships with hitherto nameless townspeople, where is the urgent concern for their souls should this be their last day on earth and where does evangelism actually happen?[269] Worse, if any serious attempt to meet the postmodern requires selfless generosity with no hidden agenda, then this means that we must let go of any utilitarian motivation whatsoever for relationship building. For this to be the case, it must be true deep within the heart of the Christian; that is, there really can be no hidden agenda even deep within our hearts—not salvation, not inviting to church, not donations, but only a desire on our parts to love our community as

---

[268] This Scale was mentioned in Mile Marker One. It is a way of understanding regeneration or conversion as a journey from being completely unconcerned with or ignorant of God, –10 on the scale, to firing on all cylinders in discipleship and Christlikeness, +10 on the scale. The center of the scale, 0, represents the heart of stone supernaturally replaced with the heart of flesh. Even this can be conceived, in terms of the scale, as a process rather than an instantaneous event in time.

[269] Stetzer's research team noticed the same dilemma: "Fifty-nine percent of the unchurched population age thirty and over said they never wondered about their eternal destiny. Eventually, an evangelistic witness to an unchurched person must deal with issues of eternity, but that may not be the best place to start." Stetzer, Stanley, and Hayes, *Lost and Found*, 41–42.

Jesus first loved us. Relationship building can no longer be considered a Trojan horse for some colonial-esque agenda of evangelism.[270]

Because the kinetic model emphasizes community projects and presence and deemphasizes making these overtly evangelistic efforts, some may fear that it is long on social justice and short on gospel proclamation. If the church prioritizes the selfless giving away of money to the community to showcase the generous love of Jesus over facility maintenance, will this be seen as an irresponsible use of donor dollars? If, in the pursuit of reclaiming a good rapport between a jaded, postchristian cultural milieu and the Bride of Jesus, it is learned that the average local townsperson will be forever unable to distinguish between churches of greatly differing doctrinal stance, how much ecumenism is the inversion model church willing to embrace? What are the consequences to that rapport if the interchurch distinction is drawn too sharply?

Church leaders who lead this inversion may face the concern that churchgoers are to be holy and separate from the world. In actual practice, in churches that have for so long operated with a modernist worldview, for the average churchgoer to think through what it means to be a vibrant, selfless blessing to the local community without planned evangelistic presentations and no reciprocal expectations is

---

[270] "Our respondents also told us they'd encountered church planters, missional pastors, and on-campus religious groups who had utilized a 'relationship first' model in which they were exhorted to make friends with people, gain their trust, and then invite them to church. Our respondents found these 'shadow missions' abhorrent. The idea of pursuing relationships or conversations with an ulterior motive was anathema to them. They ... preferred to simply reflect God's love to others. ... Their relationships are sacred to them—not because they replace God, but because it is in relationships that they find God." Josh Packard and Ashleigh Hope, *Church Refugees: Sociologists Reveal Why People Are DONE with Church but Not Their Faith* (Loveland, CO, Group, 2015), 82.

akin to them solving a complex problem in a foreign language they do not know. In actual practice, being a vibrant, selfless blessing to the local community is in a constant tension with an innate desire to advertise "we're the ones doing this for you ... aren't we the best?" The line between appropriate, necessary branding and shameless self-promotion can become impossible to know.

Relationship between the kinetic and incarnational models

The incarnational model and the kinetic model for which this chapter argues are related to one another and are perhaps two different tributaries to the same river of church renewal now flowing from the Holy Spirit.[271] Yet the difference between the two is substantive. The incarnational model was conceived as a solution to the church being stuck inside her own walls. As a result, its primary focus is churches "without walls"[272] in unconventional forms and venues and with an organic network of cell structures.

---

[271] This may be a submission to what Hirsch looks forward to: "Emergence happens when systems become sufficiently populated and properly interrelated; then the interactions assemble themselves into a new order. Complexity theory suggests that when there is enough connectivity between the different aspects of the system, emergence is likely to occur spontaneously. This is precisely what has happened in the EMC [Emerging Missional Church]. The end result is a species of organization different from the previous elements." Hirsch, *Forgotten Ways*, 269. He lists these elements as urban mission, evangelical theology, pentecostalism, radical discipleship movement, post-evangelicalism, alternative worship movement, missions to the Western world, Gospel and Our Culture Network, living systems theory, and house church movement. Perhaps, as the kinetic model is developed and improved upon, it will fall within this EMC constellation of Hirsch's imagination. Although Hirsch and Frost write from a Pentecostal perspective, for the non-Pentecostal their equation of the apostle role with entrepreneurism easily translates to change-agent leadership styles. Cf. Alan Hirsch and Michael Frost, *The Shaping of Things to Come: Innovation and Mission for the 21st-Century Church*, rev. ed. (Grand Rapids, MI: Baker, 2013), 214ff.
[272] Hirsch, *Forgotten Ways*, 38.

Harkening back to a church before Constantine, when the church was underground and lived without society's favor, the incarnational model would like to dispense with the institutional church altogether, if that were possible.[273] The kinetic model seeks to bring most of the same radical transformation to the North American church but to do so out of the strength of a redeemed, retooled, and recalibrated institutional church. Packard, based on his research projects, would seem to agree that this needs to be the case:

> They need the church, and they know it. Organizations have real power to create and maintain coordinated activity over the long haul. Without the organization, activity is extremely difficult to sustain. Meeting in small groups over meals for discussion ... is great, but it's hard to do week after week, let alone month after month and year after year. ...There's a real opportunity for churches to serve that need and offer support and coordination.[274]

The kinetic model regards the incarnational model as having too hastily given up on the value of the institutional church. Below is a comparison between the two models.[275]

Incarnational-missional model	Kinetic model
Primarily a church planting model	A church revitalization model

---

[273] "Institutional church" is used here as shorthand for the traditional concept of a church that meets in a building, a significant accrual of internal rules and process, etc.
[274] Packard and Hope, *Church Refugees*, 134.
[275] All chart page numbers refer to Hirsch, *Forgotten Ways*.

Inspired by restorationist ecclesiology first and a practical response second (17)	Inspired by a practical response first and restorationist ecclesiology second
Draws "a clear distinction between necessary organizational structure and institutionalism" (23)	Draws a further distinction of a "necessary organizational structure" between redeemable, advantageous pieces of institutionalism and an elemental organizational structure of restorationist ecclesiology
"Missional" means "how we can engage our culture on its own turf ... the missional church must seek to redeem the social pattern/rhythm of [cafés]—reinvesting it with religious significance and what it means to be a people of God in a café–bar context" (37)	"Missional" means the church focused on the effective pursuit of the Great Commission, however that may look in any culture or time
In the community, the goal is an "organic dialogue leading toward topics of faith" (38)	In the community, the goal is the start of new, long-term relationships and increasing the rapport of the collective church of Jesus

Endeavors to transform community space into "a spiritual space," or perhaps uncover that the community space is a church (38 footnote)	Endeavors to bless the existing community space and make it richer on its own terms because of church support
Not "about overt evangelism in the first instance; that, we reckoned, would come later, through meaningful relationships" (38)	Identical philosophy here—building bridges of trust that will bear the weight of Truth in the Holy Spirit's timing
The institutional church has to "come along" (40)	The institutional church acts as a rallying center for relationship building in the community
Sometimes not seated strongly in a full-spectrum discipleship plan (42)	The kinetic model is itself the full-spectrum discipleship plan
Can have a short-term expectation of traditional metrics—"to our shame, at that point we had not seen any conversions to Jesus in the preceding two years!" (42)	Tends to take a longer view of traditional metrics; ideal for using metrics based on story; more "journey" and Engel scale, less concern about counting conversions and baptisms and other such metrics
Wants "to transform from a static, geographically located church to a dynamic movement across our city" (46)	The same on this point, but considers the static, geographically located church to be an advantageous

	headquarters for such a dynamic movement
Reverses "the ratio of active to passive (from 20:80 to 80:20)" church members (46)	Identical philosophy here: "all hands on deck"
"Built on principles of organic multiplication, including operating as a network, not as a centralized organization" (46)	Grows through these same principles but sees a centralized organization as a strength
Moves some institutionalism to a cell level: "Each of these levels [tribes, cell groups, and movement-wide network] has a leadership structure appropriate to each level" (47)	Attempts to redeem institutionalism and transform it into a structure that leads adaptive change
"Rejects the concern and need for dedicated 'church' buildings" (64)	Also rejects buildings as a need, yet seeks to retain them for their advantages
"Leadership embraces a pioneering-innovative mode" and is "noninstitutional by preference" (64)	Identical except that it redemptively salvages a useful church structure

"Grassroots, decentralized movements" (64)	The geographically located church nurtures grassroots movements and insists on working through them
"Church is once again on the fringes of society and culture" (64)	Reminiscent of the "Christendom Mode," in which "church is perceived as central to society and the surrounding culture" but in a humbled, serving, and selflessly generous way (64)
"Missional; incarnational-sending; The church reembraces a missional stance in relation to culture" (64)	Identical philosophy here; mutual in its rejection of the attractional and "extractional" models (64)

Better synchrony with Jesus's model

Although any full description and analysis of the Jesus model of discipleship or of an early church ecclesiology is beyond the scope of this book, a brief summary and comparison may show that the kinetic model is as true a return to the pre-Constantinian church as the incarnational model. The bald fact is that Jesus was itinerant in his ministry, a ministry that proclaimed the kingdom of God had already come and fulfilled the joyous hope of Isaiah 42, albeit both in an already-but-not-yet sense..[276] He made use of the institutional church, so to speak, when he preached and healed in the synagogue and when he dwelt among the prenatal church gathered in a group of five hundred or

---

[276] Mat 4.17.

among the members of the prenatal house church gathered frightened behind locked doors.[277] His wayfaring ministry on the hillside of the Mount and traveling throughout Galilee and toward Jerusalem approximates the "go" aspect of the kinetic model's "serve." That wayfaring ministry also looks a lot like the belonging aspect of the "connect" step and the celebratory nature of the "gather" piece.

In contrast (to the attractional model), Jesus is never seen setting up shop in a static, geographically located institution. He did not work to attract the outside world to powerfully emotive worship experiences or to life changes through passive listening and scriptural study. Jesus's outreach" to the community would never have been a first century version of direct mail marketing or "outreach and in-drag" strategies.[278] His concern for assimilation systems, even when adjusted for a first-century Palestinian culture, extended no further than a simple ongoing spiritual maturation along his discipleship pathway of the fulfillment of Isaiah 42 throughout his target region—live, in-the-moment, and as-needed theological learning and praxis and hour-by-hour personal contact with the Master.[279]

A similar picture unfolds upon close inspection of the early church as she gained definition throughout the New Testament and pre-Constantinian eras. Evangelism occurred in the marketplace and everyday circumstances, not through programmatic outreach or come-to-our-house-church-and-see initiatives; it occurred through existing relationships and the evangelistic intentionality brought to any newly developed relationships.[280] Any advertisement of the house

---

[277] Luk 4.16–20; 1Co 15.6; Jhn 20.19–20.
[278] Hirsch, *Forgotten Ways*, 34.
[279] Jer 9.23–24.
[280] Cf. Everett Ferguson, *Backgrounds of Early Christianity*, 3rd ed. (Grand Rapids, MI: Eerdmans, 2003); Michael Green, *Evangelism in the Early Church*, rev. ed. (Grand Rapids, MI: Eerdmans, 2004).

church in the community that could end up having a "come-and-see" effect was through word of mouth, with the drawing factor usually that of the oddity, purity, or outlandish love of this people of the Way.[281] For that matter, the pragmatically necessary house church and network structure of the early church, while anticipating the possibility of guests, was nevertheless designed for the equipping, energizing, and encouraging of believers.[282] Connection in the early church was an amalgamation of the everyday "outreach" relationships and the house church weekly rejuvenation hub.[283]

It may be that in this regard, too, the kinetic model is a better approximation than the incarnational model of a return to early church ecclesiology. The house church was the first century equivalent of the church as a static, geographically located institution. The early church does not appear to have sought, for example, to request permission to make the first century "coffee house" a "spiritual space," where perhaps, for argument's sake, the members might share a communion meal in some marketplace venue in order to "take the church to them" or establish a church "without walls."[284] Rather, that communion meal was a private affair, part of the "gather" piece of the kinetic model, after which the church gathered would disband to go out and

---

[281] Cf. Justo Gonzalez, *The Story of Christianity*, 2nd ed.. Vol. 1, *The Early Church to the Dawn of the Reformation*. Vol. 2, *The Reformation to the Present Day* (New York: HarperCollins, 2010).
[282] Cf. 1Co 14.
[283] Cf. Peter Bunton, *Cell Groups and House Churches: What History Teaches Us* (Lititz, PA: House to House, 2001).
[284] Hirsch, *Forgotten Ways*, 38 footnote.

"serve," building relationships with gospel hope as they went about their daily lives in the marketplace.[285]

It took a zealous emperor and a worldwide decree of paradigmatic proportion to move the early church from such an ecclesiology to one that would gradually atrophy into the attractional model of now-waning efficacy in a postmodern and postchristian New England culture. Likewise, it will take nothing less than a supernatural paradigmatic shift in the hearts of the North American church leadership and ecclesial psyche to effect the kinetic model in a church firmly secure in the most state-of-the-art attractional methods ever seen.

If going after Neutrals is the salient point of authentic missionality, as this book has been arguing from the first, going all-in toward such missionality will invariably mean coming to a place of surrendering many of the things about church that are so precious to church members. In fact, everything not specifically mandated by Scripture and not in direct service to the goal of missionality will be on the chopping block. For example, if Sunday school is siphoning off volunteerism that could go to reaching Neutrals of the community, then even if it is an effective ministry, the church all-in for missionality will likely shut it down. This is because her all-consuming objective is to actually realize salvation and discipleship among all those around her that have no realistic pathway to a church, attractional or otherwise.

Therefore, her people will be motivated to sacrifice ministry pieces that are very dear to them and that have for

---

[285] Cf. John Mark Hicks, *Come to the Table: Revisioning the Lord's Supper* (Abilene, TX: Leafwood, 2002); I. Howard Marshall, *Last Supper and Lord's Supper* (Vancouver, BC,: Regent College, 2006); Leonard J. Vander Zee, *Christ, Baptism and the Lord's Supper: Recovering the Sacraments for Evangelical Worship* (Downers Grove, IL: InterVarsity, 2004).

time immemorial been considered a definitional part of any church, because her focus is not on the way things have always been done but on the hard-to-reach around her. Or church members may intentionally forfeit expectations of pastoral care that they would have hitherto considered their right, because their all-consuming focus on the Neutrals around them causes them to recognize that pastoral care staffing hours are needed there instead. A missional obsession with the completely uninitiated postmoderns and postchristians around the church will trump every other occupation or pursuit of the church that has chosen paradigmatic change. What makes this concentration possible, spiritually and biblically, is that the definition in Mile Marker One of discipleship and spiritual formation makes evangelism and discipleship one and the same on a continuum and makes discipleship something that happens on the go. In this way, discipleship is not ignored or devalued relative to evangelism, but is from one perspective in service to it and from another perspective is inseparably bound up in it.

This level of missional focus will mean taking the long view. The church opting for paradigmatic change in a postmodern culture will assume that the results of salvation and discipleship she longs to observe from her efforts in the community around her will be a long time in coming. She takes the view of the farmer planting his field, knowing full well that a long time will pass before the huge outlay of money and labor for planting is rewarded.[286] In fact, like the farmer, she will realize that ever seeing the reward is itself a chancy thing. Like a careful stock market investor she will do her research, place her bets, and not look for any gains in the near term. The hope of authentic revitalization and of the paradigmatic sacrifice it requires cannot be visible growth in

---

[286] Jas 5.7–8.

church attendance and giving. These may never be the result, and if they are the result they will be lagging indicators of revitalization success. The primary goal, kept constantly in central view, must be to actually connect to all those in the community who have no familiarity with the church, Jesus, or the gospel—and, as already discussed, the discipleship continuum is then a natural side benefit for all.

It will mean the church and her leaders will allow themselves to go dangerously native. There is an unsubstantiated urban legend that Heath Ledger went so native in his role as the Joker in *The Dark Night* that it contributed to his suicide. He was so good at method acting, at intimately being the character he portrayed, that it may have lethally consumed him. As already discussed, when the church goes all in for missionality and dives headlong into the paradigmatic change it requires, she will incarnate so deeply into the psyche of the postmodern and postchristian culture around her that she will surrender (to Jesus) any tight control she may have had on her own identity.

Even for Jesus, incarnating into the world he longed to reach meant emptying himself. The church has always been eager to pilgrimize society and the community around her, but in her eagerness, she has too often forgotten the prerequisite of indigenizing. Indigenizing is being the absolute best at knowing contemporary postmodern culture as intimately as possible. To adapt the thinking of C. S. Lewis, these churches "come to know their [surrounding postmodern culture] as Wellington knew Napoleon, or as Sherlock Holmes knew Moriarty; as a ratcatcher knows rats or a plumber knows about leaky pipes."[287] They do not lose themselves to the point of *becoming* their postmodern culture with little or no gospel distinction; they do lose themselves,

---

[287] C. S. Lewis, *Mere Christianity* (New York: Macmillan, 1952), 94.

however, to the hazardous point of accepting that their very identity as a church will be significantly altered by their "method acting." They think like missionaries even though they may be native to their own culture.

Aware of these bitter pills, then, the church that desires authentic missionality nevertheless forges straight ahead into the disconcerting liminal space of meaningfully altering her church model of evangelism. She determines to hold the model up, examine it anew in light of her newfound missionality, and experiment with it without inhibition or a preconceived outcome of what that model will look like when she has finished the altering. The kinetic model sketched out in this chapter is offered as one example of how such a newly missional model of church evangelistic strategy might look. There is nothing perfect, settled, or privileged about this example. It is offered instead as a template for each church's journey down a revitalization path, and it is offered as one model that has already survived the initial experimentation process in at least one setting.

Discovery Projects

1. Depending on how you write up your church budget each year, experiment with reorganizing its layout around the three steps of serve, connect, and gather. You may find that you will need to go so far as to extract individual line items from their usual placement in the budget in order to collect them under the word for which that line item is most apt. Before doing this exercise, however, you may find it helpful to labor a bit over your own concise single-sentence description of each of the three words, serve, connect, and gather. As you create a theoretical reorganization of the church budget, set aside as an "other" group those line items that don't fit very well under any of the three "steps," as well as those that

seem alien to any of the three. Finally, you can (1) shoehorn items of this "other" group back into the serve, connect, or gather category, (2) dump them into a fourth category labeled "support" or something similar, or (3) evaluate whether they are items that should be discarded altogether because they are good things that distract from the main, best thing to which God has specifically called your church. Now that you have hypothetically reorganized your existing church budget into three or four categories, put them onto a pie graph as three or four pieces. Is there one category that has the lion's share of the pie? Is there great disparity between the sizes of the pie pieces? What does it tell you about what you and your church value and consider most important? How does this finding line up with the kinetic model as promoted in this chapter? Put yourself in the shoes of a postchristian in your church's local community; if this person happened upon this pie graph, would he or she think it showcased your church as one that gave of herself sacrificially for her community or as one that used most donated dollars for herself?[288]

2. Take some time together to recount the life and ministry of Jesus with regard to his discipleship of the disciples, the Three, the Twelve, the Seventy-two, and the crowd. Consider getting creative with this on a large whiteboard. What parts of what Jesus did seem to commend the idea of inverting the attractional model of the "come and see" church? Given that there are clear examples in Jesus's life and speech of both "come and see" and "go and be," how legitimate do you think it is to say that we need to discard

---

[288] "The church can play a unique role in facilitating [community-conscious service], but it may take some painful reallocation of funding. A church willing to devote far more of their budget to mission work, both foreign and domestic, rather than their building program, will likely be a haven for young adults." Stetzer, Stanley, and Hayes, *Lost and Found*, 117.

the attractional model of doing church in favor of an incarnational or kinetic model? A number of real-life concerns and pushbacks to an inversion of the attractional model have been mentioned in this book. Are there any additional concerns from church members/attendees that you might anticipate in your setting?

3. One of the earliest stories of the church being the church in the Bible, in Acts 6, reveals how absolutely crucial it is to adapt ecclesiology to context. The Jerusalem church leaders were aware of an exploding demographic of widows and dependent elderly who had immigrated from all over the world in recent times to live out the rest of their days in the Holy City. They were wise to the natural tension between the Palestinian Jews and the diaspora Jews.[289] They appreciated the heightened contemporary need for apostolic proclamation. Their church was racially homogenous, a homogeneity that extended to worldview, ritual, and expectations. In short, they knew their zip code. They knew their zip code, they loved their zip code, and they modified their ecclesiastical structure to meet their zip code.[290] What is assumed by many to be the first instance of deacons in the church was the result. To the degree that the kinetic model is a more accurate representation of Jesus's own discipleship model and, extrapolated from that, Jesus's own model of ecclesiology, perhaps the kinetic model can be applied universally, regardless of context. How well do you know and love

---

[289] Craig S. Keener, *The IVP Bible Background Commentary: New Testament*, 2nd ed. (Downers Grove, IL: InterVarsity, 2014), 338.

[290] In Revelation 1–3, each church is symbolized by a candlestick. Each church is located by Jesus in a specific locale. When combined with Acts 1.8, it may be fair to assert, based on this symbolism, that a church should be heavily concerned with and targeted toward her specific locale or "backyard," yet without being myopic to the point of neglecting a witness to the wider world.

your church's zip code? Consider whiteboarding a description of your church's zip code together as a team, including its demographics, cultural mood, self-perceived needs, and collective attitude toward the institutional church. Looking over this description, how do you think the kinetic model can be adapted to the uniqueness of your zip code? If you put yourself in the shoes of the townspeople around you, does the postmodern critique of the attractional church described in this book match the skepticism regarding the institutional church and the sources of skepticism from the history of your area?

Mile Marker Five: The Historic Church

Why fight it?

Having considered the kinetic model of church evangelism and its close relation to the incarnational model, we pause at Mile Marker Five to wrestle with a question. The question may be asked in several ways. If the kinetic model is so similar to the incarnational one, why is it so paramount to tinker with what already works in the incarnational model? Why cling to the old church building and the traditional idea of a centralized church if a purely organic, diffused option is available? After all, as we have already noted, the former requires so much overhead. Since church planting alternatives encounter so much less headwind in terms of change to the established culture of an individual church, why be so determined to take a hard route like revitalization? Why fight the undertow of a dying historic church?

There is an answer to these questions, and it matters. A discipleship pathway inversion is the key element that differentiates the kinetic model from the attractional model. The inspiration for this change is the postmodern critique. But it is the determination to preserve the value of and reimbue value into the historic church that marks the difference between a kinetic and an incarnational model, and that begs the questions above. So an understanding of why historic churches are worth saving is crucial, because it must be the motivation for reinventing what has already been working in the incarnational model, microchurch models, and church planting options. Mile Marker Five represents a rest stop on the revitalization pathway to contemplate an answer to these questions.

As mentioned earlier, I use the term *historic church* the way many use *institutional* or *established church*.[291] In New

---

[291] E.g., Alan Hirsch, *The Forgotten Ways: Reactivating Apostolic Movements*, 2nd ed. (Grand Rapids, MI: Brazos, 2016), 30.

England what might first come to mind is the large town meeting center with rows of giant windows and a spectacular white steeple, built in the eighteenth or nineteenth century. These edifices are everywhere and it seems they are one by one being repurposed into historic societies or museums or apartments or any number of other uses.[292] An online search for "churches reused" nets all kinds of top-ten type lists for how to do it as a strategy for preserving the old structures. When I refer to the *historic church,* I am referring to the congregation of people that make up that church currently and inherited the legacy of those before them who have made up that church through the decades and centuries. But *historic church* can also refer to the building they occupy, itself a significant piece of the culture and history of the New England town in which God has placed them.

We have one of these in our small town. It sits right in the middle of town, right beside the stately town hall building, so close that a Christmas Eve fire in the church burnt down both buildings in 1877. It is a town icon. At one point, Andrew Card, President George W. Bush's advisor of 9/11 fame and a Holbrook native, pulled some strings to help the church buy a new steeple. Yet, after being the town mother for over two hundred years, the church is closing for good at the time of this writing.[293]

Although these old, stately edifices may be the first mental picture one thinks of as a historic church, what I mean by a historic church is essentially any congregation that has been around for a while. These are churches that are

---

[292] E.g., Amelia Nierenberg, "New Spirits Rise in Old, Repurposed Churches," *New York Times*, October 25, 2020, https://www.nytimes.com/2020/10/25/us/abandoned-churches-covid.html.

[293] It has a better final chapter than many historic churches in that it may be reopening as a satellite campus of a large and growing church in the next town.

or have been an important part of their communities—from their communities' point of view. They might not have the glistening steeple or the colonial look, but they have had a vibrant ministry. From some period of their existence, maybe multiple periods, they have left a large missional footprint in their area. In New England, so many of these historic churches seem to be past their prime. When they close, since New Englanders are often so parochial, the few who were attending them at the last may simply cease going to any church at all. When they close, the historic church buildings are usually repurposed. Less commonly, they are simply left to rot and fall over with the passage of time.

There is an odd confluence occurring in New England. At the very moment that many churches, both mainline and independent, dwindle and close, the buildings they once inhabited are only growing in reverence in the New England psyche. Perhaps this is in part because of the increased cultural interest in the supernatural and spirituality in general. Certainly, it is because New Englanders tend to value the old, the historic, and the native.[294] For example, in the case of the church in Holbrook already mentioned, Winthrop Congregational Church, the townspeople and the backers of the local historical society planned a fundraiser to rescue the church from closing. They may be entirely dismissive of the morality and the authority of the church itself, but the building holds a powerful reverence for them that they cannot as easily dismiss.

Perhaps this odd confluence has something to do with space. In Pennsylvania, where I lived before moving to New England, people have an entirely different concept of space. Pennsylvania roads often have wide berms for breakdowns

---

[294] J. David Jackson, *New England Culture & Ministry Dynamics: Where You Serve Makes a Difference in How You Serve*, 3rd ed. (Marlborough, MA: Screven and Allen, 2018).

and a margin of safety; in Massachusetts the berms are employed for legal lanes of travel. In Texas, where most of my family lives, a typical berm might be the width of two whole travel lanes in New England. Some avenues in Boston look like they could not accommodate a golf cart. The concept of space in New England is that it is compact and precious.[295] It has a definite "use every part of the buffalo" feel. In this context, the historic church is often a rare asset of square footage. It hoards space that might not exist anywhere else in the New England town. In Holbrook, for example, there are only two other sizable venues: the school and the second floor of the town hall. The school, for reasons of safety or ethics, is mostly off limits. The second floor of the town hall is in need of remodeling and difficult to access. The historic church, which is seemingly losing any space she ever had in the New England consciousness, by some odd twist of fate has become a great potential community resource. That she occupies a spacious physical address gives her a precious chance to function as a solid base of operations.

The confluence that gives curious value to the historic church might be, more than any other thing, a function of her own local history. By definition, the historic church has been around for a long time. For some portion of that long time she thrived, and those around her thrived because of her. Chances are she had a significant impact on her town and was an appreciated factor in the community. In the case of Winthrop Congregational, the founder and namesake of the town, and a major benefactor to the town, was a leader in that church. The postmodern tendency to revive and embrace old traditions, particularly those that are experiential or sensory rich, might serve to magnify this historical enmeshment of the church with that of the local

---

[295] Ibid.

historical narrative.[296] Here again, the historic church represents a strong link to the local psyche, self-identity, and purpose in the world. Even if the postmodern and postchristian culture now surrounding her ignores or feigns a patronizing nod toward her moral relevance, that same culture cannot bear the thought of entirely excising her from its own story.[297]

Mismatched for the present opportunity

Perhaps, even with these initial considerations, it is becoming clear that the historic church is worth fighting for. In a New England context, at least, the historic church is worth retaining and reviving for, at the very least, the leverage and opportunity offered by her facilities. This conclusion might appear at first to be shallow and trifling, but when it is understood in the context of a discipleship pathway inversion, and in juxtaposition to the incarnational model, it begins to stand out as an outsized benefit that fits perfectly with the current state of affairs. It becomes an unexpected answer to the postmodern critique of church done attractionally. It extends the strengths of the incarnational model, especially in a New England context, to include a valuing of an established church, against which so much of the incarnational model is, in part, a reaction.

As demonstrated by the previous four mile markers, New England, like similar cultural contexts, finds itself involved in a peculiar mismatch between the language the church speaks and the language the culture hears. In his book *The Five Love Languages*, Gary Chapman asserts that the

---

[296] D. A. Carson, *Becoming Conversant with the Emerging Church: Understanding a Movement and Its Implications* (Grand Rapids, MI: Zondervan, 2005).
[297] Jack L. Daniel, *Patient Catalyst: Leading Church Revitalization* (South Easton, MA: Overseed, 2018).

communication of love from one person to another sometimes encounters the same dilemma as, for example, a person who only speaks Spanish might when conversing with a person who only speaks English. They might both be doing an excellent job of communicating, but the mismatch between the mouth and the ear makes it almost as if they were not communicating at all. For example, if a husband is telling his wife "I love you" through the language of acts of kindness, but the language in which his wife has receptors for "I love you" is the language of quality time, she might hardly recognize that he loves her. She may be feeling profoundly unloved by the very man who is going to extreme lengths to show her how dearly he does love her.[298] Something similar is happening right now between the church's proclamation of the gospel and the culture's ability to hear it.

Microbiology provides another example. A given cell in our bodies has proteins that act as receptors for certain messages from other cells. These receptors can have extremely specific "antennas," so that they only receive and encode specially tailored messages that can bond with the cell and communicate effectively, or at all, with the internal "self" of the cell. Signals or messages that are a mismatch for those receptors, no matter how potent or crucial they may be, cannot be accepted by the cell's receptors. It is as if they were never sent.[299] So it is with the historic church geographically situated in a postchristian culture with only postmodern receptors.

To a large extent, this mismatch has already been addressed, particularly in the church evangelistic model proposed in Mile Marker Four. Inverting the discipleship

------

[298] Gary Chapman, *The Five Love Languages: The Secret to Love That Lasts* (Chicago: Northfield, 2015).
[299] E.g., "Cell Signaling," Scitable by Nature Education, https://www.nature.com/scitable/topicpage/cell-signaling-14047077/.

pathway of the attractional model yields an incarnational model or a kinetic model that matches with these postmodern receptors. A culture that no longer possesses attractional model receptors can now hear the gospel in its own language because of the inversion already discussed. And yet, there appears to be a danger here. If this incarnationally packaged gospel is unmoored from the historic church, there is a risk that it may still be a mismatch or that it may simply altogether miss the receptors of a culture badly in need of Jesus. This may be particularly acute in a culture like New England that still reveres places of worship, still generically values faith, and still recounts the historical contribution of the church in its communities.

Examples of potential mismatches

Judging by the array of experiments and options available for renewal of the church, some level of recognition of this mismatch has hovered at the edge of the church's consciousness for some time. Practitioners and thinkers in churches throughout North America have been concentrating on a solution to the problem through both coordinated and uncoordinated efforts. The result is a number of solutions and experiments both new and old. In some cases, it is merely a matter of context, time, and geography that makes them less than the perfect match for a culture such as that of New England. In others, it is because they only address the mismatch in part or do not press far enough. The missing ingredient that transforms so many incarnational attempts into the secret sauce that is receptor specific for New England is valuing and retaining the historic church as an integral piece of the model.

Church planting, one of the best tested and most conventional options for revitalization, may be less than ideal in a culture that values history and the old. In some cases, it may be the most indigenous possibility and the best path toward church renewal in a postchristian world. But in a place like New England, church planting may, paradoxically, struggle to be indigenous. If a church plant is the effort of a church outside of town, even if it is made up of people inside of town it may have difficulty being perceived as a natural part of the fabric of the town. This is due to the strongly parochial bent of New Englanders.[300] And church plants, by definition, lack a historical legacy in the town. Jack Daniel, something of a father of revitalizing historic New England churches as the field director of Overseed, acknowledges that church planting and replanting have their place but envisions that "the greatest opportunity for revival in America lies in the revitalization of the many thousands of existing churches in decline."[301] There are no good numbers to go on, but conceivably an attempt at revitalization might have long-term chances of success similar to those of a church plant. Likewise, a successful revitalization might reasonably require about the same amount of time as a church plant to become successful and could have just as much energy and momentum and youthfulness as a church plant upon completion of the revitalization process. Gordon MacDonald states this in the form of a dare:

> Our experience leads me to say that if you want to be part of a church that is radically different from anything you've ever known, then plant one—start one. You can create new programs, new rules, and new structures. And you'll have about a one-in-five chance that it will survive. And if that's your call, go for it.

---

[300] In fact, the well-intended church planting programs of the Southern Baptist Convention sometimes have unintended consequences. Many newly and well-established church plants in New England have church leaders with southern accents.
[301] Daniel, *Patient Catalyst*, 1.

There's a lot of nobility in planting churches. It's happening all over the countryside. But if you are willing to be patient in one of those old churches (like ours) that is pretty high up the S-curve, then put your head down and go to work. Be patient, be prayerful, seek allies, build alliances with other generations. You'll probably have to convince a lot of people, and they'll come dragging their feet like the members of our Discovery Group. But as time passes, somehow the Spirit of God will grab at hearts, and you just may see a miracle—a hundred-year-old church that acts with the spirit of an enthusiastic teenager. That's what happened to us.[302]

To be sure, church plants and replants do have the advantage of being able to freely adapt to postmodern culture. Compared with an historic church undergoing revitalization, they have considerably less in the way of sacred cows or rote traditions or other baggage with which to contend. And they are often very focused on some form of a disciple-making movement in the community as a matter of cobbling together a brand-new church out of nothing. Given these two strong advantages, why might church plants be considered a mismatch for the current evangelistic vacuum in New England? Because New Englanders tend to disdain or be suspicious of the new and the history-less. For this seemingly too-simplistic reason alone, historic New England churches are worth fighting to revive. There is a stark difference in a context such as New England between an upstart church that is doing everything right and a mother-of-the-town church that has finally begun to do everything right.[303] Viewed side by side like this, there is no competition—the revitalized historic church will have far

---

[302] Gordon MacDonald, *Who Stole My Church? What to Do When the Church You Love Tries to Enter the 21st Century* (Nashville: Thomas Nelson, 2007), 224.
[303] Cf. Jackson, *New England Culture.*

more clout in the town hall and far more acceptance on the streets and in the living rooms of the town.

A second, well-established option is some form of the emerging church.[304] Tim Conder helpfully circumscribes what can otherwise be an untamed definition:

> The emerging church seeks to be an authentic contextualization of the gospel within the values and characteristics of postmodern culture. Therefore, it envisions and expresses Christianity primarily as a way of life, rather than an adherence to a doctrinal system or organizational pattern ... the emerging church seeks to be a community that embodies and supports God's mission of establishing a present and future redemptive kingdom.[305]

Perhaps, then, the kinetic model of inverting the attractional discipleship pathway proposed in Mile Marker Four is an accidental example of the emerging church. From its early days, the emerging church movement has been highly reactionary against existing, ensconced churches, but Conder applauds a trend in the emerging church toward focusing on "creative and collaborative construction of the future

---

[304] The "emergent church" and "the emerging church" are very distinct concepts. The former is usually associated with heresy and relativism and with Brian McLaren and a few other prominent spokesmen. The latter is what Conder is referring to, which is a broad spectrum of churches that are attempting to minister incarnationally. Conder lists their core values as "The pursuit of the gospel expressed and explained in community; a passion for living out the values of Jesus's kingdom in the present; comfort with mystery and uncertainty; a spiritual holism that calls forth a radical and comprehensive discipleship; a reading of Scripture that intersects with local stories and contexts; an experiential approach to both worship and the pursuit of truth; and a ministry that honors the beauty of God's creation and the creative spirit found in humanity." Tim Conder, *The Church in Transition* (Grand Rapids, MI: Zondervan, 2006).
[305] Conder, *Church in Transition*.

church."[306] The emerging church movement might not, therefore, be anything of a mismatch for the current opportunity in cultures like New England. Instead, it may be ideally suited to seize that opportunity precisely because it has come full circle over time to value the historic church.[307] The kinetic model might offer some level of precision to the emerging church's methods, and a sightline to the emerging church's goal.

Another option that has been growing louder in a wider church renewal conversation is what has come to be called fresh expressions of church. A precise definition of what a fresh expression entails is difficult to come by, probably because it is still very much an experimental option, but Chris Backert, the Fresh Expressions U.S. National Director, frames it as "taking the church Jesus loves closer to where the people Jesus loves actually are."[308] It is difficult to tell if the fresh expressions movement is another iteration of the incarnational model, if it is church planting under a new label, or if it is a twist on church revitalization. Collins juggles all three as he attempts to define the movement:

> It's about planting new forms of church in bowling alleys, fitness centers, restaurants, recording studios, VFW halls, homes, and workplaces. It's about planting new forms of church among students, artists, scientists, the homeless, people who are deaf, rock climbers, rockabillies, and bodybuilders. It's about entrepreneurial models that house multiple businesses in a building that also houses worship and is a platform for ministry. It's about serving people, listening to

---

[306] Ibid.
[307] Cf. Conder.
[308] As quoted in Travis Collins, *From the Steeple to the Street: Innovating Mission and Ministry Through Fresh Expressions of Church* (Franklin, TN: Seedbed, 2016).

them, and figuring out by the leadership of God's Spirit what form church would take if it were planted in a particular context.[309]

Later, he distills this assortment into something more direct: "The optimal situation (from a fresh expressions perspective) is an existing church with a missional pastor sending out a handful of apostles from its membership to begin a new form of church among a particular subculture."[310]

All in all, I understand the fresh expressions movement as a broad cluster of experiments in church renewal that fill out the incarnational model popularized by Hirsch and Frost.[311] Like the incarnational model, the fresh expressions movement retains some value for the historic church. Primarily, however, the historic church has value because it is a sending agent as in Collins's "optimal situation." Indeed, Collins appears to see leading church revitalization in a historic church as something short of a full-fledged fresh expression.[312] In other words, the historic church's primary value is not because of her own presence in the community but because of the multiple smaller fresh expressions of church she plants away from her. As such, the fresh expressions movement does relatively little to extend the incarnational model, at least as it concerns historic churches, and might better be fitted within Hirsch's Emerging Missional Church (EMC) constellation of system connectivity.[313] It is a potential mismatch for the present

---

[309] Collins, *From Steeple to Street*.
[310] Ibid.
[311] Alan Hirsch and Michael Frost, *The Shaping of Things to Come: Innovation and Mission for the 21st Century Church*, rev. ed. (Grand Rapids MI: Baker, 2013).
[312] Cf. Collins, "Missional Pastors Are in Great Demand," in *From Steeple to Street*.
[313] Hirsch, 269.

opportunity at the intersection of postmodernism and postchristianity for the same reason church planting is.

The microchurch movement is another option for church renewal in the current New England spiritual climate. It is well advocated by Neil Cole and many others and extolled as a strong option for multiplication since it is based on an organic structure.[314] But it is rather indistinguishable from the incarnational model or from church planting in its treatment of the historic church. And so for the same reasons, the many microchurch variations are likely a weak match for a New England that is parched for the gospel proclaimed in a manner suitable for her receptors to receive it. In cultures such as New England's, the microchurch movement's greatest contribution may be in experimenting with smaller group connections within a kinetic model rather than standing as a model all of its own. Curiously, because the New Englander's definition of a small group is at least twice as large as most other areas of the United States, the principles of the microchurch might have more to say here than anywhere else about an effective small group ministry.[315]

In addition to the options outlined above, church health formulas have been put forth from several corners of the larger church revitalization conversation. One such is found in Thom Rainer's *Anatomy of a Revived Church*, a book offered as a positive answer to his *Autopsy of a Deceased*

---

[314] E.g., Neil Cole, *Church 3.0: Upgrades for the Future of the Church* (San Francisco: Jossey-Bass, 2010).
[315] Jackson notes that a small group in New England might be greater than 35, while 12 to 15 is usually thought of as maximum size. Jackson, *New England Culture*, 34. Cf. Nelson Searcy, with Jennifer Dykes Henson, *Fusion: Turning First-Time Guests into Fully Engaged Members of Your Church* (Grand Rapids, MI: Baker, 2008).

Church.[316] Rainer itemizes correctives such as accepting responsibility for decline, escaping the strictures of rote traditions, using more missional metrics, being devoted to prayer, enjoining conflict resolution, taking the long view, and putting a premium on a high bar of church membership.[317] With the exception of the last item, these are all very needful in church revitalization.[318] They place a high value on the historic church within church revitalization. But they lack the clarity of the kinetic model sketched out in Mile Marker Four. They also spend more time on an internal focus than on an outside-the-walls missional understanding of postmodern culture. In Mile Marker Two the importance of walking in the shoes of the postmodern for becoming missional became clear. Rainer's list may not be an ideal match for the present opportunity for these reasons and because it is a description more than it is a plan.

Another such health formula, long relied upon in church revitalization even within New England efforts, is that of Christian Schwartz's *Natural Church Development*. Taking an online survey yields a score card for any given church in eight categories that Schwartz claims mark the difference between growing and declining churches: empowering leadership, gift-based ministry, passionate spirituality, effective structures, inspiring worship services, holistic small

---

[316] Thom S. Rainer, *Autopsy of a Deceased Church: 12 Ways to Keep Yours Alive* (Nashville: B&H, 2014).

[317] Thom S. Rainer, *Anatomy of a Revived Church: Seven Findings of How Congregations Avoided Death* (Spring Hill, TN: Rainer, 2019).

[318] Rainer devotes a whole book to the value of membership: Thom S. Rainer, *I Am a Church Member: Discovering the Attitude That Makes the Difference* (Nashville: B&H, 2015). My own view is that placing a high value on church membership badly backfires in a postmodern context. Add to this that church membership has little or nothing to commend it in the Scriptures, and it can quickly be regarded as a wholly unnecessary obstruction to New England receptors. Cf. the findings of Josh Packard and Ashleigh Hope, *Church Refugees: Sociologists Reveal Why People Are DONE with Church but Not Their Faith* (Loveland, CO: Group, 2015).

groups, need-oriented evangelism, and loving relationships.[319] As helpful as NCD has been to so many, its use in revitalization efforts in contexts like New England has the potential to obstruct the revitalization pathway. Like Rainer's list, it tends to focus on inward renewal over missionality. It might even be arguable that the NCD list has a circularity to it, attempting to find the very metrics the researchers hope to prove. Like Rainer's diagnostics, the NCD categories are very needful in church revitalization. But one of those categories stands out as betraying an attractional underpinning for the others: inspiring worship service. The very presence of this category on the NCD list undercuts the primacy of the need-oriented evangelism invoked by the postmodern critique, and is thus a mismatched solution for the current opportunity.

Since the Spirit of God is clearly at work on a macro level wooing his church toward relevance and incarnationality in a postmodern culture, the options reviewed above are only representative. In every corner, and quite likely often without knowledge of one another, church leaders and church people are experimenting. They are staring down the liminal void and realizing that they must lead and walk with their culture across it. They are coming to the unavoidable conclusion that the church must be more nimble for the task. Consequently, just as this book offers an experimental revitalization template that collates the best from the revitalization conversation, so many other variations of the above options are sure to be proliferating.

---

[319] Christian A. Schwartz, *Natural Church Development: A Guide to Eight Essential Qualities of Healthy Churches,* 7th ed. (St. Charles, IL: ChurchSmart, 2006).

Smarter not harder

Despite the above review of how the other available options are a mismatch to some degree with the receptors of this postmodern and postchristian moment, a kinetic model like the one proposed here can be a very hard sell. Church members who have only ever known some form of the attractional model may feel as though the kinetic-modeled church has lost her way. When the traditional metrics decline as the church continues further down a path toward revitalization, these church members may feel that the decline in numbers proves their point. Based on their attractional upbringing, Sunday morning and other onsite programming is the prism through which they judge the health of their church, so their feeling of a loss of momentum can be palpable. The very option that is the best match for the intersection of postmodernism and postchristianity in a context like New England is the one that gives them an overpowering sense that their church is continuing in decline.

Evangelistically, they may feel all dressed up with nowhere to go—both because where they already are is the point of mission and because a dedication to a kinetic model frustrates all the ways they are used to pouring themselves into ministry. This is because of the prioritization of the community presence for which the kinetic model calls. Following a deemphasis on programming and prioritization of long-view relationship building out in the community as a core value of the kinetic model, these church members may feel a distinct lack of clarity about what they are to be doing to be good church people and part of the mission. This is likely because working to maintain face time out in the community is an uncomfortable proposition for most. Participating in attractional programming is so much easier because it happens on our turf and on our terms, and because it has buildings and systems and a geographical location that give it a crisp definition. Attractional programming also allows for a sense of Christian quality control—many uncomfortably un-Christian situations that might regularly be encountered out in the community are socially unacceptable or able to be successfully disallowed in a church setting.

If the classic incarnational model is understood as something of a halfway measure between the attractional model and a kinetic one, it too may be generally more comfortable than the kinetic model. The incarnational model gets it half right, that is, that a proper response to the postmodern critique calls the church out of her safe base and into a relationship with the mess and beauty of her community—yet the incarnational model is continuously attempting to do some version of Collins's "optimal situation." An incarnational model seeks to set up unconventional little churches in the community. This, like attractional model programming, promises church turf on church terms and the crisp definition of geographical location, albeit in the form of a public space like a coffee shop. It sacralizes a coffee shop.[320] A kinetic model is more concerned with sacralizing the whole community, through relationship building, through the historic church as a base. In this light, it may be judged a more authentic adaptation to the postmodern critique than the incarnational.

However, because a kinetic model lacks the clarity and comfortability of location-based attractionality and programming, it may feel prohibitively uncomfortable in the best case, and in the worst case overly nebulous because there is no apparent evangelistic metric as a goal. The long-term relationship building of a kinetic model may, understandably and even by design, result in no or very few

---

[320] Cf. Leonard Sweet, *The Gospel According to Starbucks: Living with a Grande Passion* (Colorado Springs, CO: WaterBrook, 2007).

salvific moments or baptisms in the short term. Indeed, the townspeople with whom the church people are relationally investing may find faith in Jesus but still never darken the door of any church building. And even if the majority of these now-in-faith townspeople find their way into an organized discipleship pathway such as a small group, that still leaves many of them who will not be a consistent part of anything organized by the church—at least not in the short term. So the hoped-for result in a kinetic model, outside of what seems like the distant future, is people in the town becoming part of the Engel-scale discipleship pathway.[321] This may be preconversion discipleship, conversion, or early postconversion discipleship, but the whole point of a kinetic model is that it is not expected to result in church attendance, or even small group attendance, in the short term. If it does, the kinetic-model church is delightfully surprised! Restoration, redemption, and healing are showing up throughout these long-term relationships, but such work of the Spirit will not necessarily show up in any way in which the church has traditionally accounted for it.

Since the results of a successful kinetic model will most likely not show up in the traditional metrics of church health, many church leaders and church people are left feeling as if the kinetic model offers no real path forward for the revitalization of their church. From their point of view, (1) the kinetic model only offers some vague knowledge of evangelistic success (and in any case, does not grow their church), (2) the incarnational model is a half response that leaves behind their historic church, and (3) the attractional model has already been proven to be a thorough mismatch.

---

[321] In Mile Marker One, the discipleship pathway is described as a continuum from completely ignorant of or malicious toward the gospel to the mature, wayfaring-with-Jesus, disciple-making disciple. All along the way God is working redemptively in big and small ways, healing and restoring as only he can do.

NIMBLE CHURCH: THE HISTORIC CHURCH

In a quandary such as this, something like the Disciple Making Movement may appear to offer hope. The Disciple Making Movement centers around Christ-followers identifying a "person of peace" in the community, someone who is not a believer but is nevertheless open.[322] From this starting point they build a group in the community comprised of both believers and unbelievers. The goal is to kick off a multiplication movement of disciples making disciples making disciples.[323] But, alas, this option has little if any advantage over the kinetic model's imprecise short-term goals.

Considering the above, perhaps the greatest advantage of the historic church, especially in a New England context, is that it has the potential to ball up into one many of the appealing elements and advantages of the options so far explored. Primarily, in a kinetic model, the historic church can act as a springboard for her people to have a major community presence, and she can leverage her facilities for community use and blessing. Secondarily, in a nod to an incarnational model, she can act as a sending agency, such as the one the Disciple Making Movement envisions from Luke 10 or the "optimal situation" of Fresh Expressions. Accidentally, she can throw a bone to those who will be forever tethered to an attractional church mindset and still capitalize on invitational evangelism. In other words, although a kinetic model may be the only model in focus, the historic church can leverage her building to accommodate anyone willing to go on-mission with her,

---

[322] The term *person of peace* derives from Luke 10.5–7. E.g., C. Anderson, "How to Know Someone Is Not a Person of Peace: Disciple-Making Movements," March 10, 2019, https://www.dmmsfrontiermissions.com/how-know-not-a-person-of-peace/.
[323] E.g., Roy Moran, *Spent Matches: Igniting the Signal Fire for the Spiritually Dissatisfied* (Nashville: Thomas Nelson, 2015).

even if the person cannot buy into the kinetic model. In short, the historic church is worth fighting for to revitalize and save, no matter how arduous and precarious that fight might be, because by virtue of her history and location she possesses vast resources to leverage and underwrite kinetic and incarnational discipleship pathways.

For quintessentially New England reasons, this leveraging and underwriting strength of the historic church can be greatly magnified by one further development. If the church can be more generous and charitable in her collaboration with other churches, her historic capital in the local community grows that much more. I realize that this may be a bridge too far for many churches, but it may be worth a reanalysis and a fresh, open-eyed evaluation because of the heightened possibilities it offers. It is outside the scope of this book to expand upon this topic in the way it deserves. It requires that the church become more nuanced in the way she distinguishes herself from other churches with regard to orthodoxy, doctrine, purity, and denominationalism. It requires the church to more graciously adopt a peacemaking motto that seems to have sprung from the trauma of the Thirty Years' War: "In essentials unity, in nonessentials liberty, in all things charity."[324]

In the specific case of Holbrook, Massachusetts, this entails finding ways to publicly collaborate at appropriate levels across the denominational lines of KJV-only independent Baptists, United Methodists, Episcopalians, Roman Catholics, Congregationals (not Conservatives), and Southern Baptists. One way to do this may be, in reference to the motto above, to whittle the "essentials" down to a bare,

---

[324] Mark Ross, "In Essentials Unity, In Non-Essentials Liberty, In All Things Charity," September 16, 2009, Ligonier Ministries, https://www.ligonier.org/posts/in-essentials-unity-in-non-essentials-liberty-in-all-things-charity/.

irreducible minimum. These six very different church traditions might be able to show the community a united front of love in Christ by reducing the "essentials" to as little as "we call brother and sister anyone who proclaims that Jesus is the Son of God and the only way to God."

A willingness along these lines to publicly collaborate with other churches while less publicly maintaining doctrinal distinctives plays well in a New England context for the Name of Christ. It magnifies the historic capital of each of these historic churches until it become a sum greater than its parts from the perspective of the townspeople. It loudly demonstrates, all the more so as the churches emphasize a community presence, that the people of Jesus are people who love one another. Given the decided postchristianity of New England towns, most townspeople do not have the capacity to understand why two churches professing Jesus would caustically distance themselves from each other over an issue such as homosexuality or any other—all the townspeople have a capacity to see is two churches professing Jesus while badmouthing or refusing to work with one another. Instead, by collaborating well as churches across disparate doctrinal and denominational lines, we show our community that the one group of people on the globe who should have the capacity to do harmony well are able to be united in love even in the most challenging circumstances.

COVID-19 is proof positive

Prior to 2020 it might have been more understandable than it would be now to judge that church planting, on the whole, is still a better option in New England than church revitalization. It may have been justifiable to regard the many incarnational variants within Hirsch's EMC constellation as more economically sound than a determination to retain the historic church. But after almost two years and counting, at the time of this writing, of pandemic fear and lockdown, the church renewal conversation has been washed with revealing light. Many have called for the church to realize the opportunities of and instructions from the pandemic and to pivot in terms of the way they understand church ministry.[325] Pivoting to a predominantly digital model of church has, for obvious reasons, received much attention. We have been living in conditions where many churches could not meet at all in person on Sundays. The basis for the attractional model was stripped away and an incarnational or kinetic model began to be the only nondigital option.

Noticing this, Alan Hirsch compared it to gaining skill in chess. Sometimes, to help a chess student learn to play with the full board, the teacher will remove the queen, the most powerful piece. The student is then forced to find other paths to victory without the piece upon which he had been most reliant. Similarly, the pandemic removed the option of a heavy attractional emphasis on weekend gatherings. Hirsch's "remove the queen" strategy suddenly became an unavoidable external constraint.[326]

COVID-19 made the prophets look good. Anyone like me saying that the attractional model was no longer going to be effective in a postmodern context saw their futuristic predictions become an overnight reality. Church leaders everywhere collectively gasped at the apocalyptic hit their attendance and giving numbers were feared to take. Without the centrality of Sunday morning corporate gatherings, it

---

[325] E.g., Carey Nieuwhof, "Eight Ways to Lead in the New Digital Default Church," https://careynieuwhof.com/8-ways-to-lead-in-the-new-digital-default-church/.
[326] "Alan Hirsch: Rethinking the Chessboard," March 20, 2020, https://redeemercitytocity.com/articles-stories/alan-hirsch-rethinking-the-chessboard.

became difficult for many of those leaders to define church. In a matter of days in March of 2020, the church found herself struggling to justify her existence in her local community. If the church was no longer able to meet corporately on Sundays, and if she had no community ground game, what relevance did she have any longer to society and what justification did she have to exist as an entity? To whatever extent tithers had understood their giving as being tied to facilities and salaries and growth before the pandemic, pastors expected giving to plummet. Churches hurried to retask their staff for pastoral care phone calling and digital production in an effort to avoid layoffs. Any form of the attractional model became, by the very definition of the label, a house of cards.

And yet, as the globe began to stagger out from her pandemic bomb shelter, an unexpected lesson emerged. "If I have to do one more Zoom meeting, I'm going to lose it" has become a common refrain.[327] As much as people have taken to attending church in their pajamas during the height of the pandemic, they are realizing ever more sharply just how much they miss human contact and closeness. Their need for connection could only be sparingly serviced by the digital platforms. Their small, socially distanced backyard get-togethers lacked the sense of greater connection they knew from Sunday mornings, and their almost nonexistent opportunity to help others lacked any contiguousness with a corporal church effort. If we have been taught anything by a year of pandemic, it is that the church based on attraction

---

[327] Recent research found that while one in twenty men were severely affected by Zoom fatigue, for women it was much higher, one in seven. Zoom fatigue was unequal in other demographic categories, as well: introverts more than extroverts, younger people more than older people, and people of color more than caucasians. Kim Elsesser, "Zoom Fatigue Is Worse for Women—Here's Why," *Forbes*, April 19, 2021, https://www.forbes.com/sites/kimelsesser/2021/04/19/zoom-fatigue-is-worse-for-women---heres-why/?sh=736d0ae45225.

really is taking its last breath but that the historic church as a geographical base of operations is more optimally situated than ever.

Carol Roman, a member of the revitalized Brookville Bible Church in Holbrook, Massachusetts, comments on being missionally nimble.

Missionally nimble

This section will talk about the inverted model of church and how it helps to make us "missionally nimble." *Inverted* for us means that rather than the usual "gather–connect–go" model of church function, we are promoting "go–connect–gather." The priority in most churches is Sunday morning—filling the pews and preaching God's Word, singing praise to him, prayer, and welcoming those we haven't met before and those we see each Sunday. Here people will find solid teaching that is applicable and feel the life and love that's so present in God's house. It's a wonderful time and spurs us on to seek the Lord all week long. After a while, the people attending on Sundays will want to make some deeper friendships, get into the Bible and prayer more, and find encouragement and support in a more intimate setting. This, of course, is about joining a small group. Again, it's a wonderful time and helps us draw closer to God and live out what he is showing us. Both "gather" and "connect" are also meant to prepare us to "go," to share the gospel with others. And they do. We are more apt to talk about the Lord with our friends and co-workers and sometimes casual acquaintances. We may end up inviting others to church and maybe even see some come.

This is all great; I mean, really and truly great. At the same time, as the last section described, the culture around us is becoming less and less open to our confident understanding of God. They don't see most things as defined or knowable. They see our assurance in Christ as just "how we feel" or maybe even arrogant. Trust is possibly even broken when we are so clear-cut about the God we know and love, about Jesus and his love for us, his sacrifice for us. Broken because they feel maybe we are only pushing our feelings and opinions on them.

So we have a couple of problems. The culture is a problem. But the culture is not going to stop changing and so, we must change in order to be heard by those living in this culture.

I guess that sort of makes the other problem us. We are not a problem in and of ourselves, but in fact God's vessels to bring a lost world to himself. There is nothing wrong with how we do Sunday mornings and how we do small groups. Like I said, they're wonderful. The problem is us putting them as priorities ahead of "go." Jesus said to go into all the world and preach the gospel. He didn't qualify this with having a strong foundation of biblical doctrine or evangelism training. But because the mission is normally "gather–connect–go," people are inadvertently made to feel they need to achieve a certain level of knowledge and spiritual growth in order to be prepared well enough to "go." And for the majority, they see themselves as less than capable next to the woman in their small group who is so godly and has such beautiful insights, or the small group leader who seems to know a passage of Scripture to go with any given situation, etc.

The other part of the problem being us is that Sunday mornings and small group times together are so good. What safety and freedom, what love and encouragement, what practical and prayerful support. Am I saying we should make them less wonderful? Of course not. It's just that we get pretty comfortable in our cocoon of sweet fellowship. And that's great, but we need to find a way to get us all "going" as well.

So how do we make "go" the priority without taking away from "gather" and "connect"? We don't want to sideline "gather" and "connect"; we want to streamline them. Before Shawn Keener or the principles of Nimble Church ever came to Brookville, the church revitalization group CRM helped us begin to pare down some of our redundant and also waning efforts. The idea was to free up our volunteers for other areas. Becoming more lean doesn't mean we're sacrificing the quality of Sunday mornings or small group times. It just means we don't have lots and lots of ministries that are focused inwardly on ourselves. It means simplifying but still having depth in our worship and our time in the Word. And it means we are not so burned out with in-house events that there's little time or energy left for the outside world that we want to connect with.

At Brookville, it took a while for us to discover the best ways to "go" into the culture around us and begin connecting with others. It is still a process and I imagine it always will be. We wanted to get to know people in our community in the most natural ways possible. We came up with ideas such as these: Why not stop by the pharmacy across from the church each week to get something you might need and get to know some of the workers there, or fill up your gas tank at the same nearby station each week, or find a new restaurant, hairdresser, dog groomer, nail salon, etc. that's in town, or join the town library's book club, or attend the concert at the town gazebo, etc., etc.? About seventy-five percent of our congregation live in other towns, but even at that, many of them took the time to try to find connections this way. It was ok but far from ideal. The connections were actually too casual and didn't provide the kinds of settings where something could grow. We also realized that asking individuals to venture out on their own, or maybe with another person, was fairly intimidating for them.

So we worked on connecting as a church body with other groups in town, such as the Council on Aging. They were in need of some sprucing up and we were able to do some yard work and landscaping with them. This went well and seemed more like what we were thinking about. The town let us know that cleaning up litter, especially near the town square, in preparation for the Memorial Day parade and ceremonies would be appreciated. We organized it along with some town members and it went fairly well. These were some first attempts, and things improved as we went along. I say this because it takes time and it takes some trial and error to get any momentum, but that you will eventually get better and better.

Once or twice in the summertime we invited the other churches and groups in town to work together to host a Family Fun Day at the town playing fields, topped off with a Movie-in-the-Park in the evening. This was very well attended by the town but was a bit much on our leadership and volunteers since we did so much of the work. And that was okay but we knew we wouldn't be able to put that kind of effort into events very often. We also had a Fall Festival with games and prizes and food one year. It was in a school that was no longer in use and went very well. The people attending remarked at how much fun it was, and they certainly enjoyed the free food—we had huge pots of homemade chowder and chili. I forgot to mention— everything we do is free of charge. We want to show selfless generosity; that we're not here to get anything from people but to give.

With these town connections, we came into contact with groups who were in need of a space to meet in. The Girl Scouts were our first—such a sweet group of leaders and girls—we love having them and they appreciate having a place to be together. We don't charge for using the church building, either. We have two AA groups, an NA group, a recovery art group, a homeschooling group, and a senior chorus group at this point in time. It's funny because our building used to be sort of a sore point for us—it's quite old with a couple of additions over the years (long ago) which make it an odd configuration, plus we had the old tile floors, cinder block walls downstairs, pipes in view, etc. It wasn't all that attractive. I'll give Shawn a good deal of credit for getting us to update and beautify. We've come to appreciate our building in a new way, even the areas that haven't seen the updating. We didn't realize we had the best spaces in the entire town for groups to meet in. What a blessing to be able to give this much-needed commodity away freely.

And so our footprint in town has begun to take shape in a positive way.

You might have noticed our events take place mostly outside of our church building. There are a few exceptions to this of course. We had Trunk or Treat one or two years in our parking lot (we realized another church in town was doing this and we were seen as competition so we stopped). We had a Christmas Wonderland one year at the church with food, games, crafts, and tons of fun decorations indoors and a Living Nativity and petting zoo outdoors—again, all free. This isn't meant to say how great it was or how great we are, just that this is our philosophy and it's becoming our reputation.

Our preference is to meet people outside of our church building. We don't want to give the impression that we are just trying to get them to come to the church, one way or the other. And we're also trying to do more collaborative things with others, so it's on town turf rather than in a church setting. It varies as far as the type of event or project. Sometimes it's Brookville hosting a fun event at the town field. Sometimes it's Brookville coming alongside a town group to help them with an event or project. What we want to do is help with things that matter to them. And then occasionally just do something nice for people to come to.

We got connected with three churches in Georgia and they decided they wanted to come alongside us in some big ways! A large group from these churches came and did much-needed work on our church building—it was amazing. But what really meant so much was that they wanted to also work together with us to bless our town. They made beautiful benches for the town park, delivered groceries and helped people in a nearby housing project, and had a big cookout for the town with bouncy houses and other fun stuff. The three pastors got to know a man from town, who came to Christ that week. He's been with us ever since and even traveled to Georgia with Shawn for a visit. This time with the people from Georgia going out to our community with us was a great "shot in the arm" for what we want to do here. Our reputation is growing more and more; we're finding favor in our town.

But the things I've mentioned are nothing new for a church to be doing. There are lots of ways to bless a community. We haven't cornered the market on the most new and exciting ideas; we just want to carry them out in ways that are not centered around ourselves. We're not doing things with an agenda in mind. We are not promoting ourselves. We're not handing out literature. We're not worried about getting credit for what we're doing. We want to show that we are FOR our town and had tee-shirts made saying FOR Holbrook, rather than our church name (from the Orange Tour, Jeff Henderson). We give them out at events with the idea that we in the town are all in this together, here to help and support each other. I'm sure many will read this and wonder how on earth does the message of the gospel get through then? Once again, it's that side door. Little by little people have come to know that they can count on us. We've had town officials, and even the firefighters, let us know about ways we can help when help is needed. So when we talk about building relationships, it's also about our corporate relationship with the town, which gives more opportunities for the personal ones. People are tasting and seeing that the Lord is good.

In fact, it was funny—there was a town-sponsored event recently and Shawn kept getting thank yous from people who assumed it was something we had done! Of course, he set them straight, but it was nice to see that this is the kind of thing the people in town have come to expect from us.

Just a couple of more things on our philosophy. The first is that we don't compete with other churches or groups in town. We don't try to duplicate what they are working on but instead find out if they'd like our help. So it's still "their baby" but we lend the support they need. For example, if another church or town group is gathering warm clothing for the homeless, we don't start our own effort, we join theirs (if they'd like us to and if the Lord leads us in that direction).

The second thing is that we weren't completely sure initially where our focus should be. We are located right near the border of a city that we could be serving as well as our smaller town—they're our neighbors too. But we realized as a smaller church, we would have more impact on our own town. The city next door has a lot more resources for people to go to, and our town is limited. So we keep our focus narrow and hopefully keep our volunteers more energized.

And even though we are making Sunday mornings the last priority, we are seeing growth there. I should add that the kinds of people who start coming are not necessarily "what you had in mind". They come from all walks of life with all kinds of backstories. It's such a blessing to look around on a Sunday morning and see the new and newer faces. Some of the old, familiar ones have left. We love them and wish them well; we are not worried about "winning them back." They need to be where the Lord leads them, and if they come back, great, and if they don't, they can bless another church where they feel more comfortable. It's not always easy, but getting out of ruts involves a bumpy ride—thankfully as a temporary measure to get to a better place. It seems we are in that better place, trusting the Lord to bring us further and further along.

But back to all of us becoming more outwardly focused. Most churches have spent years with a mainly inward focus, us included. They haven't purposed to do that; it just happens. It's about that cocoon effect I mentioned earlier. It's a wonderful place to be and mostly good for us. We cherish our Sunday morning times, small group times, larger group church events—experiencing spiritual growth and insight, experiencing connection and belonging, experiencing change and renewal in ourselves and seeing it in others—it's a beautiful thing. We want this for others but we're not sure how. We're not sure how so we stay a little longer, get a little stronger, gain a little more knowledge, snuggle into that comfort and warmth. But like the butterfly, at some point we need to make a change, a change that involves struggle and action, that involves tearing open the cocoon and emerging into the world outside.

The word picture breaks down here, especially since the butterfly is alone in the cocoon and then flies off by itself. Not for us. We've shared our cocoon with our dear brothers and sisters in Christ, and we don't have to leave it forever; in fact, it will always be there for us, always provide for us as it has. But now we have somewhere to be—out there together. We need to find the lost sheep, get to know and understand them, and watch the way the Lord brings them to Himself. And isn't it great? We're actually bringing the comfort and warmth of the cocoon with us—in each other!

So we venture out and find our way together. And we make it fun. And we make it easy. And we make it something most anyone would enjoy being part of.

Whatever the reason to be together with our community, whatever the part we're playing in it, we just need to go out there with no real expectation, no agenda, and have a nice time with others. Grab a friend or two from the cocoon and be part of the activity that day. If the church is working alongside a community group on a project, make some small talk with the people you don't know as you work with them. The same with a fun event—making casual comments about what's happening, laughing at the same things, etc. Introduce them to your friends if it seems natural. No big commitment, just the usual ways people get to know each other better. There's bound to be a common thread to connect with. And when the conversation ends, let it. Trust the Lord that there will be more later if He brings you back together.

It's kind of like, "Be out there, be normal, and trust God with what this means and where it will go."

When I say "be normal" it's because I'm reminded of something my mother-in-law said a long time ago. She came with us to our church's Thanksgiving Eve service one year. She was completely nonreligious but maybe just wanted to get out that night. We were way too early and ended up having coffee in one of the side rooms. A church member came in and joined us for a bit. She and my mother-in-law were both from Southie (South Boston) and had a nice time talking about the old days there and other things Southie girls might talk about. I'll never forget, after the other woman left the room, my mother-in-law looked at us and said, "Hey, you got regular people here!"

I laughed but also thought about how "church people" may not always seem like "regular people." Someone else I know calls it "scary" when church people get really animated and excited about God when they're talking with them. We often don't realize the things we say and do with other believers, that are normal to us, sometimes give other people a weird impression. So we'll want to be careful, that's all, and just be aware of how others may be feeling. We don't need to always try to squish God into the conversation; He's already there, and He's at work.

We also want to avoid anything that creates "us" and "them". We want others to feel fully accepted and that they belong, whether or not they ever come through our church doors. And this is part of the inverted model—that people can take their first steps toward God outside the church, right where they are. We don't need to get them to church this Sunday to hear the gospel; we don't need to just get them to come to our small group so they'll see how great it is to know Jesus; we don't need to get them to that special event or game night at the church to show them that we're fun and that God is awesome and can change their lives. God will take people as they are, where they are, and will work in their hearts in His own time. We just need to be there when He does, so they have someone to talk with about the things God is impressing on them. To be there when that happens, we need to be there beforehand, in contact and eventually connection.

And so, we can rest in the Lord. We can put ourselves and others in His capable hands—tossing aside the script, working without a net—because we know we can fully trust our Lord to use us and to bring others to Himself.

Mile Marker Six: Liminal Leadership

Leadership from where?

In a postmodern culture that claims to value teamwork and collaboration across any divide, democratic and collective leadership has grown in popularity. An offshoot of this emphasis, buoyed by inspiring examples of social justice reformers past and present, is the idea that transformative leadership may be better done from the periphery, rather than from a central, recognized position of institutional authority. After all, leaders in a central position may be prone to becoming blind to large systemic faults that may be obvious to a peripheral leader. Central leaders often fall prey to the stunted growth that results from self-preservation and defensiveness.[328]

Leaders in central positions may be tempted to rely on the authority of their institutional position alone to effect changes and to mandate such changes in a top-down fashion. Leaders on the periphery might be more likely to depend on calling upon the moral necessity of these changes and harnessing the awareness of this moral necessity in a grassroots campaign.[329] Without central, officially recognized power, these may be the only recourses. From a biblical perspective, centrally empowered leadership is more vulnerable to the creeping infections of pride and the lust for power and abuse of power, while peripheral leadership is ostensibly less so by its very nature.[330] Yet there is likely a danger here of swinging the proverbial pendulum too far.

If we can come to Mile Marker Six with two assumptions, we can narrow what would otherwise be the very broad subject of leadership to only those parts of it that pertain to

---

[328] Cf. Dan Allender, *Leading with a Limp: Take Full Advantage of Your Most Powerful Weakness* (Colorado Springs, CO: WaterBrook, 2006).
[329] Cf. Leonard Sweet, *I Am a Follower: The Way, Truth, and Life of Following Jesus* (Nashville: Thomas Nelson, 2012).
[330] Cf. Arthur Boers, *Servants and Fools* (Nashville: Abingdon, 2015).

the postmodern critique of the church. First, central leadership, peripheral leadership, or any type of leadership in between them is each valid, biblical, and necessary.[331] Second, the best leaders possess a Christ-like character, whether the environment is a secular or religious one, for-profit or nonprofit.[332] With a kinetic response to the postmodern critique in view, in Mile Marker Six we see that central leadership, wise and chastened, may be the best suited for a successful church revitalization in a New England context. Central leadership, or pivotal leadership, is what is needed for the transformational, visionary voyage across the liminal void. Specifically, in a North American church, choosing a direction and making the hard decisions required to effect that choice may be better achieved by a single, central leading unit than by a consensus of members or owners.[333] Conveniently, a case can be made for a theological underpinning for the preference of central leadership.

My life experience

The focus here is on North American churches with a significant level of autonomy or freedom in governance, and particularly on such churches in the New England states.[334] (To understand how I am intending the use of these terms, such as *leadership, follower, central unit*, and others, please refer to the section on definitions of key terms in the introductory chapter, Start Here.) In many North American

---

[331] Cf. Walter Brueggemann, *The Prophetic Imagination*, 2nd ed. (Minneapolis: Fortress, 2001).

[332] Cf. Bernice M. Ledbetter, Robert J. Banks, and David C. Greenhalgh, *Reviewing Leadership: A Christian Evaluation of Current Approaches*, 2nd ed. (Grand Rapids, MI: Baker, 2016).

[333] These are not the only two options, of course, but they may be taken to represent opposite ends of a leadership or decision-making continuum.

[334] Because this reflects the governance situation of many non-profits and employee-owned for-profit businesses, the arguments and conclusions below may be easily applied across those sectors as well.

churches, a nonmajority cultural context may dictate a different worldview regarding leadership.[335] An example might be a church defined by a partially unassimilated ethnic group. Perhaps most of the rationale in this mile marker would not fit such a church because of significant differences in cultural values.

Not only is the line of reasoning in this mile marker intended for a heavily postmodern context, it also is coming from my own contextual experiences. I spent all of my precollege years in central Pennsylvania as the child of a pastor in an independent, conservative Bible Church that was governed by a board of church elders. For the most part, this governance seems to have had a track record of moderate success in terms of governance accountability and goal setting. Lengthy board meetings, micromanagement, elder representation of member factions, and paralysis of administration and goal setting were some of the detrimental tendencies of this structure. These were overcome most of the time by the servant leadership style of the pastor, who presided as chair of the board of elders, as a first among equals.

After entering college, I began to attend a church that appeared to have a similar form of governance, as well as similarities in other attributes. I continued there for twenty-one years through the life phases of dating, marriage, children, a major medical trauma, foster care, adoption, and teenagers.[336] Over the same period, this church grew in attendance from one hundred and fifty to twelve thousand, and I was able to witness the changes in governance structure

---

[335] I am thinking primarily here of ethnic churches in the greater Boston area, but this would, of course, also be the case in theological traditions, such as anabaptist and Quaker groups, which would disallow centralized leadership on biblical grounds.
[336] This was the LCBC Church, Manheim, PA, 1991–2012.

that accompanied this growth. At approximately the twelve hundred mark on that growth track, the church transitioned in governance structure from one like my childhood church to a Policy Governance® model.[337]

For the last eight years, at the time of this writing, I have had experience in central church leadership. The first two years were spent as an associate pastor in a church in Pennsylvania with an elder board form of governance that seemed to be demoralizing, constraining, and contrary to both leadership and servant leadership as defined in this mile marker. Accompanying this was a large power distance between the pastor and the elders and a far larger one between the members and the pastor. Owing to these dynamics, this position as associate pastor proved to be a demoralizing experience of leadership from the margins.

The remaining time has been spent in a role as lead pastor of an independent, conservative church in Boston's South Shore region, affiliated with the Southern Baptist Convention.[338] This church has worked through the difficult process of transitioning from having an elder board governance like those I had previously experienced to the Policy Governance model, and is experimenting with a range of methods to deconstruct power distances and exemplify

---

[337] Policy Governance® is described in the next chapter. Policy Governance is an internationally registered service mark of John Carver. Registration is only to ensure accurate description of the model rather than for financial gain. The model is available free to all with no royalties or license fees for its use. The authoritative website for Policy Governance is www.carvergovernance.com. John Carver, *Boards That Make a Difference: A New Design for Leadership in Nonprofit and Public Organizations*, 3rd ed. (San Francisco: Jossey-Bass, 2006).
[338] This is Brookville Bible Church, Holbrook, Massachusetts.

servant leadership.[339] The results are still forthcoming on this complex transition. The move of my family to the Boston area was traumatic, and the cultural shock cemented in me an awakening to the mismatch between traditional church evangelistic models and postmodern culture. A church on a revitalization pathway as has been proposed in this book may quickly discover that without a mechanism for clear, agile decision making for the whole congregation, the radical changes necessary may not happen.

Responding effectively to postmodern culture requires radical shifts in the traditional understanding of the pastorate, the job description of the pastor, and the discharging, both inwardly and outwardly attitudinal, of the church's mission. As we have seen in previous mile markers, postmodern and postchristian culture pleads for a radical shift in how the church goes about evangelism. The infamous "Nones" have quit the church because of the church's stubborn resistance to or inexcusable ignorance of these demands and pleading.[340] And a clearer, theologically grounded model of church governance is needed to give footing to the church pastor heeding the call to meet postmodern culture. The same footing will unfetter church leaders as they attempt little less than the reconfiguration of Pangea in their church evangelism strategy. And as we saw in

---

[339] Power distance refers to how any particular culture views levels of rank within any group of people, and particularly with how those in lower ranks are able to interact with and challenge, in socially acceptable ways, those in higher ranks. Cf. Peter G. Northouse, *Leadership Theory and Practice*, 8th ed. (Thousand Oaks, CA: Sage, 2019); Mary T. Lederleitner, *Cross-Cultural Partnerships: Navigating the Complexities of Money and Mission*, (Downers Grove, IL: InterVarsity, 2010).

[340] Cf. Ed Stetzer, Richie Stanley, and Jason Hayes, *Lost and Found: The Younger Unchurched and the Churches That Reach Them* (Nashville: B&H, 2009) 54, 107ff. Of course, as James Emery White notes, there are other factors at play for the "Nones," principal among which for White is the privatization of faith. James Emery White, *The Rise of the Nones* (Grand Rapids, MI: Baker, 2014).

Mile Marker Two, a frustration with the inflexibility of traditional church governance is a primary impetus behind the church refugee crisis.[341] This governance is the focus of Mile Marker Seven. In Mile Marker Six we are considering what kind of leadership is necessary to spearhead the reconfiguration.

Practical response to the postmodern critique

Considering the postmodern critique of the church, it may be easy to see that what the typical traditional church expects in a pastor and what the typical traditional pastor expects in the duties and decorum of the job must radically change if any effective engagement of the postmodern and postchristian culture is to occur. In some churches, at some point in the past, the traditional pastor could rely to some extent upon an authority inherent in the role, and upon respect for pastoral expertise. But a response to the postmodern critique might move the pastor to go out of the way to ensure he is the lowliest of all, and while well-trained and called, is just another traveler on the journey of discipleship. Previously, the pastor may have at times been able to take recourse to position and call, pulling the pastor card when it was necessary to sway an argument or action. But the pastor in a postmodern context may need to allow for no positional leverage at all, instead persuading through strength of character, strength of relationship, and ultimate trust in the Holy Spirit's will.

In some church contexts, it may have become expected that the pastor be the center of all church ministry and pronouncement. In a postmodern context, however,

---

[341] Josh Packard and Ashleigh Hope, *Church Refugees: Sociologists Reveal Why People Are DONE with Church but Not Their Faith* (Loveland, CO: Group, 2015), 53ff.

dismantling such an expectation might clarify for others that the pastor is working out of a position of accepted powerlessness and the empowerment of others. Many other matters of decorum can be leveraged to make the same clarification. If a church has an expectation that the pastor should dress in a particular way, or sit in the front row, or always be addressed by title, etc., and the pastor instead chooses to blend in with the rest of the congregation, it may send a powerful message in a postmodern context of approachability and humility. All such adjustments begin to make sense when the postmodern and postchristian aversion to pomp, power distance, authority, and modernist certainty of knowledge are understood. In short, the leader of the church who wishes to understand the times and know what to do must be *self-emptying*.[342] He or she must be focused on wayfaring with Jesus himself in that regard.[343]

Likewise, the job description of the pastor will likely need to change. Traditionally, in the contexts from my own background, the pastor has been tasked with visitation, counseling, and other personal care. Although these kinds of pastoral care duties build connection and may contribute to a perception of relevance and diligence for the pastor, they may also have the unintended consequence of making the pastor appear indispensable in the fulfillment of church–body care. These needs that could be met from within the body life of the church might also end up consuming enough of a share of the pastor's focus that he or she can reserve little time or personal bandwidth for empowering others. A pastor wanting to capitalize on a postmodern worldview might find it better in the long run to forego this "bread and butter" for the more critical and more tedious task of heading the entire

---

[342] 1Ch 12.32; Col 4.5; Php 2.
[343] Isa 53.

organism of the church in the direction of being more uncompromisingly faithful to the Great Commission.

These kinds of adjustments may be difficult to accept, particularly given that the *shepherd* term employed by the Bible for the church pastor has long been interpreted by the western mind to mean that the shepherd personally meets the needs of the sheep. The model of shepherd certainly has much scriptural call, and as we saw in Mile Marker Three, all followers with Christ are to be deputy shepherds for the Good Shepherd.[344] But if the pastorate is understood only, or even primarily, in terms of a shepherd, this can give rise to the notion that pastoring is about care more than, or even instead of, leadership. As Larry Osborne shows, both are part of the duty of a shepherd, but the latter, leadership, is crucial.[345]

Sometimes I like to prove this point by appealing to simple arithmetic. It is not that things such as pastoral care are bad things for a pastor to be doing; it's just that the pastor cannot do much, if any, pastoral care if he is to do the things he absolutely must do at all costs. So let's say a pastor works fifty hours per week and values self-care enough to spend the rest of the time with his family. If leading is his highest priority, it ought to occupy the major part of that fifty hours. And from there it is a simple mathematical equation—the more time he spends on pastoral care, or sermon prep, or maintenance, the less he spends on his primary task of collaborating with others on healthy, proactive, future-focused leadership. Those fifty hours fill up fast, and there's only a finite fifty of them.

---

[344] E.g., Jhn 21, 1Pe 5.1–5.
[345] Larry Osborne, *Lead Like a Shepherd: The Secret to Leading Well* (Nashville: Thomas Nelson, 2018). Larry quips, "Leadership without discipleship is a waste of time. And discipleship without leadership is an idealistic pipe dream, a recipe for frustration and cynicism," 3.

NIMBLE CHURCH: LIMINAL LEADERSHIP

Additionally, understanding the pastorate primarily as a caring shepherd can lead to an unfortunate side effect of the pastor being buffeted by the explicit and implicit desires of the church membership. But if the pastor is instead guided by an audience of One, he can hear and consider the merits of those desires while still keeping the church on her unwavering mission.[346] Being guided in such a way by an audience of One may also strengthen the pastor to be obsessively focused on the subjective metrics discussed in Mile Marker Four, whereas the consuming nature of a heavy pastoral care focus can sometimes lead to the pastor being focused on the questionable and easily skewed metrics of attendance and income.[347]

Where churches in modernity may have staked a claim to fame on deep, full-throated, doctrinally framed teaching, a pastor focused on connecting preaching to the postmodern will stake that claim on real life change and real kingdom advancement above all else.[348] In short, the leader of the church that wishes to understand the times and know what to do must be *self-sacrificing*. He or she must commit to a deep soul-searching to decide how to be faithful to the Great Commission and what desperate experimentation will be required to be genuinely effective in pursuing the Great Commission.

---

[346] Of course, the pastor is also under the accountability of whatever church governance is in place, which is the subject of Mile Marker Seven.
[347] Cf. Leonard Sweet, *I Am a Follower: The Way, Truth, and Life of Following Jesus* (Nashville: Thomas Nelson, 2012); Alan Hirsch, *The Forgotten Ways: Reactivating Apostolic Movements*, 2nd ed. (Grand Rapids, MI: Brazos, 2016). Some possible examples of the subjective metrics called for by the postmodern critique might include a decrease in the number of people in the surrounding community who express a sense of loneliness, or an increase in the number of new, long-view relationships between Christ-followers and postchristians.
[348] Andy Stanley and Lane Jones, *Communicating for a Change: Seven Keys to Irresistible Communication* (Colorado Springs, CO: Multnomah, 2006).

Finally, the discharging, both inwardly and outwardly attitudinal, of the church's mission must invert. Where the traditional church sought, as the postmodern will argue, to amass for itself prestige, resources, momentum, and largess, the church of today must give it all away. It must not only be seen to be giving it all away (important on its own), it must be giving it all away at its most basic levels of heart and attitude. For example, traditionally, the pastor and church may have jumped at tax exemption and any potential income stream, such as renting the church building to outside groups. But the church willing to invert its focus might instead choose to extend itself financially in order to give money away to the community, caring for it, blessing it, with no motives, conditions, or recognition attached. She might choose to offer her building for free for community use.

In the past, the consensus may have considered it unimaginable to ignore building a church's own brand and name, but the pastor and church calibrating for the postmodern viewpoint might choose to raise the proverbial tidal water under all churches in the local community.[349] Where some conservative traditions may have fastidiously drawn distinctions between their own church and most other churches in the community over doctrinal differences, a pastor focused on gaining a hearing in a postmodern culture will be an ambassador, minimizing all distinctions outside of the smallest core of the gospel message. Postchristian townspeople will not have any appreciation for why churches with different names draw distinctions between themselves; all they will ever notice in such debates is that people who follow Jesus cannot play nice together. A church striving to be missional in a postmodern context labors to

---

[349] Cf. Mark T. Oliver, *Boycott Disunity! Release the Body of Christ to a Ministry of Community Transformation* (Morgantown, PA: Masthof, 2003). Oliver is a pastor in Brockton, Massachusetts.

present a united image of every church in the community to the postchristian.

Preaching provides yet another example. Prior to the advent of a postmodern worldview the preacher may have labored over the precision of the sermon wording to demonstrate craft as a custodian of language and austerity befitting the Word of God.[350] But in contemporary culture, the preacher might focus on navigating a single arrow of transformative truth through all the cultural misconceptions and informational white noise of the postchristian visitor or the postmodern beginner–follower. This is the way Jesus taught, using parables of farming, fishing, and items right at hand, and going straight to the point of immediately applicable, deeply transformative truth.[351]

All these changes answer the pleading of the postmodern and postchristian culture for a radical shift in how the church goes about evangelism. In short, the leader of the church that wishes to understand the times and know what to do must be *self-giving*. He must meditate on the ugly security of passing an offering plate versus the cross-like insecurity of redirecting the income stream from the church toward the community. In order to inject the proper antivenom to counteract the postmodern and postchristian presumption of the church's evangelistic self-centeredness, the self-giving pastor and church will refuse to be happy until their presence in the community raises the tidal water for every part of that community.

---

[350] Cf. Marilyn McEntyre, *Caring for Words in a Culture of Lies*, 2nd ed. (Grand Rapids, MI: Eerdmans, 2021); Stanley and Jones, *Communicating for a Change*.

[351] Yet there is one sense in which Jesus and the pastor in a postmodern context care for words. Jesus was committed to charitable dialogue with those holding opposing viewpoints so long as their hearts were not hostile to God's truth.

Central and marginal

Leadership from the margins is a universal calling, but it may be an indication that something has gone wrong, requiring an increase in peripheral voices.[352] In some cases, to whatever extent there is a vital need for leadership from the margins, to that same extent leadership from the center has failed.[353] This is not to say that leadership from the margins and leadership from the center cannot complement one another and work together when things are going well.[354] The authentic leadership theory would seem to advocate that both should always be present.[355] But when central leadership has turned a blind eye or gone off course, leadership from the margins then becomes the only lifeline. Perhaps this is how the popular phrase "everything rises or falls on leadership" should be reinterpreted.

Central leadership is the pivot upon which a tectonic shift such as the one this book is suggesting can have a good hope of happening. Central leadership and leadership from the margins should work hand in hand always, and leadership from the margins becomes indispensable the moment central leadership begins to abate. Central leadership is not the only factor in seismic organizational change—it is the pivot, and the fulcrum, upon which such change is plausible.

The triad of roles, thematic throughout the Bible, of prophet, priest, and king shows the camaraderie of central

---

[352] Cf. Boers, *Servants and Fools*.
[353] E.g., Walter Brueggemann, *The Prophetic Imagination*, 2nd ed. (Minneapolis: Fortress, 2001). Some classic examples of this might include Mahatma Ghandi, Sojourner Truth, Martin Luther, and Nelson Mandela.
[354] The codes of conduct found in the Epistles are an example of the leadership of followers of the Way from the margins of Roman society.
[355] Peter G. Northouse, *Leadership Theory and Practice*, 8th ed. (Thousand Oaks, CA: Sage, 2019); cf. Bill George, *Authentic Leadership: Rediscovering the Secrets to Creating Lasting Value* (San Francisco: Jossey-Bass, 2003).

leadership and peripheral leadership.[356] The king, whether he be a member of the monarchy or God as king in the early theocratic nation of Israel, wields massive positional power as the central leader who can effect landscape-altering change. He is the only one who is afforded that luxury of radical flexibility and decision making. The priest is the referee. The prophet exercises leadership from the margins. When times are good, the prophet has things to add. When times are bad, the prophet is the lone, frail figure marking the edge of the cliff—or the towering proclaimer of impending doom, howling in both the wilderness and the courts of the king. But the prophet on his or her best day can never approach the direct capability for necessary radical shifts in the organization that the king has always and readily at his disposal.[357] Mile Marker Seven argues for a practical one-to-one analogy between this triad and Policy Governance. For now, it may be sufficient to see that the Policy Governance model applied to church polity is an excellent platform from which to effect the radical movements inherent in the shift from an attractional model to a kinetic model in New England church revitalization.

Leaders and followers

---

[356]The author draws partial inspiration for this argument from Anthony L. Blair, Jo Ann Kunz, Steve Jeantet, and Danny Kwon, "Prophets, Priests and Kings: Reimagining Ancient Metaphors of Diffused Leadership for the Twenty-First Century Organization," *Journal of Management, Spirituality and Religion* 9, no. 2 (2012): 127–145; cf. Boers, *Servants and Fools*, Chapters 8 and 9.

[357] Gareth J. Davies and co-authors, writing about regulatory agents, a term that might describe the role of priest or even prophet, apply French and Raven's five forms of power in a way that underscores this statement. Gareth J. Davies, Graham Kendall, Emma Soane, and Jiawei Li, "Regulators as 'Agents': Power and Personality in Risk Regulation and a Role for Agent-Based Simulation," *Journal of Risk Research*, 13, no. 8 (December 2010): 961–982.

Some have argued for dispensing with the value of the central leadership position.[358] Author and theologian Leonard Sweet makes an argument similar to this from a biblical perspective, building the case that everyone is really just a follower of Jesus. Some are what he calls first followers, and the rest are followers with those first followers, but all are simply following or, more accurately, wayfaring with the Master.[359] But Sweet seems to despair of central leadership in the church, painting in broad brush fashion a picture of today's church leader as a fanatic for leadership fads and junkets, an obsessor over numerical growth, and a purveyor of diluted faith, secular leadership principles, and disingenuous humility. Per our discussion earlier in this mile marker, such a leader is separated from Jesus's example by galactic measurements, but characterizing all central leadership in the church this way and then despairing of it altogether seems unwarranted. In quintessential postmodern fashion, I suggest that both are equally true. From a biblical perspective, everyone is merely a follower of and wayfarer with the foot-washing Almighty, and it is equally true that God puts a lot of weight on the call to leadership in the fulfillment of the Great Commission.

The core advantage of followership is dependence, a concoction of surrender and helplessness, something of huge importance in the walk of faith and in the process of personal sanctification.[360] The core advantage of leadership is the high responsibility and commensurate authority for leading others through the liminal spaces that continually crop up in the fulfillment of the Great Commission. Hence, the follower–leader is a dynamo, not shrinking back from

---

[358] E.g., Boers, *Servants and Fools*; and of course, some theological traditions such as Quakers do not have any central leadership.
[359] Sweet, *I Am a Follower*.
[360] Henri J. M. Nouwen, *In the Name of Jesus: Reflections on Christian Leadership* (Pearl River, New York: Crossroad, 1992).

either calling and holding the advantages of both. Blogger and pastor Carey Nieuwhof lists what he considers some of the prerequisite qualities of a positionally central church leader: they think big, believe God can do it, see abundance rather than scarcity, think vision first and resources second, invest in personal and team development, believe the mission of the church is bigger than themselves, implement experimentation first and improve it later, accept ambiguity, risk it all without any guarantee of success, never wait for a consensus, continue to act even while their critics talk, and are not afraid to break the rules (not a reference to biblical or ethical rules).[361] Followers might not have the psychological motivation or positional permission to think and act in such an entrepreneurial fashion, but follower–leaders can.

Members of a church are a wealth of wisdom and godliness, and may possess qualities like those listed above in fits and starts, but decision making for the radical shifts demanded by the Great Commission to engage contemporary New England culture will rarely if ever occur by the consensus of those members. This kind of decision making will instead be most likely to come from a central core of leadership, whether that is a tightly defined group or a diffused leadership that gives the decision-making share to a broader group. Members are leaders from the margins, usually in the priestly or prophetic roles of the trioptic leadership mentioned above.[362] The desperate need for and calling of bold, Christ-like leaders throughout the church

---

[361] Carey Nieuwhof, "Twelve Signs You're a Spiritual Entrepreneur," https://careynieuwhof.com/12-signs-youre-a-spiritual-entrepreneur/. Also Adam Grant, *Originals: How Non-conformists Move the World* (New York: Viking, 2016); Larry Osborne, *Sticky Leaders: The Secret to Lasting Change and Innovation* (Grand Rapids, MI: Zondervan, 2016).
[362] Cf. Thom S. Rainer, *I Am a Church Member: Discovering the Attitude That Makes the Difference* (Nashville: B&H, 2015).

remains, and it is magnified with each new league into the postmodern macroworldview shift.

Trioptic interplay

The congregationalist concept of church leadership via voting of the members and consensus of the members seems to derive from historically recent western ideals of representative government and democratic majority rule. Yet even in United States politics these ideals fall below the threshold of what is required for radical change without the executive branch's central ability to act. There is scant evidence that these ideals could ever be included in a biblically supported model for the church.[363] Yet often throughout history, when the central leadership, or kingly role, has failed to adapt or lead in servant-like fashion, the change necessary has transpired despite the leader's objection, percolating up from a general acceptance of the need for that change by the people under the leader's care. Radical change *can* come about in this way, although when it does it seems to happen after the need for that change is long overdue.[364]

On the other hand, there seems to be a plethora of biblical examples of leaders from the margins and leaders from the center of power. Good and bad examples of both abound. Furthermore, if one were to make the case that only one of these two forms of leadership is commanded by Scripture, the case for leading from the center would likely be easier to build.[365] In the theocracy of Israel, God was in the kingship role until the demise of the last judge, Samuel.

---

[363] But perhaps these are examples: 1Sa 8.6, Act 6.5, and Rev 4.4.

[364] Cf. Brueggemann, *Prophetic Imagination*.

[365] Sweet's statement that "It is impossible to maintain the category of leader and simultaneously engender the fellow-follower dynamic" appears to lack grounding from the New Testament. Sweet, *I Am a Follower*, 85.

Following this period, God put that mantel on the kings of the united and subsequently divided monarchy to effect the changes, large and small, necessary for God's designs and grand redemptive plan.

It is not as though, however, the roles of priests and prophets were only stopgaps in God's redemptive plan. The tripotic model gives continuous value to all three roles. But the prophetic role in particular may have been at its zenith when the kingly role failed in fulfilling the mission of God, and during the Exile when central leadership was nonexistent. Nevertheless, the role that usually possesses the most direct ability to effect organization-wide transformative change is that of the king.

Jesus, of course, is the epitome of strong, assertive, responsible, risk taking, and called leadership as the Kinsman Redeemer and the Sustainer of All Things, while simultaneously exemplifying self-emptying, self-sacrificing, self-giving, and called leadership as the Sacrificial Lamb.[366] The apostles are commanded to lead the church, and did so throughout their lifetimes, collectively but as a single, central unit.[367] The epistles command church leaders to lead, serving faithfully as overseers of the flock God has placed under their care.[368] The ancient near-eastern shepherd, a motif for godly leadership throughout the Scriptures, had as a primary duty the leading of the flock from one soiled resting place and depleted pasture to new and fresh places, and to keep

---

[366] Of course, it could also be argued that Jesus wielded marginal leadership as a despised and rebel rabbi working to bring Jewish faith back to the person of God from a warped manipulation of Torah.
[367] Mat 16.18–19; e.g., Act 15.
[368] 1Pe 5.1–4.

that flock on task by defending it from distraction and molestation.[369]

The relevance of the church seems to be weakening every day amidst the sheer volume of the world's hollow offerings. And the effectiveness of the church's evangelistic proclamation is every day more blunted by the mismatch between the postmodern critique and the church's carried-over, evangelistic model. Those churches awakening to this situation and mismatch are confronted with a seemingly insurmountable task: exhaustively inverting the model and comprehensively retooling the priesthood of all believers. Therefore, the need for decisive, called leadership from the center to lead the church through this harrowing new liminal space has seldom been more striking. The confluence of rich theological theories underpinning pivotal servant leadership, radical church evangelistic model shifts, and competent governance gives shape to an urgent and critical application to practice. We have discussed the first two; the third, competent governance, is the concern of the next mile marker.

If the missional church, incarnating among and hearing postmoderns, is to attempt the radical inversion of Mile Marker Four, she must be adaptive and agile. If she is to do so speedily, or even remotely concurrently with the cultural change around her, she must be nimble. The kind of leadership envisioned in this mile marker may be her best hope of possessing this kind of alacrity. But without clear governance in place, this central leadership will be stymied, frustrated, or comparatively unaccountable.

---

[369] Jack W. Vancil, "Sheep, Shepherd," in *The Anchor Bible Dictionary*, Vol. 5, ed. David Noel Freedman (New York: Doubleday, 1992); Osborne, *Lead Like a Shepherd.*

Mile Marker Seven: Clarified Governance

Why good governance matters

As we saw in Mile Marker Three, a prominent reason why nondenominational, Bible, Baptist, and other independently governed churches are autonomous and independent is their heritage. They come out of or stand in the legacy of the Puritan and Congregational churches of the seventeenth and eighteenth centuries in Massachusetts and the other New England colonies. This independence was a necessity. Without a pope, king, or bishopric to establish churches, ordain clergy, and arbitrate disputes in a wooded frontier far from the ecclesiastic civility of their English homeland, the early colonists defaulted to a form of governance that may be taken for granted today: they handled all these matters independently within their own local churches and parishes.[370] The early necessitating factors leading to the autonomous church tradition are now largely forgotten, a consequence of which is the temptation to view local church autonomy, and congregational polity, as a New Testament prescription. In Mile Marker One, we explored why such a view may be an overreach.[371] There it was argued that church governance structure, because of a lack of New Testament prescription, should be in the service of mission, not the other way around.

Mile Markers Two and Three detailed a massive cultural shift, one so seismic it may be viewed as an event on the world history timeline in the years to come. This is an epistemological shift from modern, empirical worldviews to postmodern, relativistic ones. It is a wave that catches the

---

[370] Cf. Nathan O. Hatch, *The Democratization of American Christianity* (New Haven, CT: Yale University Press, 1989).

[371] Grudem states unequivocally that "the form of government adopted by a church is not a major point of doctrine." Wayne Grudem, *Systematic Theology: An Introduction to Biblical Doctrine,* 2nd ed. (Grand Rapids, MI: Zondervan, 2020), 936.

church fully in its curl, stripping her of the cultural dominance on which she has based her evangelistic strategy for centuries, even back to the time of Constantine.[372] The attractional model, heavily reliant on this cultural dominance now lost, is the wrong tool to bring the gospel of Jesus to a world that has shifted from modernism to postmodernism and from Christian hegemony to postchristianity. Consequently, this book has proposed an experiment to precisely invert the attractional model so that what may be dubbed a kinetic model is formed, one that places community value and outreach as the main attractants to church and Jesus—and the Sunday worship experience at the tail.

Though this inversion may be demonstrated on paper to be an absolute necessity for the New England church caught in this massive cultural wave, inverting the attractional model in an established church through a church revitalization effort is in reality a nearly impossible feat. Why? Because people are predisposed to resist change until the point at which staying where they are is more painful than undergoing the trauma of change would be. But they often arrive at that point too late. The rule is that old habits die hard, and not only is the church no exception to the rule, but she may be especially vulnerable to it because of her love of sacralized tradition. For this reason, good leadership is crucial, and good governance, which supports it, becomes the difference between talking a lot about church revitalization and courageously starting down the revitalization pathway as a whole church body.

A theology of good governance

---

[372] Alan Hirsch, *The Forgotten Ways: Reactivating Apostolic Movements,* 2nd ed. (Grand Rapids, MI: Brazos, 2016), 58.

To a discerning eye, the Bible is replete with examples of the value of governance, so much so that governance stands out as a baked-in part of the natural order of creation. The redemptive story begins with bad governance of the human responsibility in Adam and good governance of a vast, unruly people in Moses. The Law written out by God's own hand on Mount Sinai was a masterpiece of clear governance oriented around proximity to God and the mission of God.

The New Testament is itself something of a governance manual for the church. It stresses, more than any other piece of governance, the proactive, future-oriented mission of bringing all people to God, as speedily as possible, because the time is short, as we saw in Mile Marker One. Based upon that mission, the New Testament also proscribes those things that hinder us from realizing that purpose or entangle us in hurdles along the way.[373] There are even glimpses into such governance details as clear lines of authority and unified proclamations from a central leading unit made up of multiple people.[374]

One of the clearest of examples of this may be in Acts 15. A dispute arose in the church over whether or not it was possible for Gentiles to follow Jesus without converting to the rules of Judaism. Paul and Barnabas, the church's messengers, brought the issue to their governing authority, the Jerusalem elders. This did not merely represent a matter of arbitration, for which good governance may also at times be needed. Rather, it cast in sharp relief a moment of major decision for the future of the church. As Andrew Walls points out, this was the first time the gospel was transmitted from

---

[373] Heb 12.1–2.
[374] Paul is free to hand out directives in the epistles that he expects each respective church to follow.

one culture to another.[375] This issue, one that may seem to our ears a matter of legalism and nitpicking, was actually a make-or-break one for the spread of the gospel throughout time and space from that day to this. It represented a moment when the central leading unit of the church at that time had to choose between being reactive or proactive.

The group of elders that deliberated on the matter could have chosen to be reactive, that is, to charge and penalize the new Gentile believers for not conforming to the Mosaic legal code. They could have written new rules for how, specifically, the Mosaic rules would be translated for the contemporary Gentile culture. But the Spirit of God led them instead to exemplify proactivity for us. That is, the mission of God and of his church was fully in their view and it was their highest priority. Reminding us of our discussion in Mile Marker One, they recognized that the highest goal of orthodoxy was that "everyone [might] come to repentance."

They arrived at this emphasis carefully and after much debate and prayer. Peter is recorded as one who stood up and expressed his own opinion on the matter, but his was understood by the rest to be just one opinion among others. Then, although they came to the decision collectively, they made a single pronouncement: "It seemed good to the Holy Spirit and to us not to burden you with anything beyond the following requirements: You are to abstain from food sacrificed to idols, from blood, from the meat of strangled animals and from sexual immorality. You will do well to avoid these things."[376]

Finally, they effected their decision, or rather delegated their authority, through their messengers, Paul and

---

[375] Andrew Walls, *The Missionary Movement in Christian History: Studies in the Transmission of Faith* (Maryknoll, NY: Orbis, 1996).
[376] Act 15.28–29.

Barnabas. As overseers of God's Church, they were careful not to establish multiple avenues of pronouncement, or permit multiple differing decisions on the matter to stand. They recognized that, true to what Peter himself would urge later, to be shepherds of God's flock in a manner deserving the crown of glory that will never fade away, they needed to oversee the growing and disparate elements of the church with proactive vision, decisive pronouncements, and unmuddied lines of authority.[377] Conceivably, in the aftermath of Acts 15, they also monitored and corrected against factions of the church that ran afoul of their decision, as we see in other areas of the New Testament.[378] In so doing, they thoroughly and cleanly carried out their responsibility to lead the church across a giant liminal void of the time and into whole new life and advancement of the mission.

One good governance expansion

In Mile Marker One, I sketched the outlines of the style of church governance with which I am most familiar. Briefly, in the Baptist, Bible, and nondenominational traditions in which I have worshipped and worked, there is some mix of congregational decision making and plural-elder governance. Typically, each elder is tasked with oversight of his share of specific ministries.[379] This oversight can be as unobtrusive as praying for the ministry(ies) and acting as a liaison for the body of elders. But more often it involves reporting from that ministry to the assigned elder and the obtaining of permissions in decision making from that elder. The pastor is usually an elder and considered "first among equals." Deacons or trustees, if there are any, are often tasked with facility maintenance or church finance.

---

[377] 1Pe 5.1–4.
[378] E.g., 2Tim 4.2.
[379] All of these churches with which I am familiar are complementarian.

A basis for the legitimacy and value of this style of governance can be found in Scripture, as was noted in Mile Marker One. Although, as noted there, it might be inappropriate to find a biblical prescription or mandate for this style of governance, it has much to recommend it both biblically and philosophically. For example, it provides for an advisory council, in the form of the body of elders, to support the pastor and staff and to keep them accountable to God and the church. Often, it ensures something of a deep bench of experienced men who can preach or make emergency decisions. More than anything else, it makes possible a church structure independent of outside hierarchy. An expansion on this style of governance, one that originated in the nonprofit world but that can bring extra clarity to elder-polity governance, is John Carver's Policy Governance.

The Carver Policy Governance® model, adapted as a tool to serve the autonomous, elder-led church, provides for the agility and stability necessary for a radical inversion of the attractional model.[380] This comparatively new model has found wide acceptance in nonprofits, charities, and public elementary school systems. In autonomous churches, however, it is rarely known and even more rarely understood or implemented. I propose that Carver's Policy Governance is an excellent tool for the clarification of church governance in churches desiring to revitalize.

Often, when someone in a church leadership context speaks of policy governance, what they may be thinking of is governing primarily through policy. Carver's Policy Governance is a tightly defined system that takes the concept

---

[380] John Carver, *Boards That Make a Difference: A New Design for Leadership in Nonprofit and Public Organizations*, 3rd ed. (San Francisco: Jossey-Bass, 2006). Carver Policy Governance is copyrighted not to monetize it but to preserve it. Hull, *Focusing Your Church Board*.

of governing through policy to an entirely new and sophisticated level. In Policy Governance, just as is often found in nondenominational, Baptist, Bible, and similar churches, the trust and authority of the church membership are placed in a subset of their own number, a governing body of elders. Taking this a step further back, these elders are not members who represent factions of the church but are instead the conduits through which the guidance of the Spirit of God flows into church decision making and direction taking. This governing body then governs *solely* through policy it has written.

Bound by the parameters of some comparatively immutable documents of the church, such as bylaws and a constitution,[381] the governing body writes down its own policies, can change these policies easily at its discretion, and holds itself and the church and church leaders accountable against these written policies. It does not hold itself, the pastor, or the church accountable against any other criteria, formal or informal. The governing body writes policies in four areas: the vision for the church, proscriptions against what the pastor and the church cannot do,[382] the line of authority and communication from the governing body to the church (referred to by Carver as the board–pastor

---

[381] Incidentally, in a denominational context, Policy Governance may still be an appropriate fit, bounded by the proscriptions and defining documents of the denomination. Prescriptions tell someone what to do; proscriptions tell someone what they cannot do.

[382] Some may object that proscriptive writing seems difficult and prone to gaps in coverage. In my experience, the opposite is true. Prescriptive writing is much more difficult to accomplish in any exhaustive way. Many governing bodies of autonomous churches, if they write policy, do so in a prescriptive manner, which serves to be constraining to the pastor and staff, encourages micromanagement from the governing body, and tends to be unimaginative in planning for all possible scenarios.

linkage),[383] and conduct of the governing body itself.[384] Typically, the governing body is delegating most of its authority to a single person, usually the pastor, who then further delegates the authority to other staff and volunteers.

The policy written in these four areas covers *every* possible eventuality within the function of the church, because it is written as an exoskeleton, offering total accountability and containment of all possible decisions and actions. In traditional elder-led governance, comprehensive accountability is difficult to attain. What the governing body might conceive of as comprehensive accountability is often, upon further inspection, very spotty. It may even in many cases turn out to be fickle, haphazardly applied, inconsistent, unintentionally neglected, reactionary, hastily drawn under duress, or accidentally dispiriting.

The four areas of Policy Governance provide for an accountability that is proactive, visionary, and complete, deftly mitigating most of these unfortunate deficiencies in traditional autonomous church governance. I have witnessed at least one traditional elder body that appeared to be proactive and visionary, and to have achieved complete accountability. To maintain these qualities, this governing

---

[383] Many elder-led autonomous churches assign areas of oversight to each individual governing body member. This creates multiple, unnecessary problems, chief among which is confusion for the ministry staff regarding where their orders are coming from and to whom they are accountable. It is a conflation of governance and management.

[384] Intriguingly, Miriam Carver, in a private conversation with me, asserted that this fourth area is the one that most often decides the fate of Policy Governance survival and implementation in an organization. It is an unfortunate fact that in many elder-led autonomous churches, the real power is wielded by people who have no affirmed leadership, or little background or education in the matters they affect, or are themselves governed consciously or subconsciously by their own pride or greed for power. When correctly applied, all of Carver Policy Governance, particularly this fourth area, frustrates or makes impossible these unhealthy situations.

body met for frequent and lengthy meetings and each member was responsible for a significant amount of work between meetings. Carver's Policy Governance, when applied to a church setting, achieves the same results with far less labor while still honoring the tradition of elder-led governance.

Typically, the church pastor wears two hats: one as a voting member of the governing body and one as the leader of everything that goes on at the church, for which the pastor is accountable to the governing body. Typically also, the members of the governing body wear two completely separate hats: one as a voting member of the governing body and one as a volunteer leader responsible to the pastor. In Policy Governance, the governing body has no hierarchy within it. All are equal, though the pastor is typically understood to be a spiritual leader to the governing body.[385] The governing body only ever speaks (outside of its own meetings) as one voice and only through its carefully considered *written* word. A governing body member has no distinction or special status singly but only when deliberating and speaking together with the other members as a body.

One of my favorite analogies for Policy Governance is football. This analogy is purely to help someone else understand the concepts of Policy Governance and not as any replacement for the New Testament's outline of church elders. As with many analogies, it is quite imperfect, but it seems to make the Policy Governance concepts understandable. (Unfortunately, the Brady–Belichick dynasty is now only a memory, but it can live on as an explanation of

---

[385] Grudem claims: "we must agree that a system of plural elders in which all have equal authority does not prevent one elder (such as the pastor) from functioning as a sort of 'first among equals 'and having a significant leadership role among those elders." Wayne Grudem, *Systematic Theology*, 937.

Carver's Policy Governance.) This is especially fun, given this book's focus on New England churches. The reader may think, very loosely and for the sake of the analogy, of the Kraft family, Patriot fans, and others as the church membership and then roll up Belichick, the Patriots' coaching team, the referees, and the NFL rules committee into one ball that represents a church's governing body (admittedly, this is a weak spot in the analogy). The Greatest of All Time, the quarterback Tom Brady, can represent the church's lead pastor, and the other players on the field and on the bench represent the church staff and volunteers. There is one solitary goal: to get the ball into the end zone. Carried over from football to the church, the end zone is the mission of the church and moving the ball toward the end zone is the pursuit of that mission.

In Policy Governance, the governing body's far-and-away most important duty is to define and name the end zone, what it is, and what it looks like when the church has gotten there. They do this with as much abandonment to the Holy Spirit and with as much clarity as possible. The second duty of the governing body is to define and name acts that would be out of bounds or deserving of a yellow flag. The reader may recall here, and this is crucial to Policy Governance, that the governing body is not writing *prescriptive* policy to tell Brady *et al* how to get the ball into the end zone. Rather, the governing body is writing only *proscriptive* policy that says, "Here you shall not go."

This proscriptive policy also says, "Even if a particular play or strategy is *effective* at getting the ball into the end zone, it is nevertheless forbidden and out of line with this team, and with this league." In other words, not everything that may seem to work from the perspective of the pastor or the church is allowable by the governing body. Inseparable from the naming and defining of the end zone and the out-of-bounds actions is the governing body's duty to hold the team accountable to these written policies that are currently in place. Just like in the NFL, sometimes the governing body finds it necessary to slightly adjust the rules of play going forward, and they adjust their written policy accordingly.

Here is the genius of Carver's Policy Governance model. As can be easily understood from the Brady–Belichick analogy, Brady and team are liberated to call audibles or to act or strategize in any way that does not fall afoul of the rules or sidelines. They have a free hand to dream and experiment. In fact, crucial to the Policy Governance model is the recognition that, following this analogy, *everything* the Brady-and-team scheme about or do is automatically *preapproved* simply because it stays between the sidelines and is oriented toward the right end of the field. The football field becomes a liberated, innovative playground. The no-no's are crystal clear. They are written down as policy and indisputable within the range of any reasonable interpretation.[386] The pastor, staff, and volunteers do not ever have to worry about stepping on informal or unstated land mines. Creativity is thereby platformed and systemically encouraged. Empowerment with the protection of clear and written accountability reigns.

However, the Brady–Belichick analogy, while still a good one, breaks down at one key point. Integral to Carver's Policy Governance is the precise linkage between the governing body and the lead pastor and church. In the model, the governing body has no direct authority, and, technically, no

---

[386] "Any reasonable interpretation" of policy by those to whom the governing body delegates its authority is a key element of Carver's Policy Governance. Some may regard "any reasonable interpretation" as so difficult to define that it renders the policies worthless. In my experience this is not the case because the governing body has the right and obligation to challenge any such interpretation by asking for justification. If the justification is unsatisfactory, the governing body has only to write another layer of more explicit policy on the matter in question.

direct communication, with any leadership or volunteer in the church except the lead pastor alone.[387] In Policy Governance, if the analogy is continued, any and all connection between the governing body and the Patriots players flows solely through Brady. While this would make zero sense in Gillette Stadium, it is supported by excellent reasoning in a church context: it is incredibly difficult for church staff and volunteers to authentically and faithfully follow more than one authoritative voice concurrently. (This authoritative voice may come from a single person or from a single leading unit in the form of more than one person in shared leadership.)

Another, very different analogy that may be useful for understanding Policy Governance is Hull's timepiece analogy.[388] He pictures the four areas, or "quadrants," of policy writing as completely inseparable from one another. Just as a beautiful heirloom watch ceases to function if a single gear is removed, so it is with Policy Governance. If a church implements the Policy Governance model but declines to clearly define outcomes, or insists on prescriptive staff rules, or assigns governing body members individual clout, or retains direct lines of authority from the governing body to the staff or volunteers, the entire Policy Governance house comes crashing to the ground and is of little use. Just as any half-measure implementation of the attractional

---

[387] The reader may recall here that this is the typical arrangement—the governing body delegates its authority to the pastor in a church context. Though typical, this is not the only scenario. Depending upon the church context, the governing body's authority might be delegated to a leading unit comprised of more than one person, or it may delegate several segments of its authority to separate leading units, or it may prefer some other arrangement.

[388] Ted Hull, *Focusing Your Church Board: Using the Carver Policy Governance Model* (Winnipeg, MB: Word Alive, 2015).

model inversion returns poor results, so it is with Policy Governance.

Hull adds another valuable reason for recommending Policy Governance to churches: it provides real, not illusory, control and accountability. Even well-running, elder-led, autonomous churches might have accountability that is less than satisfactory. In even the best functioning of these governance structures, informal and unwritten expectations and codes may proliferate, lines of authority and responsibility might be ill-defined or undefined, and accountability actions may be infrequent or inconsistently applied. Institutional memory of the governing body that might otherwise mitigate these flaws may become a casualty of term limits and turnover. When implemented as intended, Policy Governance rectifies each one of these weaknesses, so that genuine and predictable accountability becomes achievable.

At this point, the theologically minded reader may balk at Policy Governance because of its polish, because of its copyright symbol, and because of its secular business-arena feel. But to those whose hearts are pure, everything is pure.[389] Simply because Policy Governance was created and refined in a nonchurch context does not mean that it is foreign to the will of God or biblical precedent. In fact, the opposite seems to be the case. It may be that Carver only seems to have invented a healthy, precise model of governance in a twenty-first-century North American nonprofit context—when in reality he may have merely uncovered or rediscovered an inherently biblical model for governance in the nonprofit world. If Policy Governance is a clarification of church elder-led polity, then Carver really only reinvented the church's wheel. Policy Governance

---

[389] Tit 1.15.

appears to be a well-articulated blueprint for executing elder-led polity with excellence.

First, Policy Governance seems to make good sense of New Testament teaching regarding church leadership and eldership. Hull's writing has demonstrated that New Testament descriptions of elder and pastor and deacon can be naturally aligned with Carver's Policy Governance.[390] Even if, against the arguments of Mile Marker One, the reader claims a New Testament prescription for an elder-led governance structure, Policy Governance would only serve to clarify that structure and protect it from inconsistencies and vagaries. In his thorough, biblically exegeted discussion of "Forms of Church Government," Grudem returns repeatedly and with preference to the principles behind the Policy Governance model, though he does not appear to recognize this.[391]

Second, Policy Governance appears to be rooted in the same spirit or philosophy as the Old Testament legal code, even if the latter was often interpreted or practiced contrary to God's intent.[392] In the theocracy "church" that was the chosen people, the God of Israel established an end zone of loving "the LORD your God with all your heart" and loving "your neighbor as yourself" and being "a light to the Gentiles" to provoke them to jealousy and bring them back to the one true God.[393] Then in the Ten Commandments and

---

[390] Hull, *Focusing Your Church Board*, Chapters 3 and 4.

[391] Grudem could not have been aware of the Carver model for the 1994 printing of his *Systematic Theology*, and it appears he was not aware of it in the 2008 revision. Wayne Grudem, "Church Government," in *Systematic Theology*. He seems to be dismissive of the Policy Governance category (p. 935), yet seems to argue for its underlying principles (pp. 933–934).

[392] I am indebted on this point to Jeffrey Krebs, a governing body member at Brookville Bible Church.

[393] Deu 6.5; Lev 19.18; Mat 22.38–39; Isa 42.6, 49.6; Zec 8.20–23; Jhn 5.39–40; Gal 3.8.

the voluminous code of the Pentateuch, God established proscriptive sidelines and spirit-of-the-Law penalty calls. In effect, God is saying, "Pursue my consuming glorious obsession for drawing all humanity unto me, and know that you are empowered to use all the creativity and ingenuity latent within you by virtue of you bearing my own image, but do so by avoiding the limitations I have placed on you, for good, not for harm."[394] God's real intention as revealed in the New Testament is that his people have hearts of flesh, not of stone, for whom the tedious proscriptions of the Old Testament are almost unnecessary because their love for God and hunger for the prize drive them naturally to stay on the green turf and get creative about moving the ball.[395]

Third, Policy Governance can be a perfect incubator for a return to a biblical trioptic leadership culture.[396] Trioptic leadership, valuing the offices of prophet, priest, and king in leadership structure, decision making, and institutional reform, may be the biblical antidote to the excesses and abuses of contemporary leadership failures. Where central leadership in the church may veer toward pride, incompetence, or self-interest, or be plainly tone deaf, or where the leadership seminar circuit has become faddish and secular, a trioptic leadership model provides inherent checks and balances to keep the church on track with God's call and will and mission.

The trioptic model values the king for his ability and flexibility to act and decide (typically the pastor and staff in the Policy Governance model as applied to the church); the

---

[394] Cf. Jer 29.11.
[395] Eze 36.26; Eph 5.16; Col 4.5; 2Pe 3. Cf. Patrick Lencioni's discussion of "hungry" in *The Ideal Team Player* (Hoboken, NJ: Jossey-Bass, 2016).
[396] Cf. Anthony L. Blair, Jo Ann Kunz, Steve Jeantet, and Danny Kwon, "Prophets, Priests and Kings: Re-Imagining Ancient Metaphors of Diffused Leadership for the Twenty-First Century Organization," *Journal of Management, Spirituality, and Religion* 9, no. 2 (2012), 127–145.

priest for his authority under God to legitimize, counsel, and correct the king (the governing body in the Policy Governance model, made up of elders with the priestly-esque duties attributed to them throughout the New Testament[397]); and the prophet, the outsider and peripheral leader, for his ability to smack the ship aright when it has collectively conspired to tack off course (the church membership as a whole or as individual prophets).[398] Given that one of the many strong arguments for Policy Governance in the church is the consistency of accountability regardless of tenure, it is intriguing to note that this is the same strength of the priesthood, of the Aaronic, but far more so of the Melchizedek-Messianic priesthood, that "because Jesus lives forever, he has a permanent priesthood. Therefore he is able to save completely those who come to God through him, because he always lives to intercede for them."[399] In Policy Governance, the governing body, through its policy writing, is a stable, constant voice, similar to the priesthood in the trioptic model of leadership. Kings may come and go, and prophets may pop up or go silent, but the priesthood is a consistent, stable measure.

Fourth, Policy Governance epitomizes the *modus operandi* of God with his people. God desires that his people graduate from milk to solid food, not stay satisfied with milk only. In

---

[397] Act 2.42, 6.1–7; 1Ti 5.22; Jas 5.16.

[398] A parallel may possibly be drawn here, also, to the genius of the founding fathers of the American Republic in designing three branches of government that resemble the trioptic model, with the executive branch as the kingly role, the legislative branch as the priestly role, and the judicial branch as the prophetic role. Interestingly, as an aside to Policy Governance, compare Gorsuch on the proscriptive nature of the United States Constitution toward government, telling it what it cannot do and being comparatively quiet about what it should do. Neil Gorsuch, *A Republic if You Can Keep It* (New York, Crown, 2019).

[399] Heb 7.24–25.

spiritual maturity, milk equates to legalism, simple formulas, and the fear and guilt that keeps God's children threading the needle between the do's and don'ts, while solid food equates to much higher motivations such as walking by faith and not by sight, or gratitude and love, or hope and joy in what is certainly to come but is not here yet.[400] The typical elder oversight relied upon in traditional autonomous churches can be reactive and backward looking. Reports of the month just past are scrutinized. Difficulties, discipline issues, heresies, and conflicts that have already arisen are addressed. The health of the church and even the next year's budget are understood almost entirely by looking *back* at the last twelve, twenty-four, or thirty-six months. Of course, this may not always be the case, but those governing bodies that are forward looking and missional may discover that Policy Governance facilitates these postures.

One of the many singularly great coups of the Policy Governance model is its ability to nurture proactivity in a governing body. Policy Governance encourages the members to be primarily fixated on the end zone, having it rightly defined and analyzing the church and the lead pastor's ministry almost exclusively through that lens.[401] The

---

[400] Heb 6.1–3. The whole argument line of Hebrews is rest and faith, rest from the particulars of obedience to the law and faith in the prize set before us, the end zone, the place where all our focus and hope are centered. Paul's schoolmaster analogy in Galatians 4 is relevant here as well, illustrating that the law is only in place until the child is mature enough to operate without need of it. Similarly, Paul says that in Christ, everything is "Yes" (2Co 1.20). And John reminds us that "there is no fear in love. But perfect love drives out fear, because fear has to do with punishment" (1Jn 4.18).

[401] The reader may object to a job performance evaluation being biblical. In my opinion, this objection is difficult to maintain. For example, throughout Scripture, when God delegates his authority to kings, judges, or others, he clearly also demands an accounting of their use of that authority. This is simply a longer way of saying "job performance evaluation."

Policy Governance body of elders spends relatively little time in their meetings or in meeting prep pouring over, questioning, and critiquing reports from the last month. Decisions do not constantly have to be made anew regarding how to handle conflicts or other problems because the guidance of response has already been clearly expressed in a written policy. The governing body is free to spend the bulk of its time educating themselves together, communing and praying together, and seeking to peer around the corner of the cultural future to faithfully prepare and guide the Bride of Christ for what is ahead. Under Policy Governance, the church governing body is empowered to lead the church to partake of the solid food of proactive action, faith, and vision and to leave behind the milkish elementary teachings of red tape.[402]

Some (mostly) New England examples

I am closely familiar with three examples of Policy Governance being used in autonomous, elder-led churches, two of which are in New England. Somewhere around 2003, the LCBC Church in Manheim, Pennsylvania, began to implement the Carver model.[403] The LCBC elder body had

---

[402] Heb 5.12–13. Daniel Akin describes the state of some elder-led autonomous churches when he says that "Single-pastor Congregationalism is often a sight to behold. It is not necessarily a pretty one. A somewhat paranoid autocrat as pastor, monthly business meetings dedicated to senseless issues that only eat up time, a committee structure that looks like the Department of Education and is about as efficient, and a deacon board that functions like a carnal corporate board. My fellow contributors, I am sure, will be quick on the draw and point out how unbiblical such a model is. They are 100 percent right! It is unbiblical, but this is not what the Bible teaches about Congregational church government. What we discover in God's Word is altogether different." Chad Owen Brand and R. Stanton Norman, eds., *Perspectives on Church Government: Five Views on Church Polity* (Nashville: B&H, 2004).

[403] *Saturdays at LCBC*, unpublished document from LCBC Church, Manheim, PA, 2010.

been recognizing that their traditional elder oversight model was plagued by "fuzzy lines of authority" and an "evolving function of [the] elder board" in a rapidly growing church. Because they desired "to be more purpose driven," "to be better positioned for growth," "to lead proactively, not reactively," and "to have real, not perceived, oversight," the church leadership traveled to Atlanta to meet firsthand with John Carver and his consulting and training teams, and through that relationship became an early adopter of the model in a church setting.

The LCBC leadership cites these benefits of Policy Governance as primary reasons for their interest in the model: "clearly defined relationships and job descriptions for senior pastor and board," focus "on ends not means," "flexibility for [the] senior pastor to lead with his staff," "complete accountability of the senior pastor and staff to the board," and positioning of "the board in front of the organization providing vision/direction." The elder board designated the first year for what is termed a "policy blast" by some consultants, an intentionally hasty project of getting good-enough policy in place so the church could function well under Policy Governance.[404] Later, through yearly cycles of methodical review, these initial policies were, and are, honed and refined as necessary. LCBC leadership credits Policy Governance in part for the growth of the church, from approximately one thousand in attendance at the time of adoption to an approximate eighteen thousand in attendance

---

[404] Terry Hippenhammer, a Policy Governance consultant based in Seattle, Jeffrey Krebs, a Policy Governance writer at Brookville Bible Church in Holbrook, Massachusetts, and Phil Dearborn, a *pro bono* Policy Governance coach for churches in Lancaster, Pennsylvania, are a few examples of consultants who recommend this.

in 2019.[405] LCBC is referenced in the Carver books as a model of a church implementing Policy Governance.[406]

Somewhere around 2010, Christ Community Church in Taunton, Massachusetts, retained an outside church revitalization firm to improve their governance structure and leadership culture. This consulting group, CRM (now renamed VitalChurch), included an adoption of the Policy Governance model among their recommendations. Over the years since then, the church leadership has worked to fully implement Policy Governance, but the process is currently incomplete. The body of elders operates with a written policy in the areas of staff limitations and governance-staff linkage, with partially complete policy in the other areas.[407]

After observing the successes of some of the CRM recommendations at Christ Community Church, Brookville Bible Church retained the same consulting group for its own ministry realignment. Following a deliberative survey and analysis period, CRM offered a series of recommendations to the Brookville leadership in June 2014, one of which was a move toward a church structure based on Policy Governance.[408] CRM supplied the church leadership with a template of policies for two of the four areas, those of governance-staff linkage and governance body behavior, and these templates were subsequently adopted with little alteration in January 2015. For the next four years, the governance body members and leaders worked through the

---

[405] Phil Dearborn, handout from a private consulting meeting. I am not implying here that successful implementation of Policy Governance leads to ballooning attendance numbers, or even that such a ballooning is in line with God's will for a church, only that LCBC finds a partial connection.

[406] E.g., Carver, *Boards That Make a Difference*, 96.

[407] From conversations with the Lead Pastor of Christ Community Church, Matt Thornton.

[408] Gregg Caruso, Tom Wilkins, and Chet Ainsworth, *Final Report: Brookville Baptist Church, Holbrook, MA*, reTurn/CRM, July 2013.

realities of the governing model they had adopted, slowly gaining in their understanding and appreciation of it, yet with only half of the policy areas codified, and those only in a borrowed form. In October 2018, after meeting with a private consultant familiar with Policy Governance applied to church contexts (someone who had been on the LCBC body of elders during that church's adoption of the model), the Brookville body of elders drafted a completely rewritten set of policies for all four areas, finally voting them into service in October 2019. This process might have been four months long instead of a year had it not been necessary to amend an outdated church constitution and bylaws in order to properly implement Policy Governance as originally voted in the January 2015 business meeting.[409]

The LCBC example illustrates that Policy Governance can work well in a church context and has for nearly twenty years at the time of this writing. The Christ Community and the Brookville Bible examples illustrate that it may be viable in a New England autonomous church context. These latter two also indicate that converting from traditional elder-led governance to Carver's Policy Governance, though a short step in theory, can be contentious and arduous in practice. Further, these latter two examples highlight the value of a comprehensive adoption of the Policy Governance model's components.

Effecting an inversion of the attractional model is improbable in light of the paradigmatic change it requires. But the trail toward its attainment is crucial to plot out in advance. This book has already called for a renewed pastor, well-adjusted (in his relationship with Jesus), who

---

[409] I became the current lead pastor of Brookville Bible Church in August 2015, and in this capacity can attest anecdotally to the significant insufficiency and frustration of partial implementation of the Policy Governance model.

understands that he must nurture a flat-structured, kinetic, decisive leadership that stands in contrast to the shepherd image of pastoring and all that comes along with that portrayal. Without a full appreciation for the indispensability of this kind of decisiveness, principled and usually unpopular, a successful inversion may be unlikely. A paradigmatic shift of this magnitude seems to be unrealistic in traditional elder-led, congregational-voting, committee-structured church governance models. The pain of change and the mutinous spirit that can accompany decisive direction setting may present obstacles that are simply too high for such models. And due to the deliberation inherent in elder-led and congregational governance models, if inversion were to be pursued through them, they may move too slowly for revitalization to take hold—the New England autonomous church, already far behind cultural adaptation in a rapidly cycling culture, would be gaining a step of progress here and there while consistently falling further behind by a net of multiple steps.

Critiques of policy governance

Policy Governance has been around long enough now to garner a few common critiques. When churches consider the model, there is often concern that it was developed in the secular sphere, albeit for nonprofits.[410] Because Carver does not tie the foundation blocks to biblical citations, it is often assumed that the model is unbiblical, or at least extra-biblical. But, as we have already seen, Policy Governance can easily align with a biblical elder-led polity and bring to it precision.

---

[410] Dearborn, handout.

Church leaders new to Policy Governance often view it as cumbersome, rigid, and tedious.[411] This seems to be an outsider-looking-in perception not shared by church leaders who have worked under the model for any length of time. This perception is analogous to preparing for mass production and assemblage of a complex toy yet regarding the preparatory task of writing a careful step-by-step assembly guide as an onerous, laborious, and constraining thing. Once church leaders have worked under the model, however, they usually recognize it for the time- and grief-saver that the policy corpus is.

A companion critique here is that Policy Governance does not allow for flexibility owing to its requirement for doggedly following written policy. This misses the point that the church's body of elders can change any of their own written policy on a whim, at will, in a matter of minutes. Written, voted-in policy provides stability and consistency even while encouraging flexibility and creativity in governance and problem solving.

Some have noted that the entire Policy Governance model stands or falls contingent upon the self-discipline of the body of elders and the quality and character of the lead pastor.[412] Though this is admittedly the case, and though some will categorize it as a negative critique, it may also be viewed as a positive one. Without a leader, or a shared leadership, of integrity and competence in Policy Governance, the model will fall apart of its own weight. Of course, if the lead pastor, or shared leadership unit, does not possess the requisite integrity and competence, the function

---

[411] Hull, "What Are the Drawbacks to Policy Governance?" in *Focusing Your Church Board*.
[412] Carver, *Boards That Make a Difference*, 327.

or efficacy of Policy Governance is least among much larger worries.

Nor will Policy Governance function well in a church that wants to protect its pastor from the mantle of leadership, defining the role instead by heavily weighting it with the concepts of pastoral care and preaching. As we have already seen throughout this book, the critical need for the New England church as she stands on the edge of the postmodern and postchristian liminal void is for pastors who will understand that their role is primarily donning the mantle of leadership.

All of this is likewise true of the individual members of the governing body. If they are not committed to following their own written policy, if they are not principled and stout enough to hold one another accountable to their own written policy, or if they are inattentive, Policy Governance, or for that matter *any* governance system, will implode. Some have complained that Policy Governance sets up an insulting situation for the body of elders and the lead pastor—that a trustworthy leader should not need parameters, written "staff limitations," or active monitoring, and that such a requirement is belittling.[413] I struggle to find the logic in this critique.[414] With such a strong core value as brotherly and sisterly accountability in the Bride of Christ, this should not be seen as an insulting situation but a communal and loving one. A seminal strength of Policy Governance is its provision for actual, verified, truly comprehensive accountability between a body of elders entrusted with the church and a lead pastor (and, through the pastor, all other staff, and

---

[413] Hull, "What Are the Drawbacks to Policy Governance?" in *Focusing Your Church Board*.
[414] A quip from my upbringing may be apropos here: "Strong fences make good neighbors."

volunteers) to whom the governing body has delegated nearly all of its authority.

Related to the critique of the necessity of a self-disciplined body of elders is another common critique that the requirement for governance body holism of Policy Governance restricts the freedom of individual elders in fulfilling all the biblical duties of an elder.[415] The concern here is that individual members of the governance body cannot provide direct oversight to individual ministries of the church, or exert power in the decision making within those ministries. The voice of an individual elder who disagrees, maybe very passionately, philosophically, and based on Scripture, with something the governance body has thus said may be hidden within a vote. And Policy Governance also forces individual elders to give up the direct control of areas of the church over which they may have been accustomed to having significant control in the past. It restricts all oversight, and clout, of an individual elder in church ministries to the one voice of the governing body as a whole, written in the form of policy and then delegated only through the pastor.[416] This can be a nearly impossible pill for the traditionally minded elder to swallow. Nevertheless, this indispensable requirement of Policy Governance is the very piece that guarantees clear and indisputable lines of authority and protection against the innocent and not-so-innocent power plays that may otherwise result.[417]

Finally, there are competing critiques of Policy Governance that the model puts too much weight on a

---

[415] Hull, "What Are the Drawbacks to Policy Governance?" in *Focusing Your Church Board*.
[416] Dearborn; Carver, *Boards That Make a Difference*.
[417] Dearborn; it is interesting to note here that another critique of Policy Governance, that the model institutionalizes a top-heavy, top-down organizational chart, is precisely what Policy Governance is designed to avoid. Carver, *Boards That Make a Difference*, 325.

business-style value of numerical results for the church and, alternately, that the vision area of policy writing is too "nebulous" and disdains "measurable objectives."[418] The double-mindedness of this critique might provide its own rebuff. It may be noted, however, that the vision area of policy writing has a quality and clarity proportional to the deliberation, prayer, and research that went into debating and composing it. It may also be noted that a clearly written, thoroughly researched, and prayerfully deliberated vision policy paints a picture for all of an end zone brightly lit, worthy of attaining, impossible without the Spirit, achievable, and, with regard to traditional numeric metrics, inspiring, lofty, and scalable.[419]

What must come after

This book has argued that an inversion of the attractional model is required to effectively engage with and witness to contemporary New England culture, that pivotal leadership is required to effect such a radical inversion, and that Policy Governance is a powerful tool to execute such an inversion in an orderly, future-looking, and timely manner. Policy

---

[418] Hull, "What Are the Drawbacks to Policy Governance?" in *Focusing Your Church Board*; Carver, *Boards That Make a Difference*, 323.

[419] Hull states, "In the event that your board concludes that: 1) It is accountable to its legal and moral owners, 2) It doesn't exist to advise or tell the qualified pastor it has hired how to do his or her job, 3) It's unacceptable for renegade board members to seek to undermine official board decisions, 4) The church doesn't exist to employ people and administrate programs, 5) It should be disciplined and principled rather than random and arbitrary, 6) It has hired a competent pastor who shouldn't be confused by directions from individual board members, 7) Its policies should be clear, consistent, comprehensive, and sequential, 8) There should be no confusion as to who is responsible for operations, 9) Micromanaging is never a good idea and always an impossible task, or 10) If it's important enough to have expectations, then it's important enough to make sure the expectations are met... ...then why not implement Policy Governance?" Hull, *Focusing Your Church Board*.

Governance, therefore, is no silver bullet and is categorically insufficient on its own to effect such an inversion.

Policy Governance, or any other form of church governance, has as its greatest goal and contribution the nurturing of a church aura and leadership culture conducive to such radical, future-anticipating, liminality-accepting shifts in church evangelistic strategy. Yet even in the nurturing of such a culture, clear governance is only one of at least three key players. The other two, addressed in the next chapter, are a deconstructing of the pastoral pedestal and a core value of open-source experimentation.

Carol Roman, a member of the revitalized Brookville Bible Church in Holbrook, Massachusetts, comments on being structurally nimble.

Structurally nimble

As the culture changes around us, we need to be able to pivot to whatever new (biblical) method is necessary to reach those around us for Christ. Adaptive changes may entail uprooting long-standing traditions, ministries, and mindsets—possibly a restructuring that is all-encompassing, rather than what Shawn calls technical changes, which may seem significant but are really just add-ons to how the mission is already being done. If we are not nimble or agile, it will be pretty much impossible to effect this kind of truly necessary, adaptive change.

So how do we become nimble? It seems that the first step, the most important step, is having a church governance that takes decision making out of long, drawn-out business meetings, committees, elder meetings, and the like, into a more efficient place, allowing ideas to take flight in a much smoother, much much quicker way. Having worked in ministry for many years and then on staff as well, I found the process under a democratic, deacon-and-trustee–led system to be extremely slow, frustrating, and morale killing, and it usually ended up nowhere. Ideas were brought to the boards or to business meetings (only when they were going to meet, which meant it could be weeks before something could even be proposed) and then went to the various groups before a decision was made. The bigger the idea, the longer it would take, to the point that it would eventually be moot or forgotten by the time it was brought up to the surface again, having been suffocated sufficiently in these meetings. And I should say not intentionally, just the way it often went.

Policy Governance has changed this dramatically. Teams can run with ideas as long as they stay within the bounds of our mission. The pastor is responsible for the teams. Ideally, the pastor gives great leeway to his leaders, encouraging them to use their own creativity and use whatever methods they envision to accomplish their goals—goals that push the mission forward. This ownership and trust bring tremendous motivation and excitement to leaders and their teams. They aren't waiting for permission to "play the game"; they can take the ball and move it toward the goalpost with the strategies and actions they've chosen. The pastor isn't hoping for buy-in to his ideas; he is watching the team fulfill their own plan to win the game. He is there to coach and to help, always—giving guidance, making sure they stay on point, yet making the joy of success theirs. But I'm getting caught up in the excitement of how fun and freeing this makes our work for Jesus! I'm getting away from the point—that this governance enables a church to be nimble.

Another step toward "nimble" has to do with speed. Policy governance clears the path, but going forward seems to be a separate learned behavior. It would seem only natural that once the obstacles are removed and the way forward is open, that we would move in that direction with great enthusiasm. But if we've been stuck in the usual pattern of eight meetings and three months before even getting approval for an idea, it's almost foreign to have this newfound freedom and takes some getting used to. This sounds a little ridiculous but I experienced it for quite some time before I started doing things "now" rather than waiting for the tedious process that no longer existed! The feeling of "open field ahead" is inspiring and lends itself to new ideas, new methods, and maybe even greater dependence on the Lord as we seek His guidance along some very new paths.

This is not meant to sound like "and then everything was perfect." There are always going to be obstacles of some sort; there are always going to be people who decide to work against the grain; there is no perfect. But when it comes to obstacles, the way the church is structured needs to be off that list. Church structure instead needs to be the very grease to the skids of moving forward with our mission.

And that was how I started this section, that it seems this is the first step for a church to become nimble. I almost forgot I said that and that it implies there are more steps. It's just that it seems like the biggest and most important step, and that the other steps probably won't happen without it.

So, for the next step, I would say it is having only two to four goals that the whole church is involved in fulfilling through their various teams. For us, we say, "We do three things, and three things only, at Brookville. There are so many good things we could do, that other churches may do, but everything we do needs to fit into one of these areas. Why? Having only three things keeps us lean and focused. It helps prevent overburdening Brookvillers. This way we avoid distraction and stay on mission." Our three things are CARE, CONNECT, CELEBRATE. This will be explained later when we talk about inverting the attractional model. Each church will have its own two to four goals. Having just a few goals rather than many helps as mentioned in the quote but also helps in deciding what needs to be a priority and what needs to be put aside. There are lots of wonderful ministry ideas but if you try to do too many, you and your volunteers will be stretched too thinly, and as they say, "If everything is a priority, then nothing is". One of the problems that comes with too many areas of focus is that your church ends up with "silos," something CRM (a church revitalization group) taught us to be aware of. Silos are when ministries exist seemingly apart from everything else going on at a church. They don't interact much with other ministries, or overlap activities or events with them. They don't seem to have any mutual accountability with other leaders. Silos tend to happen with ministries that have been around forever, but they can happen in any area of ministry, especially those which involve age- or issue-specific members. How do you avoid, or more importantly, dismantle silos? As with anything, avoiding is relatively easy and dismantling can be quite difficult. Also, how do you become a church with fewer ministries, which sounds backwards but actually creates a more nimble church? And this is where I'd say step three comes in.

The third step, in my mind, is to really mean it when you decide to do only two to four things to fulfill your mission. This takes some fortitude, an honest process, and kindness. These are needed not only when you first choose your two to four things but as you go forward in the years to come. Each ministry or activity will be looked at carefully to see which ones fit and which ones don't. If a ministry doesn't really fit and is dwindling anyway, it's sort of a no-brainer, but if it's been around for a long time and Mr. So-and-So runs it, it may be harder than it looks. Ministries which serve similar purposes can be combined, or the one that best fits your mission can go on while the others are put aside.

For Brookville, CRM saw redundancy and too few volunteers to staff both Sunday School (before the church service) and Children's Church (during the church service). We needed to stop having children's Sunday School and focus on the time frame during the church service, when more kids attended and especially when visitors with children would attend. This meant stopping adult Sunday School as well. Otherwise, it would mean we're only having adult Sunday School for those without children. And our small groups during the week could fill that need for adults studying, praying, and supporting each other. It also should be said that we had very few children in our Sunday School at that time—classes had two or three grades in them, and even then we had trouble finding teachers. It was a very unpopular decision because the adults enjoyed their time together. But there was no surge of volunteers to keep children's Sunday School going, and so they both ended. But even if there had been a surge of volunteers, the right thing would be to close it down—it was redundant, and volunteers would be needed for other areas.

Looking at how your volunteers are distributed among your ministries will tell you something too. It's helpful to you and your members if you list your two to four things in the order of their priority. It doesn't mean the other goals are unimportant; it's just that the first one is your prime focus and so on. If your volunteers are more apt to serve outside your number one priority, you will want to adjust the kinds of ministries you have to be more in keeping with that main priority. This most likely means cutting back something that's not in your prime focus in order to free up volunteers for that prime focus. Again, easier said than done, but so vital if you are to take on the task God has put before you. No one wants to upset or disappoint our church family, but if we aren't willing to make the changes needed to go forward, the church family will have little purpose and eventually die on the vine. Tradition, comfort, and complacency will lull us into a false sense of fulfilling God's mission by keeping us busy with gathering knowledge and lots of fun fellowship. Of course, we need to know God's Word and know the sweet communion we have together as His children, but if the world around us isn't why we're here, then it's all for naught. All of this is to say, it is definitely worth the pushback, the accusations, and even the loss of members, as hard as that is.

To summarize, the three things most needed structurally to become a Nimble Church are:

- Adopt a church governance structure that enables leadership to advance with as few restrictions as possible, with the freedom to use whatever biblical methods necessary to fulfill the mission of the church.

· With the guidance of the Holy Spirit, find the two to four goals that make up your church's specific mission.

· Be willing to narrow your church focus by cutting and adjusting your ministries to fit into and accomplish your specific mission.

Brookville: The change to Policy Governance has been difficult but so worth it. It's the hardest step in some ways, but it makes every step after it a pleasure. It's hard for people to go from doing things a certain way for generations and then doing something new. And for Christians, maybe more especially Baptists, somehow if it's new it should be suspect. Not to say we should just accept without checking something out—just that the checking out needs to be fair and honest, without preconceived judgments or five hundred unlikely "what if" scenarios to scare off any takers.

Without going into too much detail and background, our story of adaptive change began when Brookville voted to hire CRM, a church assessment and revitalization group, which brought Policy Governance to us along with other major changes. The assessment was that Brookville was dying, and so we committed to having them work with us to help us see the issues we couldn't see and make the changes that were needed. Our intentional interim pastor was a CRM member who did well in guiding us but not too heavy-handedly, so that our own leaders were the ones bringing us through much of the process.

It didn't take long for some to leave. Some just didn't want any change at all, and some didn't like the kind of change that started to happen. CRM was accused of using church health and strategy books instead of the Bible. This was certainly not true. The intentional interim pastor and our own elders used some CRM-recommended books to guide us into changes we needed to make in the way our church was set up but also changes we needed to make in our hearts.

Making Peace by Jim van Yperen was one of the books, and it brought us to a Sunday where we held a "sacred assembly," a time when Brookvillers could stand and ask forgiveness for some of the sins and attitudes that had been more prominent.[420] It was incredibly moving as we watched person after person go to the front, sincerely confess, and ask forgiveness. It seemed to me that the CRM members there that day were surprised by just how many got up and how long it went on. I would venture to say that all of the leadership and maybe seventy-five percent of the others participated. It was really beautiful. I think CRM had to end it eventually because it went on for so long. I remember one of the usual naysayers remarking that beforehand he thought it would be "hokey" to do this, and afterward admitted that he found it to be something very special.

In spite of this very special moment in our transition, and in spite of our voting that we would embrace and follow CRM's recommendations, within a few years there were a number of long-standing members who "just wanted to go back to the way things were." They had a hard time realizing that the victories of the past were, in fact, in the past. Quite a long time in the past, actually. The victories of the past were wonderful. They should be remembered, and God will always have glory from them. But God is about "creating a new thing" and had new victories in mind for us. So it was difficult at times—respecting the past and the people who wanted to go back to it, but also knowing God had a future for us and that we needed to follow Him into it. Sadly, when these kinds of situations arise, there are those who believe that new methods are somehow unbiblical and that suddenly leadership doesn't care about, you name it, prayer, solid Bible teaching, missionaries, evangelism, and anything

---

[420] Jim van Yperen, *Making Peace: A Guide to Overcoming Church Conflict* (Chicago: Moody, 2002).

else that, of course, they really do care about. CRM encouraged us to streamline much of what we were doing, to look at what was redundant in our ministries, and therefore to cut anything that was already dwindling but also things that were overburdening our small number of volunteers. This was hard, but we were dying and were committed to working with the revitalization group God had sent to us. And I should say here that CRM did not treat our church with a one-size-fits-all attitude. They worked to find out about our church and our people to help us to change our structure and methods but not our essence, what made us Brookville.

Shawn Keener entered the picture in the midst of this. He grabbed the baton and ran with it. He worked to continue what had been started and to make teams to carry it out. With so few people, it wasn't easy. Our teams have never actually been what we planned on paper, what we'd ideally want, but it's just a work in progress even now. I remember Shawn saying it would take five years to make things really happen, and here we are at six, and I can see why he said that. I mention this because anyone reading this who wants revitalization in their church will need to be patient and flexible in their expectations. Like a little baby, it takes years to grow and looks very different along the way! Almost unrecognizable if you compare someone's picture now to a baby picture, but that's how it's supposed to be. We'd all look pretty strange if we looked just like our baby picture, only taller.

I could get into more details, but I don't want us to get bogged down in them here. If more are helpful as we go, I'll share them with you then. But I will say this one other thing—just as I mentioned that leadership will need to be patient and flexible while going through this very worthwhile process of revitalization, I will also give fair warning to the pastor in particular. Policy Governance gives the pastor a great opportunity to be a true overseer of the church, to be the leader the flock needs, who keeps us all on mission and out of the thorns, but also out of fields that are good but not for us right now. He has a great opportunity to unify the flock in this, to keep them working together for only a few goals rather than many ministries, each with its own goals. He has a great opportunity to lovingly guide and direct the flock into the future God has in store for them. I could go on. But there often is a price to this, an unfair price, but one you may experience.

Those who misunderstand Policy Governance (and especially those who can't accept that the church was never meant to be a democracy) may accuse the pastor of "changing things for the sake of change," not caring about certain types of ministries, and acting as a dictator (and yet accused of not caring enough to be at every meeting and event). I'm sure there are more. Even with the way Shawn works together with others in decision making, even with the way he is very open to new ideas and others' input, and even with the way that Shawn is kind and gentle as he leads, he has still been accused of all manner of intentions and motivations. I won't get into particulars, but it hasn't always been easy on him. Thankfully there were enough of us who understood, supported, and trusted this special man and his heart for God and for us. I will add that much could be said about his wonderful wife, who, as you may realize, would feel the hurt of this even more than he did, but kept her eyes on Jesus and His purpose for them here.

Mile Marker Eight:
Leadering Hacks

In sight of the finish line

It is not difficult to see why a groundswell of distaste for some forms of strong leadership in church contexts can be detected in arenas of leadership studies and in pastoral conferences over recent years. Two of the churches with the largest profiles in the country have experienced precipitous drops in attendance and budget over the last few years solely because their respective high-profile pastors were found to be living double lives.[421] Spiritualized forms of toxic masculinity expressed in authoritarian leadership styles and shielded by debatable biblical prescription have not only sullied the Name of Christ in our society but have also left many in church leadership circles cringing at some of the consequences of assertive leadership in the church.[422]

Moving from "where we are to where we need to be" in New England churches requires leaders who are willing to risk it all on faith and to take team-generated, difficult, decisive directions. These directions increasingly align with something like a kinetic model of church evangelistic strategy in predominantly postmodern and postchristian areas of the country. Although church structure may play an outsized role in effecting this strategy, as we saw in Mile Marker Seven, the spiritual stability of the pastor sets the tone for the volunteer body of the church. Mile Marker Eight explores practical methods of altering the typical pastorate in

---

[421] Ruth Graham, "How a Radio Shock Jock Helped Bring Down a Megachurch Pastor," *Slate,* March 1, 2019, https://slate.com/human-interest/2019/03/mancow-muller-james-macdonald-harvest-bible-chapel.html.
[422] Joel Connelly, "The Return of Mark Driscoll: A New Church in Arizona and Gigs on the Road," *SeattlePI,* May 31, 2016, https://www.seattlepi.com/local/politics/article/The-return-of-Mark-Driscoll-A-new-church-and-7955134.php.

the local autonomous church tradition in order to retrain the pastor and the church for greater spiritual stability for all.

In *The Ideal Team Player*, Patrick Lencioni unveils the results of a lengthy study by his consulting group on the question of what qualities underlie the greatest probability that a person will smoothly and powerfully collaborate with other members of a team. His conclusion is that these qualities are three and that their overlap is the definition of an ideal team player: humble, hungry (passionate, self-driven, eager), and smart (emotionally intelligent and possessing excellent social skills).[423] This same three-sphere Venn diagram may work well in describing and understanding God's ideal team player. The pastor or Christian leader who ranks high in all three may be a tiny piece of the antidote for cynicism against assertive church leadership. He may also be a blunt powerhouse for moving the church in New England from an attractional to a kinetic strategy.[424]

By experimenting with the phrase "spiritually stable pastor," I am attempting to coin a label for a pastor (or any leader of any type who is leading to please an Audience of One) who is humble, hungry, and smart in the execution of that role. Unlike in Mile Marker Six, which focused on the capability of decisiveness, here we are examining the leader's ability to set an internal culture. A spiritually stable pastor is one who successfully sidesteps the many idolatries that

---

[423] Patrick Lencioni, *The Ideal Team Player* (Hoboken, NJ: Jossey-Bass, 2016).
[424] As the reader may recall from Mile Marker Four, a kinetic model fully inverts the common attractional model. Where the attractional model places an exceptionally well done weekend gathering experience in the first priority, a kinetic model places the activity of church people out in the community (selflessly, without agenda, and with an eye toward long-term relationship building) in the first priority.

frequently seduce anyone in the pastorate.[425] He is capable of the greatest possible reach, stability, courage, and depth because of a solid footing of his own identity in Jesus.

Often in the emotionally difficult job of pastoring, results and up-and-to-the-right movement are the points of greatest encouragement, courage, reassurance, and strength. But the spiritually stable pastor is capable of foregoing all such results because of a firm basis in the habit of walking by faith and not by sight. He has the spiritual leverage, because of this basis and footing, to act and to lead counterintuitively when mobilization for mission calls for this, even in situations where he is thoroughly misunderstood and uniformly opposed.

Humble

The spiritually stable pastor is humble, and in a determined manner, gravitates toward personal powerlessness. I am borrowing the concept, and the term itself, of *powerlessness* from Henri Nouwen.[426] One of my readers suggested replacing powerlessness with *internal strength disciplines* since the former has an unavoidably negative connotation. It also connotes, at least to some degree, a deficiency in competence or aptitude or ability. It hints of restriction or the restriction of oneself from utilizing effective options that rely inherently on power. Without intending to be contrarian, these are precisely the reasons I like the word. The pastor who commits to leading in powerlessness will be incessantly reminded of its negative connotations. He will be consistently viewed as less than

---

[425] Carey Nieuwhof, "Are You Worshipping Idols in Church?" https://www.charismanews.com/culture/45949-pastor-are-you-worshipping-idols-in-church.
[426] Henri J. M. Nouwen, *In the Name of Jesus: Reflections on Christian Leadership* (Pearl River, NY: Crossroad, 1992).

capable because of his unwillingness to rely upon power to lead. But the up side is that he will find joy, and effect in a postmodern culture, in doing just that. For others, the pursuit of powerlessness can be romanticized because it is something for which we may hunger, but practicing it and grappling with the collateral damage powerlessness causes in our lives can be untenable and undesirable. The pastor who sets his heart on living out the nexus of servant leadership, authentic leadership, and transformational leadership may discover that the Christ-followers he works to collaboratively lead will unwittingly revert to some primal instinct of a hunger for power.

If a pastor is determined to be a servant leader, his church often senses in him a lack of initiative, an inappropriately low level of assertiveness, and incompetence. If a pastor is determined to be an authentic leader, members of his church may at first feel demoralized because of having a pastor who is in the same boat as they are in everyday life. They may have been subconsciously hoping for a more messianic pastor who could be viewed as in some sense above all the mess of everyday life. The lived-out powerlessness of the pastor may be intended to model authenticity and confession one to another for the church, but initially what may happen is that church members bring charges against the pastor in subtle or public ways as he intentionally maps out for them the chinks in his own armor.

As the pastor illustrates with his own life the transformational nature of being all together on a journey with the Master, church members may in some cases be quite put out that their leader is so far from arrival. Seasoned Christ-followers may be offended that the basic steps of faith are what they are still being cajoled to take. Certainly these reactions are not universal, and for many church attendees, intentional pastoral powerlessness will be a wholly unanticipated draft from the nectar of the gods. In a New

England context, one of the surest ways to elicit a swift and nasty visceral reaction from otherwise normal and kind people is to assert the authority of the pastoral role. Instead, the pastor who lives in powerlessness will adopt the prayer of the LORD's obedient servant in Isaiah 50.4–9.[427]

Living in powerlessness as a front-of-mind thing tends to require conscious self-limiting on an hour-by-hour basis and on an all-of-life basis. In *Range: Why Generalists Triumph in a Specialized World*, David Epstein argues that the most successful specialists do not specialize early.[428] They acquire broad and general experience, skill, and erudition early in their life or career and only later specialize in the area in which they excel.

The one who leads by powerlessness is like this. Such a leader first grows deep and wide in the spiritual journey with Jesus, sometimes through great trial and heartache. He learns the call to rest that is inherent in the gospel and the satisfaction that only comes from faith tested and rewarded. This kind of deep and wide basis gives him the firm footing and consequent ability to leverage this early training to lead through powerlessness, unbeguiled by the metrics and compliments to which he would otherwise turn for comfort

---

[427] " The Sovereign LORD has given me an instructed tongue, to know the word that sustains the weary. He wakens me morning by morning, wakens my ear to listen like one being taught. The Sovereign LORD has opened my ears, and I have not been rebellious; I have not drawn back. I offered my back to those who beat me, my cheeks to those who pulled out my beard; I did not hide my face from mocking and spitting. Because the Sovereign LORD helps me, I will not be disgraced. Therefore have I set my face like flint, and I know I will not be put to shame. He who vindicates me is near. Who then will bring charges against me? Let us face each other! Who is my accuser? Let him confront me! It is the Sovereign LORD who helps me. Who is he that will condemn me? They will all wear out like a garment; the moths will eat them up." Isa 50.4–9.

[428] David Epstein, *Range: Why Generalists Triumph in a Specialized World* (New York: Riverhead, 2019).

and confirmation. His strength in powerlessness now derives from his relationship with God, freeing him to focus on the particular calling God has given him.

For example, a pastor who has first generalized with God may then be called by God to specialize in one or more focused areas in his role as pastor. For the sake of example, maybe these areas are visioneering, church-wide communication, and team building. He may largely forego some of the generalist duties so often assumed to be required of his role, such as counseling and visitation, in order to specialize in his particular gifting and calling.[429]

This outworking of powerlessness can also be shared, meaning that the whole church body, not just the pastor, may specialize as a matter of leading through powerlessness. The import of the popular book *Simple Church* is that a singular organizational focus can function as a plumb line for the alignment, acceptance, and expulsion of programs and ministries of the church.[430] This type of specialization, whether individual or corporate, derives from the self-limiting requirement of powerlessness and comes full circle by making powerlessness stand in stark relief.

For some, it may be concerning to think of a pastor who divests of the laundry list of duties thought to be incumbent upon that role so that he can specialize within the role of pastor as God has called him. Or again, when a church uses a plumb line such as "We do three things and three things only: community value, connecting spaces, and collective worship," someone may be concerned about all the

[429] Speaking to leaders about delegation, Andy Stanley concisely quips, "Only do what only you can do," in *Next Generation Leader: Five Essentials for Those Who Will Shape the Future*, 2nd ed. (Colorado Springs, CO: Multnomah, 2006), 17.
[430] Thom S. Rainer and Eric Geiger, *Simple Church: Returning to God's Process for Making Disciples*, 2nd ed. (Nashville: B&H, 2011).

truly good and excellent programs such a declaration necessarily places out of bounds for that particular church as God has uniquely called her. The self-limiting requirement and result of leading in powerlessness deepens the humility of the pastor and of the congregation, too, if they joyfully embrace such an intentional focus.

The spiritually stable pastor in a New England context seeks to dismantle the power distance that has grown large in North American churches. Ironically, while the power distance has remained large in churches of all varieties, the power distance in the New England culture has been steadily shrinking for decades with the influence of postmodernism. A power distance speaks of a relational distance between a leader and that leader's followers. An excellent, perhaps apocryphal, example of a very large power distance is the story of a missionary in China who was driving a car of pastors to a conference several hours away. He thought he knew the way but early on took a wrong turn. Only after driving an hour or so in the wrong direction, and only after he asked "Are we going the wrong way?" did his car mates tell him of his early wrong turn. Because they considered him an authority above themselves, they would never dare to personally question or openly speak against his early turn despite knowing full well it was in the wrong direction.[431] In the midst of a New England cultural context that is postmodern and postchristian, the humble pastor weaves a common thread of rationale through everything he does, great or small—dismantling the power distance between him and those he serves in his role as pastor.

One method of dismantling a power distance is a readiness to display a lack of answers. The pastor who is

---

[431] This story was related in a Masters of Divinity missionological class at an evangelical seminary. In comparison, the popular culture in the United States falls on the low end of a spectrum of power distance.

quick to admit that he cannot claim finality on an answer, or that he is still journeying toward an answer, or, best of all, that he needs to work in collaboration with his hearers toward an answer, is a pastor who understands how powerfully such a stance works to undermine a power distance. He is quick to answer searchingly and slow to answer absolutely. Displaying a lack of answers has the additional benefit of piercing the jaded armor of postmoderns allergic to modernist certainty in black-and-white detail.

Dismantling the power distance comes with a host of milestones. It subliminally reinforces a thoroughly authentic "priesthood of all believers" concept as a reality and in the process irons into the church psyche the falsehood of the dependence on excellent preaching and expert Bible teaching. It tears down the myth that the seminary graduate is the Bible knowledge wizard and the earthly arbiter of doctrinal dilemmas. When pastors and leaders display a lack of answers, permission to do likewise seeps into those they lead, resulting in a softer, arguably more mature, presentation of God's truth wrapped in gospel. It results in a presentation to those around them in everyday life that diverges from a more rigid maintenance of black-and-white lines.

Despite these benefits, living out humility by displaying a lack of answers comes with great cost to the pastor or leader. He is no longer as necessary, or central, to church functions—or at least he *feels* much less necessary. Here I think of one of my favorite descriptions of a leader as "one who is constantly working himself out of a job." And the joy and satisfaction of bringing his expertise to bear in public settings and being respected for doing so might be rarely experienced. Those he might normally lead, relying on power or authority as a last resort, may now interpret his living in powerlessness as half-hearted, indecisive, weak, uneducated, or inept.[432]

A second potent way to dismantle a power distance in the church is to dispense with many of the safeties and controls that accrue over time like barnacles on a hull. The very safety and control that may be considered a desirable facet of responsibility actually result in sluggishness, lack of agility, and bulkiness. As with a ship with those barnacles (maybe think of a ship trying to outrun Black Beard), removing them can mean the difference between thriving and surviving, and even between surviving and dying. In a modernist context, safety and controls may have been invigorating, a virtual challenge for people to achieve and thereby attain higher levels within the church. Paradoxically, in a postmodern context, they virtually guarantee that few will aspire to try.

For example, if a millennial wants to try out for the music team but is required to attend for a certain amount of time and become a member first, she will likely feel that there is too much protectionism in place to make it worth it for her. She sees it as hierarchical and discriminatory. If the same church were to insist on keeping safety and controls to an absolute minimum, she and others generationally like her might see the first step of getting involved as a small and manageable one rather than a restricted and elitist one. In decades past, the consensus was that holding volunteers to a higher bar of expectation created a more robust core of volunteers in the long run. With millennials and Generation Z, this may be changing.[433] They may see the modernist high bar of expectation as an emphasis on performance at the cost

---

[432] Dan Allender, *Leading with a Limp: Take Full Advantage of Your Most Powerful Weakness* (Colorado Springs, CO: WaterBrook, 2006).
[433] Ed Stetzer, Richie Stanley, and Jason Hayes, *Lost and Found: The Younger Unchurched and the Churches That Reach Them* (Nashville: B&H, 2009).

of healthy, authentic, spiritual growth. Something very similar seems to be occurring with regard to high expectations of church membership.[434]

Pastors and church leaders have a great opportunity to set a culture of humility in their churches. The leader who embraces humility through powerlessness is capable of leading collaboratively and strongly forward without regard to what the trajectory of attendance and giving numbers looks like. Such a leader, tentatively labeled a reluctant leader or an accidental leader by Allender, is prepared to embrace declining metrics while still rolling the proverbial boulder of change uphill.[435] While the helpfulness of Allender's labels may be debatable, they get at the heart of what humble leadership looks like. Such a leader may tend to be less beholden to performance or a need for affirmation because he tends to think of his leadership in the sense of a call for a particular purpose. He tends not to consider himself particularly qualified for the job, a feeling that may push him toward being solely focused on pleasing the one who called him for a particular purpose.

Hungry

The spiritually stable pastor is hungry, obsessed with achieving God's definition of effectiveness. We may define *effectiveness* briefly here as the ongoing qualitative fulfillment of the two halves of mission discussed in Mile Marker One. Sometimes church leaders may argue that the concept of

---

[434] Recently, a very typical millennial with a postmodern worldview asked me about becoming a church member. When I responded that at our church, if you have already been baptized, you only need to write three brief essays and submit them to the body of elders to become a member, and that the value of being a member is belonging and commitment and voting, he responded, "That seems like a lot of work to become a member. What's the point?"
[435] Allender, *Leading with a Limp*.

effectiveness in ministry is a secular one that skews ministry toward a utilitarian use of the church and away from a contemplative quality of life with Christ. Yet Jesus extols effectiveness and expects it.[436] The safety for the hungry pastor yearning to be effective is a recognition and acceptance that God's definition of effectiveness is a case-by-case, person-by-person affair and wholly other than the commonly assumed definitions that rely on church growth metrics.[437] The spiritually stable pastor embraces powerlessness at the same moment he embraces a voracious drive to be about his Father's business. I mean this to be intentionally paradoxical. Spiritually stable and powerlessness can never mean "inert" for the pastor or church leader who is hungry. He may never have chosen leadership, or would not have done so with an eye to gaining a position of authority. Often he may simply be "thrown into the mess by being discontent."[438]

One avenue through which the hungry pastor can exhibit an obsession with God's version of effectiveness is an insistence on handing over responsibility to those who have been disenfranchised from power or involvement in the church. This may take various forms, including men giving room for women in church leadership or racially homogenous churches intentionally embracing culturally diverse expressions of the church.[439] In an attempt to address

---

[436] Mt 13.3–8; 18.23–35.

[437] Lk 12.48.

[438] Allender, *Leading with a Limp*. This is where the prophetic aspect of the spiritually stable pastor looms large—a hungry urge to accept a mantle of leadership across the liminal void.

[439] Lincoln and Mamiya two decades ago called out a crisis of youth in black churches. This point aligns with the aspect of removing safety and controls discussed in the section above. C. Eric Lincoln and Lawrence H. Mamiya, *The Black Church in the African American Experience* (Durham, NC: Duke University Press, 2003); cf. Dwight Perry, ed., *Building Unity in the Church of the New Millennium* (Chicago: Moody, 2002).

the church's lag behind postmodernism, this insistence on handing over responsibility may be most conspicuously concerned with older, mature Christians handing over control to younger, less-tested believers.[440]

A common shorthand phrase for this is "giving away the keys." The hungry church pastor intuits that placing an extensive training path between an eager young person and a responsibility she wishes to assume is not ideal. Instead, a hungry pastor offers on-the-job training as early in the process as the young person wishes, buddying her up with an experienced mentor if relationally possible.[441] The hungry pastor recognizes the maxim that responsibility must always come with commensurate authority.

The "giving away the keys" word picture illustrates the difference between this maxim and the tendency to demand that someone earn responsibility before they can be given it. It is a dad handing the keys of his shiny new car to his newly licensed teenage driver and saying, "I trust you to use good judgement. Drive safely. I'll see you when you get home. Call if you need me and I'll be there." Alternative scenarios that are too often relied upon include the dad insisting on a list of do's and don'ts that communicate a lack of trust, asserting himself as perpetual chauffeur and holding tightly to the keys, or only allowing his teen to drive the junker out back that has no value to him. The hungry pastor, insistent on

---

[440] Haydn Shaw has written excellently on this subject in *Generational IQ: Christianity Isn't Dying, Millennials Aren't the Problem, and the Future is Bright* (Carol Stream, IL: Tyndale, 2015).

[441] Hatch argues that this "giving away the keys" was a hallmark of the Second Great Awakening, where the revival leaders were "inviting even the most unlearned and inexperienced to respond to [a] call to preach." Nathan O. Hatch, *The Democratization of American Christianity* (New Haven, CT: Yale University Press, 1989), 55. "The inherent power of these decentralized movements springs from their ability to communicate with people at the culture's edge and to give them a sense of personal access to knowledge, truth, and power." Hatch, 212.

handing over responsibility to the disenfranchised, will give away the keys to the church and ministry in a way that intones, "We are with you in this, and we are your support, but we want this to be yours, right now, and we're prepared for the messes that are going to happen. Don't fear them." This type of trust statement is never fully warranted, and yet the confidence it imbues is like Miracle-Gro to a younger generation thinking about getting more involved in church.[442]

This kind of intentionally exhibited trust in newcomers to church leadership allows for the exponential expansion of latent, undiscovered talent and passion, and comes with messiness and high risk. There may be an extended lag time before prospective volunteers believe the pronouncement of trust and no longer suspect a trick in it. Because so many church cultures are steeped in a large power distance, and because "giving away the keys" schools them into having a comparatively flat and organic organizational structure, the hungry pastor may taste powerlessness by, in effect, agreeing to a loss of that momentum considered so critical to nurturing in church leadership.[443] The level of excellence in church ministry, so lauded today in church leadership, may suffer, at least initially, as a result of this handover. But the hungry pastor considers the cost well worth the eventual reward.

---

[442] This concept applies across generations as well, particularly for prospective volunteers and leaders who have experienced a church context and leadership path with significant control and restrictions.

[443] As Allender puts it, "savvy connoisseurs of leadership know that good leaders don't rely on power; they don't impose their will on a group as a fiat. Instead, the process of exercising authority is far more complex—more consensual and interactive. But after all the fluff is stripped away and the group processes of discussion and receiving input and feedback come to a close, someone must decide. Leadership will always require one person to stand closest to the edge and say, 'Let's jump.'" Allender, *Leading with a Limp*.

The hungry pastor may have little choice but to overstate the point in order to force the church culture to stay out of old ruts. At a construction site where multiple trucks and site equipment are driving repeatedly over a section of dirt that was not firmly packed down to make a solid road, the vehicles serve as mud pumps. With the passing of each vehicle, the wheels cause deep ruts to form that threaten to entrap the next vehicle in line. The solution is for the next vehicle to carefully align its tires with the pumped-up mud to either side of the just-formed rut. The hungry pastor understands the necessity of doing something similar in a church revitalization atmosphere. He may often find that he must overplay his hand to keep his people out of the old ways of doing things that would inexorably pull them in and get them stuck once again. "This is just the way we have always done it" can have such a powerful and long-lived pull.

In some cases, merely changing the name of an old but effective program can grant it a current alertness and focused missionality, which, with a little maintenance, can keep it free of getting mired in a former rut. An example of this might be to change "Bible Study groups" to "community groups" or "connection groups" or the like. Little may change in the way such Bible Study groups conduct their meetings, but a significant change in purpose and outcome is made front-and-center by a simple name change.

A spiritually stable pastor obsessed with God's standard of effectiveness insists on developing and working through healthy teams, even if this insistence translates into leaving key tasks undone until such a time as a team is in place.[444] While this can contribute to the loss of momentum already mentioned, it loudly reinforces the point that the hungry pastor is limiting himself in a practice of powerlessness, determined to work only through a flat and broad organizational structure of "the priesthood of all believers" and freely handing over trust to his volunteers and attendees to carry on all work outside of his own unique calling.

As mentioned above, he recognizes the importance of not only limiting himself to his unique calling and gifting but doing likewise as a whole local church. Here overplaying his hand might take the form of a careful decision against establishing any ministries or programs through the local church that do not nicely align with the uniquely stated mission. By choosing a comparatively small, well-aligned number of programs, the hungry pastor and church are deciding against otherwise excellent and other-place-crucial ones in order to protect against them competing for the availability and passion of volunteers and attendees.[445]

An obsession for God's standard of effectiveness derives from and is informed and sustained by contemplative living. Kenneth Gates defines contemplation as living continually in the awareness of the immediate

---

[444] Pat MacMillan names the characteristics of high-performance teams as a circular list, beginning with a clear, common purpose, then crystal-clear roles, accepted leadership, effective team processes, solid relationships, and excellent communication. Pat MacMillan, *The Performance Factor: Unlocking the Secrets of Teamwork* (Nashville: B&H, 2001). Patrick Lencioni offers a similar list negatively, as an absence of trust, fear of conflict, lack of commitment, avoidance of accountability, and inattention to results. Patrick Lencioni, *The Five Dysfunctions of a Team* (San Francisco: Jossey-Bass, 2002).

[445] Osborne discusses protecting against ministry competition in an accessible way. Larry Osborne, *Sticky Church* (Grand Rapids, MI: Zondervan, 2008).

presence of God.[446] And worship, for by this definition contemplation is lived worship, is clearly happening when God has his child's heart and his child has God's heart. Hunger in the spiritually stable pastor springs from surrender of his heart to God and being consumed continually with God's heart for others. This continuous process may be understood as the practical reality of Paul's "pray continually."[447]

Within the context of the contemplative life that guides, nudges, safeguards, and energizes hunger in the church leader, a clear and continual choice to die to self is required for sustaining hunger in a leadership through powerlessness. There is love and vulnerability inherent in "giving away the keys," insisting on working through teams in a flat organic structure, and enduring the blowback from holding a church firm on a missional alignment and out of old ruts. The love of Jesus on his way up the *Via Dolorosa* was a conscious choice of wound-inviting love. He modeled for his followers that the truest love knows that betrayal and cruel injury are surely coming and yet still purposefully drops its guard. Following Jesus's example, the spiritually stable pastor is drawn ever more deeply into the One who inspires his hunger and holy discontent, and who strengthens him for it.

"*Smaht*"[448]

Working from a platform of powerlessness and obsessing over the goal of God's version of effectiveness, the spiritually stable pastor is politically and relationally savvy in his leadership role. Speaking of witnessing in a society estranged from God, Jesus called for his disciples to be

---

[446] Kenneth Gates, in an unpublished paper.
[447] 1Th 5.17.
[448] A little fun for New Englanders: "Smaht" is New Englander for Smart.

"shrewd as snakes and innocent as doves," wisdom that may be adapted also to the humble and hungry pastor.[449] Being smart, in the sense used here, is not a wink at slick sales gimmicks, questionable ethics, or saving one's own skin, but about situational awareness and wisdom, what has increasingly been called EQ, or emotional intelligence.[450] The smart church leader knows which "hills to die on" and "when to hold 'em and when to fold 'em."[451] As Solomon said, "those who are wise will find a time and a way to do what is right, for there is a time and a way for everything, even when a person is in trouble."[452]

The smart church leader may employ a number of tools. One of these is rooting out triangulation. So much unnecessary turmoil and heartache in local churches is perpetrated by triangulation, a big word for gossip and back-stabbing. The smart pastor models and works to carefully construct a church culture that discourages and shames this activity. He insists that anyone who is offended by a brother or sister, whether in church leadership or not, take the complaint directly to the offender, rather than to another party.[453] And in those exceptions in which a true power differential exists, he creates safe spaces for the processing of genuine wrongs. An end run that is often seen in the face of this insistence is the offended party claiming fear or shyness or something else as an excuse to go to someone else first,

---

[449] Mt 10.16.
[450] Travis Bradberry and Jean Greaves, *The Emotional Intelligence Quick Book: Everything You Need to Know to Put Your EQ to Work* (New York: Fireside, 2005).
[451] Don Schlitz, "The Gambler," 1976.
[452] Ecc 8.5–6.
[453] Mat 18.15–17.

perhaps someone in leadership.[454] A twin principle to rooting out triangulation is that of always giving one another the greatest benefit of the doubt within the family of God.[455]

Another way the pastor may exhibit smart-ness is by removing barriers wherever they may be found along the church pathway. This may be in line with fast-tracking prospective volunteers as already mentioned, or removing any church traditions that unnecessarily restrict travel along the Engel scale road of discipleship.[456] A common example of such a barrier is that of a church taking public political stands, such as endorsing or decrying particular candidates or functioning as a platform for party planks such as *Roe v. Wade* or homosexual civil unions.

Barriers accrue readily, can be hard to recognize, and take different forms. They may come in the ostensibly laudable form of verifying that someone truly has crossed the line of faith, yet eventually they tend to petrify into unnecessary speed bumps on the discipleship pathway. The spiritually stable pastor works determinedly to identify and summarily eradicate all such barriers despite the political price he may have to pay. He has the wherewithal to do this because he has his eye on the prize of fostering a church culture that has a singular goal: introducing people to a deeper relationship with the person of Jesus.[457] Allender says of this kind of pastor, "We should expect anyone who

---

[454] Of course, there are also instances where this is not an excuse at all. In some cases, a true power differential is present between the two parties, and a third party must provide a safe space for processing wrongs. And there are traumatic situations where going directly to a third party would be legitimate, such as in the case of criminal abuse.

[455] Cf. Eph 4.2; the NLT-SE translates this verse "make allowance for each other's faults."

[456] For one version among many of the Engel scale, see https://irp-cdn.multiscreensite.com/2988a589/files/uploaded/the-engel-scale.pdf

[457] Larry Osborne, *Sticky Teams: Keeping Your Leadership Team and Staff on the Same Page* (Grand Rapids, MI: Zondervan, 2010), 52.

remains in a formal leadership context to experience repeated bouts of flight, doubt, surrender, and return. Why would this be God's plan? Why does God love the reluctant leader? Here is one reason: the reluctant leader is not easily seduced by power, pride, or ambition."[458]

The smart pastor seeks to model stability. He plants asparagus in the parsonage garden.[459] He discharges his duties and approaches conflict and drama with a calculated unflappability and stoicism. Once again, the strength and stamina to live day to day in the public eye in this way derives from a solid footing of his own identity in Jesus. He plods along, committing himself to his faithful Creator and continuing to do good.[460] He demonstrates that the long-range mission to which Jesus uniquely calls his local church requires a correspondingly long-range attitude of daily life within the church. By living in unpresumptuous obedience to the next revealed step of God's call and will, the smart pastor becomes an integral part of mentoring his church culture to value the tortoise over the hare. Ironically, modeling a steady-as-he-goes temperament includes fostering a culture of constant change. As the savvy pastor consistently reintroduces his church to purposeful, missional change and flexibility, he subliminally reiterates that stability in no way equals equilibrium or stagnation.[461]

---

[458] Allender, *Leading with a Limp*, 18.

[459] This is a fable based on the fact that asparagus is a vegetable that produces nothing for the first few years after planting but then produces a rich crop for the decades that follow. By planting asparagus, whether literally or figuratively, the pastor indicates to all who are watching that he intends to be around for the long haul.

[460] 1Pe 4.19.

[461] Leonard Sweet, *SoulTsunami: Sink or Swim in New Millennium Culture* (Grand Rapids, MI: Zondervan, 2009). Hirsch, *The Forgotten Ways*, phrases this wonderfully as "foster relentless discomfort," 265.

The spiritually stable pastor understands how to radically reorient his church family toward a zero-agenda discipleship. And he grasps the crucial aspect of zero-agenda discipleship as a recalibration of the proclamation of the gospel in a culture of postmodernism and postchristianity. Zero-agenda discipleship is discipleship that draws people closer to Jesus and Jesus-likeness regardless of where they may fall on an Engel scale and with no angle for the church's gain. In fact, zero-agenda discipleship is calculated to disallow any such manipulation or coercion, real or implied, direct or indirect. Examples can be drawn from previous mile markers but include intentionally prioritizing community value over collective worship so that church resources are spent heavily out in the community as a long-term, relational investment and comparatively lightly on well-orchestrated weekend gatherings. Allen Bingham describes the motivation for zero-agenda discipleship when he states:

> My current work as a pastor is driven by Jeremiah's challenge to the captives in Babylon to "seek the prosperity [*shalom*] of the city where I have sent you and pray to the Lord on its behalf, for in its prosperity [*shalom*] you will find your prosperity [*shalom*]." The notion that God's *shalom* (salvation, welfare, or prosperity) is tied to the broader society is antithetical to much of American experience of church and its life together.[462]

The savvy pastor expends whatever capital necessary, both corporate and personal, to effect this cultural shift within his church.

Autonomous churches in New England, typically those of Baptist, Congregational, or nondenominational traditions, have a freedom to alter church culture and procedure on the

---

[462] Allen Bingham, in a doctoral class online discussion.

local level that would be nearly impossible in many mainline churches. Although this freedom may be magnified in churches that adopt the Policy Governance model for the reasons detailed in the previous mile marker, it is nevertheless possible for any autonomous church that is willing to discover how to get out of its own way, structurally and philosophically speaking. This mile marker has attempted to draw something of a straight line between a humble, hungry, and smart disposition in church leaders and some of the key church-culture changes necessary to value the postmodern critique.

Discovery Projects

1. Take some time together as a church leadership team to make a list of "sacred cows" at your church. Ask this question: "What changes, if we were to make them, would result in people threatening to leave our church, redirect their giving dollars, or accuse us of acting against Scripture or disingenuously?" Perhaps you recognize a need to change the rationale for which missionaries the church supports and how they are supported. Or you may see a need for a greater assumption of risk for the church in allowing less vetting and preparation for aspiring leaders and volunteers. After listing and prioritizing such potential changes, tease out from the list the few you consider crucial for positively altering your church culture in significant ways. Identify realistic fallout from making each of these changes and ask God for courage and wisdom in timing the changes.

2. What is the short list of nonnegotiable priorities for your church? Force yourself to limit the list to three or four. Consider allowing yourself the freedom to conceive of this short list without dependence on

verses such as Acts 2.42. Now estimate the weekly and monthly calendar of the average attendee at your church, perhaps breaking this step into age groups. Consider especially those who are parenting their grandchildren, working two or more jobs, managing a single-parent household, and chauffeuring school-aged children to extracurricular activities. How many program offerings is your church tacitly stating you want them to commit to whether by participation or volunteering? Assign a weekly or monthly hourly figure to these tacit expectations. Finally, using a side-by-side comparison of all three (short-list priorities, current program offerings, and typical attendee availability), prayerfully determine what activities of your church may fall outside of the short-list priorities and/or typical attendee availability. For the protection of your volunteers and staff, and out of concern for margin and family time for your typical attendee, should you end the church activities that fall outside?

Conclusion

Carol Roman, a member of the revitalized Brookville Bible Church in Holbrook, Massachusetts, concludes with the following comments:

If I've given any kind of impression that we think we have all the answers, let me be clear—we don't. And we can't, not only because we're far from perfect, but also because the questions are constantly changing and the answers are too. And the questions and answers will be different from church to church, because each church will be going out to its own unique community, which will have its own flavor, its own quirks, its own priorities.

But being nimble does seem to be a quality we'll all need to have going forward in this ever-changing world. Yes, the world has "always been ever-changing," if we want to be a little redundant, but leaving the Christian era, and even the modern era, is a real sea change. It sets the stage for a domino effect of change that we can't predict or imagine. We will need to get our sea legs. Being nimble means we keep "shifting our weight," adjusting, adapting, and finding the best methods for the culture and time we find ourselves in.

Which means "being nimble" isn't something we try to do at some point and then "relax"; it's for the long haul. We will need to assess and reassess on a regular basis and be in a position to change our methods to best impact our community for that current season. And being in that position will require being structurally, culturally, and missionally nimble. We don't want to wait on action because of structural roadblocks. We don't want to find out we're relating poorly with the culture around us because we haven't kept up with their mindset and priorities. We don't want to be wondering why the community isn't knocking our door down because our methods are the last thing they would care about.

Nimble Church is meant to help as a practical guide rather than a one-size-fits-all "how-to." The philosophy and ideas are general, and there will be exceptions to every "rule" I have talked about in this summary. I hope this qualifier makes the book that much more useful, so you know its ideas are to be tailored to your particular church family and local community. Our prayer is for churches to be free of unnecessary encumberment, free to venture together into a foreign culture in need of Christ's love, and free to find the methods that will truly serve your church's mission rather than what may seem to be expected.

Bibliography

Allen, Roland. *Missionary Methods: St Paul's or Ours?*
http://www.onthewing.org/user/Allen_Roland%20-%20Missionary%20Methods.pdf

Allender, Dan. *Leading with a Limp: Take Full Advantage of Your Most Powerful Weakness*. Colorado Springs, CO: WaterBrook, 2006.

The Anchor Bible Dictionary. New York: Doubleday, 1992.

Anderson, C. "How to Know Someone Is Not a Person of Peace: Disciple-Making Movements." March 10, 2019. https://www.dmmsfrontiermissions.com/how-know-not-a-person-of-peace/

Arnold, Clinton E. "Early Church Catechesis and New Christians' Classes in Contemporary Evangelicalism." *Journal of Evangelical Theological Society* 47, no. 1 (2004): 39–54. https://www.etsjets.org/files/JETS-PDFs/47/47-1/47-1-pp039-054_JETS.pdf

The Baptist Faith and Message 2000, https://www.namb.net/wp-content/uploads/2020/06/Baptist-Faith-and-Message.pdf.

Barna Group. "The Most Post-Christian Cities in America: 2019." June 5, 2019. https://www.barna.com/research/post-christian-cities-2019/

Barna Group. "The State of the Church 2016." September 15, 2016. https://www.barna.com/research/state-church-2016/

Barr, James. *The Semantics of Biblical Language*. Eugene, OR: Wipf and Stock, 2004.

Bebbington, David W. *Evangelicalism in Modern Britain: A History from the 1730s to the 1980s*. London: Routledge, 2005.

Belleville, Linda L., Craig L. Blomberg, Craig S. Keener, and Thomas R. Schreiner. *Two Views on Women in Ministry*. *Rev. ed*. Grand Rapids, MI: Zondervan, 2005.

Blair, Anthony L., Jo Ann Kunz, Steve Jeantet, and Danny Kwon. "Prophets, Priests and Kings: Re-Imagining Ancient Metaphors of Diffused Leadership for the Twenty-First Century Organization." *Journal of Management, Spirituality, and Religion* 9, no. 2 (2012): 127–145.

Blanchard, Bill. *Church Structure That Works: Turning Dysfunction into Health*. 2nd ed. Sisters, OR: VMI, 2010.

Boers, Arthur. *Servants and Fools*. Nashville: Abingdon, 2015.

Bolsinger, Tod E. *Canoeing the Mountains: Christian Leadership in Uncharted Territory*. Downers Grove, IL: InterVarsity, 2018.

Borden, Paul D. *Hit the Bullseye: How Denominations Can Aim the Congregation at the Mission Field*. Nashville: Abingdon, 2010.

Bosch, David J. *Transforming Mission: Paradigm Shifts in Theology of Mission*. 20th anniversary ed. Maryknoll, NY: Orbis, 2011.

Boston Globe. "Church Allowed Abuse by Priest for Years." January 6, 2002. https://www.bostonglobe.com/news/special-reports/2002/01/06/church-allowed-abuse-priest-for-years/cSHfGkTIrAT25qKGvBuDNM/story.html

Bradberry, Travis, and Jean Greaves. *The Emotional Intelligence Quick Book: Everything You Need to Know to Put Your EQ to Work*. New York: Fireside, 2005.

Bradford, William. *Bradford's "History of Plymouth Plantation"
1608–1650.*
https://archive.org/details/bradfordshistor00bradgoog/
page/n54 as etched on the William Bradford statue in
Plymouth, MA.

Brand, Chad Owen, and R. Stanton Norman, eds. *Perspectives
on Church Government: Five Views of Church Polity.*
Nashville: B&H, 2004.

Breen, Mike. "Obituary for the American Church." Verge
Network. February 2, 2012.
vergenetwork.org/2012/02/02/obituary-for-the-
american-church-mike-breen

Bremer, Francis J. *The Puritan Experiment: New England Society
from Bradford to Edwards.* Lebanon, NH: University Press
of New England, 1995.

Brown, Brene. "The Power of Vulnerability." Lecture,
TEDxHouston, Houston, TX. June 2010.
https://www.ted.com/talks/brene_brown_the_power_of
_vulnerability?language=en

Brueggemann, Walter. *The Prophetic Imagination.* 2nd ed.
Minneapolis: Fortress, 2001.

Bunton, Peter. *Cell Groups and House Churches: What History
Teaches Us.* Lititz, PA: House to House, 2001.

Burr, George Lincoln, ed. *Narratives of the Witchcraft Cases,
1648–1706.* C. Scribner's Sons, 1914.
https://archive.org/stream/narrativeswitch00burrgoog#
page/n221/mode/1up

Busemeyer, Stephen, and Kelly Glista. "How Often Do We Go
to Church? Not That Much." *Hartford Courant.* February
20, 2015.
https://www.courant.com/news/connecticut/hc-how-
often-do-we-go-to-church-not-that-much

Caldwell, Larry. *Doing Bible Interpretation: Making the Bible Come Alive for Yourself and Your People.* Sioux Falls, SD: Lazy Oaks, 2016.

Carpenter, John B. "A New Definition of Puritanism: A Cross-Disciplinary Approach." *Evangelical Journal* 36 (2018): 1–17.

Carson, D. A. *Becoming Conversant with the Emerging Church: Understanding a Movement and Its Implications.* Grand Rapids, MI: Zondervan, 2005.

————. *Christ and Culture Revisited.* Grand Rapids, MI: Eerdmans, 2008.

————. *Exegetical Fallacies.* 2nd ed. Grand Rapids, MI: Baker, 1996.

————. "Matthew." In Matthew & Mark. Vol. 9 of The Expositor's Bible Commentary. Rev. ed. Tremper Longman III and David E. Garland, eds. Grand Rapids, MI: Zondervan, 2010.

Caruso, Gregg, Tom Wilkins, and Chet Ainsworth. *Final Report: Brookville Baptist Church, Holbrook, MA.* reTurn/CRM, July 2013.

Carver, John. *Boards That Make a Difference: A New Design for Leadership in Nonprofit and Public Organizations.* 3rd ed. San Francisco: Jossey-Bass, 2006.

Catmull, Ed. *Creativity, Inc.: Overcoming the Unseen Forces that Stand in the Way of True Inspiration.* New York: Random House, 2014.

"Cell Signaling." Scitable by Nature Education. https://www.nature.com/scitable/topicpage/cell-signaling-14047077/

Chapman, Gary. *The Five Love Languages: The Secret to Love That Lasts.* Chicago: Northfield, 2015.

Cherry, Constance M. *The Worship Architect: A Blueprint for Designing Culturally Relevant and Biblically Faithful Services*. Grand Rapids, MI: Baker, 2010.

Cheyney, Tom. *Thirty-Eight Church Revitalization Models for the Twenty-First Century*. Orlando, FL: Renovate, 2014.

Christopherson, Jeff. "5 Benefits of Cultural Opposition." *On Mission Magazine* 22 (2019): 10–11.

Clapton, Ben. "A Salvationist Perspective on the Sacraments." *Ben Clapton* (blog), May 3, 2012. https://benclapton.id.au/2012/05/03/a-salvationist-perspective-on-the-sacraments/

Clifton, Mark. *Rubicons of Revitalization: Overcoming 8 Common Barriers to Church Renewal*. Littleton, CO: Acoma, 2018.

CliffsNotes. "Critical Essays: Emerson, Unitarianism, and the God Within." https://www.cliffsnotes.com/literature/e/emersons-essays/critical-essays/emerson-unitarianism-and-the-god-within

Cohen, Steve M., and Richard M. Biery. *Ministry Mess Management: Solving Leadership Failures*. Bloomington, IN: AuthorHouse, 2014.

Cole, Neil. *Church 3.0: Upgrades for the Future of the Church*. San Francisco: Jossey-Bass, 2010.

————. *Organic Leadership: Leading Naturally Right Where You Are*. Grand Rapids, MI: Baker, 2009.

Collins, Travis. *From the Steeple to the Street: Innovating Mission and Ministry Through Fresh Expressions of Church*. Franklin, TN: Seedbed, 2016.

Conder, Tim. *The Church in Transition: The Journey of Existing Churches into the Emerging Culture*. Grand Rapids, MI: Zondervan, 2006.

Connelly, Joel. "The Return of Mark Driscoll: A New Church in Arizona and Gigs on the Road" *SeattlePI.* May 31, 2016.

https://www.seattlepi.com/local/politics/article/The-
return-of-Mark-Driscoll-A-new-church-and-
7955134.php

Crosby, Francis J. Rescue the Perishing. William H. Doane,
1870.

Crouch, Andy. *Culture Making: Recovering Our Creative Calling.*
Downers Grove, IL: InterVarsity, 2013.

Daniel, Jack L. *Patient Catalyst: Leading Church Revitalization.*
South   Easton, MA: Overseed, 2018.

Davies, Gareth J., Graham Kendall, Emma Soane, and Jiawei
Li. "Regulators as 'Agents': Power and Personality in Risk
Regulation and a Role for Agent-based Simulation."
Journal of Risk Research 13. no. 8 (December 2010): 961–
982.

Dearborn, Phil. Handout from private consulting meeting.
October 2018.

De Blasio, Marlon. *Discerning Culture: Knowing the Depths of
Scriptural Christianity in a Culture of Scriptural Indifference.*
Toronto, Ontario: Canadian Evangel, 2019.

Dever, Mark. *Nine Marks of a Healthy Church.* 4th ed. Wheaton,
IL: Crossway, 2021.

Donovan, Vincent J. *Christianity Rediscovered.* 25th ed.
Maryknoll, NY: Orbis, 2003.

Dorrien, Gary. *The Making of Liberal Theology: Imagining
Progressive Religion 1805–1900.* Louisville, KY:
Westminster, 2001.

Draper, Mark. "A Church Historians [sic] Look at the Same
Sex Marriage Debate."
https://markwdraper.wordpress.com/2013/03/28/a-
church-historians-look-at-the-same-sex-marriage-
debate/

Dunbar, Paul J., and Anthony L. Blair. *Leading Missional Change: Move Your Congregation from Resistant to Re-Energized.* Eugene, OR: Wipf and Stock, 2013.

Elsesser, Kim. "Zoom Fatigue Is Worse for Women—Here's Why." *Forbes* (April 19, 2021). https://www.forbes.com/sites/kimelsesser/2021/04/19/zoom-fatigue-is-worse-for-women---heres-why/?sh=736d0ae45225

Epictetus. "Book II, Chapter 17." In *The Discourses.* Translated by Internet Classics Library. http://classics.mit.edu//Epictetus/discourses.html

Epstein, David. *Range: Why Generalists Triumph in a Specialized World.* New York: Riverhead, 2019.

Epstein, Greg M. *Good Without God: What a Billion Nonreligious People Do Believe.* New York: Harper, 2009.

Evans, Rachel Held. "A Non-Zero-Sum Conversation Between the Traditional Church and the Gay Community" (November 11, 2011). https://rachelheldevans.com/blog/richard-beck-traditional-church-gay-community

Farhadian, Charles E., ed. *Christian Worship Worldwide: Expanding Horizons, Deepening Practices.* Grand Rapids, MI: Eerdmans, 2007.

Ferguson, Everett. *Backgrounds of Early Christianity.* 3rd ed. Grand Rapids, MI: Eerdmans, 2003.

Finke, Roger, and Rodney Stark. *The Churching of America, 1776–2005: Winners and Losers in Our Religious Economy.* 2nd ed. Piscataway, NJ: Rutgers University Press, 2005.

Fitch, David. *The Great Giveaway: Reclaiming the Mission of the Church from Big Biusiness, Parachurch Organizations, Psychotherapy, Consumer Capitalism, and Other Modern Maladies.* Grand Rapids, MI: Baker, 2005.

George, Bill. *Authentic Leadership: Rediscovering the Secrets to Creating Lasting Value.* San Francisco: Jossey-Bass, 2003.

Gibbons, Dave. *The Monkey and the Fish: Liquid Leadership for a Third-Culture Church.* Grand Rapids, MI: Zondervan, 2009.

Gladwell, Malcolm. *David and Goliath: Underdogs, Misfits, and the Art of Battling Giants.* New York: Little, Brown, 2013.

Gonzalez, Justo. *The Story of Christianity.* 2nd ed. Vol. 1. *The Early Church to the Dawn of the Reformation.* Vol 2. *The Reformation to the Present Day.* New York: Harper Collins, 2010.

Gorsuch, Neil. *A Republic if You Can Keep It.* New York: Crown, 2019.

Graham, Ruth. "How a Radio Shock Jock Helped Bring Down a Megachurch Pastor." *Slate.* March 1, 2019. https://slate.com/human-interest/2019/03/mancow-muller-james-macdonald-harvest-bible-chapel.html

Grant, Adam. *Originals: How Non-conformists Move the World.* New York: Viking, 2016.

Green, Don. *Developing a Church Leadership Transition Process That Adapts the Policy Governance® Principles of John Carver in Middle-Size Churches Associated with Christian Churches and Churches of Christ.* semanticscholar.org/paper/Developing-a-church-leadership-transition-process-Green. doi: 10.2986/tren.006-1603

Green, Michael. *Evangelism in the Early Church.* Rev. ed. Grand Rapids, MI: Eerdmans, 2004.

Greer, Robert C. *Mapping Postmodernism: A Survey of Christian Options.* Downers Grove, IL: InterVarsity, 2003.

Groeschel, Craig. *It: How Churches and Leaders Can Get It and Keep It.* Grand Rapids, MI: Zondervan, 2008.

Grudem, Wayne. *Systematic Theology: An Introduction to Biblical Doctrine*. 2nd ed. Grand Rapids, MI: Zondervan, 2020.

Guinness, Os. *The Call: Finding and Fulfilling the Central Purpose of Your Life*. Nashville: Thomas Nelson, 2003.

Haddad, Mimi. "Cultural Preferences or Biblical Absolutes?" November 11, 2009. https://www.cbeinternational.org/resource/article/mutuality/blog/magazine/cultural-preferences-or-biblical-absolutes Haid, Charles, director. *Iron Will*. Walt Disney Pictures, 1994. 1 hr., 49 min.

Harrell, James S.. *Church Replanter*. South Easton, MA: Overseed, 2014.

Harrison, Nonna Verna. *God's Many-Splendored Image: Theological Anthropology for Christian Formation*. Grand Rapids, MI: Baker, 2010.

Hatch, Nathan O. *The Democratization of American Christianity*. New Haven, CT: Yale University Press, 1989.

Heifetz, Ronald A., and Marty Linsky. *Leadership on the Line: Staying Alive Through the Dangers of Leading*. Boston: Harvard Business School, 2002.

Hicks, John Mark. *Come to the Table: Revisioning the Lord's Supper*. Abilene, TX: Leafwood, 2002.

Hirsch, Alan. *The Forgotten Ways: Reactivating Apostolic Movements*, 2nd ed. Grand Rapids, MI: Brazos, 2016.

Hirsch, Alan. "Rethinking the Chessboard." City to City. March 20, 2020. https://redeemercitytocity.com/articles-stories/alan-hirsch-rethinking-the-chessboard

Hirsch, Alan, and Michael Frost. *The Shaping of Things to Come: Innovation and Mission for the 21st-Century Church*. Rev. ed. Grand Rapids, MI: Baker, 2013.

Hirsch, Alan, and Mark Nelson. *Reframation: Seeing God, People, and Mission Through Reenchanted Frames*. 100 Movements, 2019.

Howell, Brian M., and Jenell Williams Paris. *Introducing Cultural Anthropology: A Christian Perspective*. Grand Rapids, MI: Baker, 2019.

Hull, Ted. *Focusing Your Church Board: Using the Carver Policy Governance Model*. Winnipeg, MB: Word Alive, 2015.

Hunter, George G., III. *The Celtic Way of Evangelism*. 10th ed. Nashville: Abingdon, 2010.

Hybels, Bill. *Courageous Leadership*. Grand Rapids, MI: Zondervan, 2002.

————. *Holy Discontent: Fueling the Fire That Ignites Personal Vision*. Grand Rapids, MI: Zondervan, 2007.

Jackson, J. David. *New England Culture & Ministry Dynamics: Where You Serve Makes a Difference in How You Serve*. 3rd ed. Marlborough, MA: Screven and Allen, 2018.

————. *ReNEW: Traveling the Forgotten Path*. Marlborough, MA: Screven and Allen, 2018.

Jenkins, Dallas, director. *The Chosen*. 2017; Provo, UT; Loaves and Fishes Productions, Angel Studios. TV Series.

Joiner, Reggie. *Zombies, Football and the Gospel*. Cumming, GA: Orange, 2012.

"July 6, 1988: The Piper Alpha Disaster." *The Maritime Executive*., https://www.maritime-executive.com/article/july-6-1988-the-piper-alpha-disaster.

Keener, Craig S. *The IVP Bible Background Commentary: New Testament*. 2nd ed. Downers Grove, IL: InterVarsity, 2014.

Kelly, Gerard. *RetroFuture: Rediscovering Our Roots, Recharting Our Routes*. Downers Grove, IL: InterVarsity, 2000.

Kelly, Stewart E., with James K. Dew, Jr. *Understanding Postmodernism: A Christian Perspective.* Downers Grove, IL: InterVarsity, 2017.

Kinnaman, David, and Mark Matlock. *Faith for Exiles: 5 Ways for a New Generation to Follow Jesus in Digital Babylon.* Grand Rapids, MI: Baker, 2019.

Kraemer, Hendrick. *The Christian Message in a Non-Christian World.* 2nd ed. New York: International Missionary Council, 1947. https://archive.org/details/christianmessage00krae

L'Amour, Louis. *Westward the Tide.* New York: Bantam, 1977.

Ledbetter, Bernice M., Robert J. Banks, and David C. Greenhalgh. *Reviewing Leadership: A Christian Evaluation of Current Approaches.* 2nd ed. Grand Rapids, MI: Baker, 2016.

Lederleitner, Mary T. *Cross-Cultural Partnerships: Navigating the Complexities of Money and Mission.* Downers Grove, IL: InterVarsity, 2010.

Lencioni, Patrick. *The Five Dysfunctions of a Team.* San Francisco: Jossey-Bass, 2002.

————. *The Ideal Team Player.* Hoboken, NJ: Jossey-Bass, 2016.

Lewis, C. S. *The Last Battle.* New York: Macmillan, 1978. First published 1956 by The Bodely Head.

Lewis, C. S. *Mere Christianity.* New York: Macmillan, 1952.

LifeWay Research, "New Churches Draw Those Who Previously Didn't Attend." 08DEC2015 https://lifewayresearch.com/2015/12/08/new-churches-draw-those-who-previously-didnt-attend/

Lincoln, C. Eric, and Lawrence H. Mamiya. *The Black Church in the African American Experience.* Durham, NC: Duke University Press, 2003.

Lockridge, Kenneth. *A New England Town: The First Hundred Years: Dedham, Massachusetts, 1636–1736 (Norton Essays in American History).* New York: W. W. Norton, 1985.

Love, Jeffrey Alan. *Lord of the Fries: It's Not About Your Money, It's About Your HEART.* n.p.: 2911 Publishing, 2016.

Macchia, Stephen A. *Crafting a Rule of Life: An Invitation to the Well-Ordered Way.* 3rd ed. Downers Grove, IL: InterVarsity, 2012.

MacDonald, Gordon. *Who Stole My Church? What to Do When the Church You Love Tries to Enter the 21st Century.* Nashville: Thomas Nelson, 2007).

MacDonald, Mark. *Be Known for Something: Reconnect with Community by Revitalizing Your Church's Reputation.* Houston: High Bridge, 2017.

MacMillan, Pat. *The Performance Factor: Unlocking the Secrets of Teamwork.* Nashville: B&H, 2001.

Malphurs, Aubrey. *Advanced Strategic Planning: A New Model for Church and Ministry Leaders.* 2nd ed. Grand Rapids, MI: Baker, 2005.

Mancini, Will. *Church Unique: How Missional Leaders Cast Vision, Capture Culture, and Create Movement.* San Francisco: Jossey-Bass, 2008.

————. *Innovating Discipleship: Four Paths to Real Discipleship Results* (Church Unique Intentional Leader Series). 2013.

Mancini, Will, and Cory Hartman. *Future Church: Seven Laws of Real Church Growth.* Grand Rapids, MI: Baker, 2020.

Marsden, George M. *Fundamentalism and American Culture.* 2nd ed. New York: Oxford University Press, 2006.

Marshall, Colin, and Tony Payne. *The Trellis and the Vine.* Kingsford, Australia: Matthias, 2009.

Marshall, I. Howard. *Last Supper and Lord's Supper.* Vancouver, BC: Regent, 2006.

May, Tom. "Column: Counting the Blessing of Those Who Minister." *News and Tribune.* May 4, 2019. https://www.newsandtribune.com/opinion/column-counting-the-blessing-of-those-who-minister/article_edb5df9e-6dbc-11e9-9f42-4ff9e3f0b24b.html

McDowell, Josh, and Sean McDowell. *Evidence That Demands a Verdict: Life-Changing Truth for a Skeptical World.* Nashville: Thomas Nelson, 2017.

McEntyre, Marilyn. *Caring for Words in a Culture of Lies.* 2nd ed. Grand Rapids, MI: Eerdmans, 2021.

McHugh, Adam S. *Introverts in the Church: Finding Our Place in an Extroverted Culture.* Downers Grove, IL: InterVarsity, 2009.

McIntosh, Gary, and R. Daniel Reeves. *Thriving Churches in the 21st Century: 10 Life-Giving Systems for Vibrant Ministry.* 2nd ed. Grand Rapids, MI: Kregel, 2006.

McIntosh, Lia, Jasmine Smothers, and Rodney Thomas Smothers. *Blank Slate: Write Your Own Rules for a 22nd Century Church Movement.* Nashville: Abingdon, 2019.

McNeal, Reggie. *Missional Renaissance: Changing the Scorecard for the Church.* San Francisco: Jossey-Bass, 2009.

————. *The Present Future: Six Tough Questions for the Church.* San Francisco: Jossey-Bass, 2003.

Metcalf, Sam. *Beyond the Local Church: How Apostolic Movements Can Change the World.* Downers Grove, IL: InterVarsity, 2015.

Miller, Sue, with David Staal. *Making Your Children's Ministry the Best Hour of Every Kid's Week.* Grand Rapids, MI: Zondervan, 2004.

Minear, Paul S. *Images of the Church in the New Testament.* Louisville, KY: Westminster John Knox, 2004.

Moran, Roy. *Spent Matches: Igniting the Signal Fire for the Spiritually Dissatisfied.* Nashville: Thomas Nelson, 2015.

Murrow, David "Why Is Church Attendance Declining–Even Among Committed Christians?" March 7, 2016. https://www.patheos.com/blogs/churchformen/2016/03/why-is-church-attendance-declining-even-among-christians/

Mwaura, Maina, Moderator. "What Should Pastors Know About Generation Z? Five Experts Discuss the Ways This Emerging Demographic Is Helping Them Rethink Preaching, Parenting, and Service." *CT Pastors Special Issue: The Integrated Pastor. Christianity Today* (Spring 2019).

New International Dictionary of New Testament Theology. Ed. Colin Brown. Grand Rapids, MI: Zondervan, 1986.

Newbigin, Lesslie. *The Gospel in a Pluralistic Society.* Grand Rapids, MI: Eerdmans, 1989.

Nierenberg, Amelia. "New Spirits Rise in Old, Repurposed Churches." *New York Times*, October 25, 2020. https://www.nytimes.com/2020/10/25/us/abandoned-churches-covid.html

Nieuwhof, Carey. "Are You Worshipping Idols in Church?" https://www.charismanews.com/culture/45949-pastor-are-you-worshipping-idols-in-church

————. "Avoid This Big Mistake: Stepping Back into the Past when You Step Back into Your Building." https://careynieuwhof.com/avoid-this-big-mistake-stepping-back-into-the-past-when-you-step-back-into-your-building/

————. *Didn't See It Coming.* Colorado Springs, CO: WaterBrook, 2018.

————. "Eight Ways to Lead in the New Digital Default Church," https://careynieuwhof.com/8-ways-to-lead-in-the-new-digital-default-church/

_____. "Five Reasons Charismatic Churches Are Growing (and Attractional Churches Are Past Peak)." https://careynieuwhof.com/5-reasons-charismatic-churches-are-growing-and-attractional-churches-are-past-peak/

_____. "In-person attendance v. online attendance and the emerging trap of doing nothing well." https://careynieuwhof.com/in-person-services-v-online-services-and-the-emerging-trap-of-doing-nothing-well/

————. "Ten Reasons Even Committed Church Members Are Attending Church Less Often." https://careynieuwhof.com/10-reasons-even-committed- church-attenders-attending-less-often/

————. "Twelve Signs You're a Spiritual Entrepreneur." https://careynieuwhof.com/12-signs-youre-a-spiritual-entrepreneur/

————. "The Western Church Needs a New Evangelism Strategy: Five Promising Options." https://careynieuwhof.com/the-western-church-needs-a-new-evangelism-strategy-5-promising-options/

North American Mission Board. "Who's Your One?" WhosYourOne.com

Northouse, Peter G. *Leadership Theory and Practice.* 8th ed. Thousand Oaks, CA: Sage, 2019.

Nouwen, Henri J. M. *In the Name of Jesus: Reflections on Christian Leadership.* Pearl River, NY: Crossroad, 1992.

Oliver, Mark T. *Boycott Disunity! Release the Body of Christ to a Ministry of Community Transformation.* Morgantown, PA: Masthof, 2003.

Olson, Roger E. *The Mosaic of Christian Belief: Twenty Centuries of Unity and Diversity.* 2nd ed. Downers Grove, IL: InterVarsity, 2016.

Osborne, Larry. *Lead Like a Shepherd: The Secret to Leading Well.* Nashville: Thomas Nelson, 2018.

————. *Sticky Church.* Grand Rapids, MI: Zondervan, 2008.

————. *Sticky Leaders: The Secret to Lasting Change and Innovation.* Grand Rapids, MI: Zondervan, 2013.

————. *Sticky Teams: Keeping your Leadership Team and Staff on the Same Page.* Grand Rapids, MI: Zondervan, 2016.

Packard, Josh, and Ashleigh Hope. *Church Refugees: Sociologists Reveal Why People Are DONE with Church but Not Their Faith.* Loveland, CO: Group, 2015.

Packwood, Allen. "Sir Winston Churchill: A Biography." Churchill College Cambridge. https://www.chu.cam.ac.uk/archives/collections/churchill-papers/churchill-biography/

Parke, Caleb. "'Secret Church' Event Hit by 'Cyberattack' Preventing People from Watching It Live." April 28, 2020. https://www.foxnews.com/us/secret-church-cyberattack-coronavirus-online-virginia

Parker, Priya. *The Art of Gathering: How We Meet and Why It Matters.* New York: Riverhead, 2018.

Perrin, Nicholas. *The Kingdom of God: A Biblical Theology.* Grand Rapids, MI: Zondervan, 2019.

Perry, Dwight, ed. *Building Unity in the Church of the New Millennium.* Chicago: Moody, 2002.

Pew Research Center. *In U.S., Decline of Christianity Continues at Rapid Pace.* October 17, 2019. https://www.pewforum.org/2019/10/17/in-u-s-decline-of-christianity-continues-at-rapid-pace/

————. *The Religious Typology: A New Way to Categorize Americans by Religion.* August 29, 2018. https://www.pewforum.org/2018/08/29/the-religious-typology/

Poe, Harry Lee. *Christian Witness in a Postmodern World*. Nashville: Abingdon, 2001.

Powell, Kara, Jake Mulder, and Brad Griffin. *Growing Young: Six Essential Strategies to Help Young People Discover and Love Your Church*. Grand Rapids, MI: Baker, 2016.

Rainer, Thom S. *Anatomy of a Revived Church: Seven Findings of How Congregations Avoided Death*. Spring Hill, TN: Rainer, 2019.

————. *Autopsy of a Deceased Church: Twelve Ways to Keep Yours Alive*. Nashville: B&H, 2014.

————. *I Am a Church Member: Discovering the Attitude That Makes the Difference.*. Nashville: B&H, 2015.

————. "The Number 1 Reason for the Decline in Church Attendance." *Facts & Trends*. December 17, 2018. https://factsandtrends.net/2018/12/17/the-number-1-reason-for-the-decline-in-church-attendance/

————. "Seven Things We Can Learn from Attractional Churches." https://churchanswers.com/blog/seven-things-we-can-learn-from-attractional-churches/?utm_source=ThomRainer.com%2520Subscribers&utm_campaign=31a48115f8-EMAIL_CAMPAIGN_07_29_2019_COPY_01&utm_medium=email&utm_term=0_00de77e553-31a48115f8-81979101

Rainer, Thom S., and Eric Geiger. *Simple Church: Returning to God's Process for Making Disciples*. 2nd ed. Nashville: B&H, 2011.

Reader's Digest Association. *Back to Basics: How to Learn and Enjoy Traditional American Skills*. New York: Reader's Digest Association, 1981.

The ReThink Group, Inc., church publication, 2016, www.thinkorange.com

Rochford, James M. "Church Polity."
http://www.evidenceunseen.com/theology/ecclesiology/
church-polity/

Ronald Reagan. January 5, 1967: Inaugural Address.
https://www.reaganlibrary.gov/archives/speech/january-
5-1967-inaugural-address-public-ceremony

Ross, Mark. "In Essentials Unity, in Non-Essentials Liberty, in
All Things Charity." September 16, 2009. Ligonier
Ministries. https://www.ligonier.org/posts/in-essentials-
unity-in-non-essentials-liberty-in-all-things-charity/

Saturdays at LCBC. Unpublished document from LCBC
Church, Manheim, PA, 2010.

Scazzero, Peter. *The Emotionally Healthy Church: A strategy for
Discipleship That Actually Changes Lives.* Grand Rapids, MI:
Zondervan, 2013.

————. *Emotionally Healthy Spirituality: It's Impossible to Be
Spiritually Healthy While Remaining Emotionally Immature.*
Grand Rapids, MI: Zondervan, 2017.

Schwarz, Christian A. *Natural Church Development: A Guide to
Eight Essential Qualities of Healthy Churches.* 7th ed. St.
Charles, IL: ChurchSmart, 2006.

Searcy, Nelson, with Jennifer Dykes Henson. *Fusion: Turning
First-Time Guests into Fully Engaged Members of Your
Church.* Grand Rapids, MI: Baker, 2008.

"Seven Startling Facts: An Up Close Look at Church
Attendance in America." *Outreach Magazine,* April 10,
2018. churchleaders.com/pastors/pastor-articles/139575-
7-startling-facts-an-up-close-look-at-church-
attendance-in-america.html

Shaw, Haydn. *Generational IQ: Christianity Isn't Dying,
Millennials Aren't the Problem, and the Future Is Bright.*
Carol Stream, IL: Tyndale, 2015.

Shellnutt, Kate. "Why Missions Experts Are Redefining 'Unreached People Groups.'" *Christianity Today* (April 22, 2019). https://www.christianitytoday.com/ct/2019/may/redefining-unreached-people-groups-frontier-unengaged-missi.html

Shults, F. LeRon. *Reforming Theological Anthropology: After the Philosophical Turn to Relationality*. Grand Rapids, MI: Eerdmans, 2003.

Silva, Moises. *Biblical Words and Their Meaning: An Introduction to Lexical Semantics*. Rev. ed. Grand Rapids, MI: Zondervan, 1995.

Simmons, Annette. *The Story Factor: Inspiration, Influence, and Persuasion Through the Art of Storytelling*. 2nd ed. Cambridge, MA: Basic, 2006.

Sire, James W. *The Universe Next Door: A Basic Worldview Catalog*. 5th ed. Downers Grove, IL: InterVarsity, 2009.

Smith, James Bryan. *The Magnificent Story: Uncovering a Gospel of Beauty, Goodness and Truth*. Downers Grove, IL: InterVarsity, 2017.

Smith-Dalton, Maggi. *A History of Spiritualism and the Occult in Salem: The Rise of Witch City*. Charleston, SC: History, 2012.

Stanley, Andy. *Deep and Wide: Creating Churches Unchurched People Love to Attend*. Grand Rapids, MI: Zondervan, 2012.

————. *Next Generation Leader: Five Essentials for Those Who Will Shape the Future*. 2nd ed. Colorado Springs, CO: Multnomah, 2006.

————. *Visioneering: God's Blueprint for Developing and Maintaining Vision*. Colorado Springs, CO: Multnomah, 1999.

Stanley, Andy, and Lane Jones. *Communicating for a Change: Seven Keys to Irresistable Communication*. Colorado Springs, CO: Multnomah, 2006.

Stetzer, Ed. "New England: New Research and Analysis on America's Least Religious Region." *The Exchange* (blog). March 21, 2013. https://www.christianitytoday.com /edstetzer/2013/march/new-england-new-research-and-analysis-on-americas-least.html

Stetzer, Ed, Richie Stanley, and Jason Hayes. *Lost and Found: The Younger Unchurched and the Churches That Reach Them*. Nashville: B&H, 2009.

Stoesz, Edgar. *Doing Good Even Better: How to Be an Effective Board Member of a Nonprofit Organization*. Intercourse, PA: Good Books, 2007.

Strauch, Alexander. *Biblical Eldership: An Urgent Call to Restore Biblical Church Leadership*. Colorado Springs, CO: Lewis & Roth, 1995.

Sweeney, Douglas A. *The American Evangelical Story: A History of the Movement*. Grand Rapids, MI: Baker, 2005.

Sweet, Leonard. *From Tablet to Table: Where Community Is Found and Identity Is Formed* (Colorado Springs, CO: NavPress, 2014).

————.*The Gospel According to Starbucks: Living with a Grande Passion*. Colorado Springs, CO: WaterBrook, 2007.

————. *The Greatest Story Never Told: Revive Us Again*. Nashville: Abingdon, 2012.

————. *I Am a Follower: The Way, Truth, and Life of Following Jesus*. Nashville: Nelson, 2012.

————. *Post-modern Pilgrims: First Century Passion for the 21st Century World*. Nashville: B&H, 2000.

————. *Rings of Fire: Walking in Faith Through a Volcanic Future*. Colorado Springs, CO: NavPress, 2019.

————. *So Beautiful: Divine Design for Life and the Church*. Colorado Springs, CO: David C. Cook, 2009.

————. *SoulTsunami: Sink or Swim in New Millennium Culture*. Grand Rapids, MI: Zondervan, 2001.

————.*The Well-Played Life: Why Pleasing God Doesn't Have to Be Such Hard Work*. 2nd ed. Issaquah, WA: Salish Sea, 2021.

————. *What Matters Most: How We Got the Point but Missed the Person*. Colorado Springs, CO: WaterBrook, 2012.

Sweet, Leonard, and Frank Viola. *Jesus: A Theography*. Nashville: Thomas Nelson, 2012.

Thornton, Matt. *Engage*. Unpublished document from Christ Community Church, Taunton, MA, 2018.

————. *Editor Copy of Grow*. Unpublished document from Christ Community Church, Taunton, MA, 2018.

————. *Facilitator's Guide, Intro Class CCC*. Unpublished document from Christ Community Church, Taunton, MA, 2018.

"Thriving in New England: A Report of Interviews with New England Pastors and Evangelical Leaders by the Cecil B. Day Foundation." March, 2018. https://thrivingne.org/stories-%26-stories

Towns, Elmer L., Ed Stetzer, and Warren Bird. *Eleven Innovations in the Local Church: How Today's Leaders Can Learn, Discern, and Move into the Future*. Ventura, CA: Regal, 2007.

"Transformational Discipleship: A Report of Interviews with New England Pastors and Evangelical Leaders by the Cecil B. Day Foundation." December, 2018. https://thrivingne.org/stories-%26-stories

Tripp, Paul David. *Dangerous Calling: Confronting the Unique Challenges of Pastoral Ministry*. Wheaton, IL: Crossway, 2012.

United States Department of Labor. *Economic News Release.* https://www.bls.gov/news.release/atus.t04.htm

Vander Zee, Leonard J. *Christ, Baptism and the Lord's Supper: Recovering the Sacraments for Evangelical Worship.* Downers Grove, IL: InterVarsity, 2004.

van Yperen, Jim. *Making Peace: A Guide to Overcoming Church Conflict.* Chicago: Moody, 2002.

Vogl, Charles H. *The Art of Community: Seven Principles for Belonging.* Oakland, CA: Berrett-Koehler, 2016.

Volf, Miroslav, and Matthew Croasmun. *For the Life of the World: Theology That Makes a Difference.* Grand Rapids, MI: Brazos, 2021.

Walls, Andrew. "The Ephesians Moment in Worldwide Worship: A Meditation on Revelation 21 and Ephesians 2." In *Christian Worship Worldwide: Expanding Horizons, Deepening Practices.* Ed. Charles E. Farhadian. Grand Rapids, MI: Eerdmans, 2007.

————. *The Missionary Movement in Christian History: Studies in the Transmission of Faith.* Maryknoll, NY: Orbis, 1996.

"What Is the Engel Scale?" *Evangelical Alliance.* https://www.eauk.org/what-is-the-engel-scale

White, Heath. *Postmodernism 101: A First Course for the Curious Christian.* Grand Rapids, MI: Brazos, 2006.

White, James Emery. *The Rise of the Nones: Understanding and Reaching the Religiously Unaffiliated.* Grand Rapids, MI: Baker, 2014.

Willard, Chris, and Jim Sheppard. *Contagious Generosity: Creating a Culture of Giving in Your Church.* Grand Rapids, MI: Zondervan, 2012.

Wilson, Jared C. "Ten Surprising Realities of Mission in New England." May 26, 2017. The Gospel Coalition. https://www.thegospelcoalition.org/blogs/jared-c-wilson/10-surprising-realities-of-mission-in-new-england/

Winthrop, John. "John Winthrop's 'City upon a Hill,' 1630." https://www.gilderlehrman.org/sites/default/files/inline-pdfs/Winthrop%27s%20City%20upon%20a%20Hill.pdf.

Wiseman, Liz. *Rookie Smarts: Why Learning Beats Knowing in the New Game of Work.* New York: HarperCollins, 2014.

Wright, Christopher J. H. *The Mission of God: Unlocking the Bible's Grand Narrative.* Downers Grove, IL: InterVarsity, 2018.

Yancey, Philip. *Vanishing Grace: Brining Good News to a Deeply Divided World.* Grand Rapids, MI: Zondervan, 2014.

About the Author

Shawn Keener is the husband of Pam, a dad to five, a dad-in-

law to two, and a "poppy" to two. Jesus and these are my life's devotion. We live in Holbrook, Massachusetts. My hobbies are strategy games and hiking in the nearby state forest of Ames Nowell.

I'm a quintessential INTJ.

My Doctor of Theology is from Evangelical Theological Seminary in Myerstown, Pennsylvania (the best seminary on earth), which is now becoming part of the Kairos network.

We used to live in Lancaster County, Pennsylvania, and seven years ago God moved us to Massachusetts to pastor at Brookville Bible Church.

If you would like to know more about anything in this book, or to enjoy a thoughtful discussion on any of it with me, or to have me meet with your church regarding this book, please contact me at shawnkeener@me.com.

CPSIA information can be obtained
at www.ICGtesting.com
Printed in the USA
BVHW081142140322
631400BV00007B/252